AF705600

Groupwork Volume I

In this series

Published Spring 2007

Groupwork: Volume 1
ISBN 9781861770554

Groupwork: Volume 2
ISBN 9781861770561

Groupwork: Volume 3
ISBN 9781861770578

Groupwork: Volume 4
ISBN 9781861770585

Groupwork: Volume 5
ISBN 9781861770592

Groupwork: Volume 6
ISBN 9781861770608

Groupwork: Volume 7
ISBN 9781861770615

Groupwork: Volume 8
ISBN 9781861770622

Groupwork: Volume 9
ISBN 9781861770639

Groupwork: Volume 10
ISBN 9781861770646

Groupwork: Volume 11
ISBN 9781861770653

Groupwork: Volume 12
ISBN 9781861770660

Groupwork: Volume 13
ISBN 9781861770677

To be published Autumn 2007

Groupwork: Volume 14
ISBN 9781861770684

A full contents list for volumes 1-13 will be found at the back of this volume

Groupwork

An Interdisciplinary Journal for Working with Groups

Volume One

edited by

Allan Brown & Andrew Kerslake

Whiting & Birch Ltd
1988
Reprinted 2006

Notes from the Publisher

Citation

This volume comprises, without any amendment, all material published in *Groupwork* Volume 1, 1988. It is advised that authors citing material in this volume should recognise this original date and journal provenance in the manner indicated by the house style of the publication for which they are writing, either by citing material as the original periodical article, or, if citing this volume, by clearly indicating the original date of publication of the material both in text references and in the bibliography.

Reproduction

For technical reasons, the typesetting files of some early volumes of *Groupwork* are no longer usable. We have therefore scanned early volumes in this series from the original journals. This inevitably results in reproduction which is less than ideal. Material is available in some other formats.

Editorial contact details

We have reproduced volumes in their complete original format including notes to contributors and advertising. It should be remembered that editorial contact details and manuscript preparation requirements have changed. Current contact details and notes for contributors are available at www.whitingbirch.net.

© Whiting & Birch Ltd, 1988 and 2006
Published by Whiting & Birch Ltd,
Forest Hill, London SE23 3HZ

ISBN 9781861770554
ISSN 0951-824X
Printed in England and the United States by Lightning Source

Groupwork
An Interdisciplinary Journal for Working with Groups

Volume 1, 1988

Contents

Preface

Since its first issue in 1988, much interesting and inspiring material has been published in *Groupwork*. Most of this still says much of use to today's groupworkers. We are therefore delighted that back volumes of Groupwork will in future be readily available in convenient form.

Mark Doel and Pam Trevithick
Co-Editors *Groupwork*

GROUPWORK

Volume 1 | Number 1 | 1988

Editors: Allan Brown and Andrew Kerslake

CONTENTS

EDITORS:
Allan Brown, Andrew Kerslake

EDITORIAL BOARD
Jo Campling, Editorial Adviser.
Ken Heap, (International Editorial Advisor), Director, School for Advanced Training, Norwegian Lutheran School of Social Work, Oslo.
Nano McCaughan, Principal Groupworker, Croydon Social Services.
Rick Morgan-Jones, Consultant and Lecturer in Groupwork, National Institute for Social Work.
David Ward, Lecturer in Social Work, University of Nottingham.

ASSESSORS AND ADVISERS, Lucy Ball, Margot Breton, John Burton, Brian Caddick, Derek Carter, Tom Douglas, Sheila Ernst, Eric Ferron, Charles Garvin, George Getzel, John Harper, Peter Hawkins, John Hodge, John Hughes, Norma Lang, Jenny Lumley, Oded Manor, Harold Marchant, Catherine Papell, Michael Preston-Shoot, Sandra Regan, Kenneth Reid, Dudley Roach, Beulah Rothman, Paul Senior, Lawrence Shulman, Peter Smith, Theo Sowa, Christine Stones, Ann Walford, Dorothy Whitaker.

SUBSCRIPTION, ADVERTISING AND OTHER BUSINESS ENQUIRIES
should be addressed to the publishers, Whiting & Birch Ltd, 90 Dartmouth Road, Forest Hill, London SE23 3HZ. Telephone 01-699-0914 (Int'l +441 699-0914). Telex 8950511 ONEONE G. Quote Mailbox 39000001.

SUBSCRIPTION RATES
British Isles £27.50 Elsewhere US$60
Special reduced rates apply as follows:
Individuals to private address: £15 British Isles $30 Elsewhere
Groupwork is published three times per year.
Two and three year, and multiple copy rates on application to the publishers.

PAYMENT
Should accompany order. Cheque or banker's draft (made payable to Whiting & Birch Ltd) may be in any convertible currency to the relevant amount. Direct transfer can be made to either our Girobank account (no. 5440564), or bank account (Midland Bank, 20 Wimbledon Hill Road, London SW19 7BX, sort code 40-07-30, account number 91109693 78). The following credit cards are also accepted: Access/Mastercard, Visa, Diners Club, American Express. Quote card number, expiry date and give cardholder's name and address if different from delivery address.

REPRODUCTION OF ARTICLES
© Whiting & Birch Ltd. All copyright reserved by Whiting & Birch Ltd. Enquiries regarding rights of reproduction should be addressed to the Publishers in the first instance.

PUBLISHED BY WHITING & BIRCH LTD, LONDON **ISSN 0951-824X**
Printed by Antony Rowe Ltd, Chippenham.

GROUPWORK (1988) 1, 3–4

EDITORIAL

Welcome. – Starting any new journal is an exciting and daunting task. As part of this process we consulted many colleagues for their views on the possible success of our proposed venture. Their answers varied from the delighted to the dispiriting. An example of the latter, from a leading academic, was the disturbing comment *'Goodness no, surely we don't need a specialist publication, and isn't groupwork rather "old hat".'* Whilst the relegation of the subject to the status of outdated millinery provides a tempting starting point for a first editorial, extolling the virtues of groupwork as a mainstream method of social work, we have decided to resist this temptation and leave it to our contributors to speak about what groupwork has to offer. However, the first part of the comment is an important one to answer.

During the last year social work as a profession rarely seems to have left the headlines in the national press. Whilst most of that attention has focussed on social work's difficulties in implementing statutory duties and procedures, it has become increasingly apparent that social work as practised often lacks clear methodological implementation, although such methods undoubtedly exist. Like many other trainers, we are continuously involved in talking, demonstrating and writing about methods. If social work is to gain credibility, then it needs to prove that it's theoretical bases and models are valid and not just conceptual 'tricks' learnt in training, then abandoned after qualification to what is often misleadingly described as 'common-sense'.

Our expectation is that this journal will be one way of bridging the gap between theory and practice. By discussing different methods and approaches under the diverse themes and practical activities that comprise groupwork, we hope that it can add to the body of practice knowledge. To be useful, any method of work has to be capable of replication. Reading about the work of others should encourage workers to improve and vary their own practice creatively. In this way we think that *any* specialist journal has a vital role to play in the development of social work as a profession, and in improving the quality of service to users.

We are very pleased to include in this issue two articles from authors overseas, one from North America and one from Norway. Whilst the journal is primarily intended as a forum for the development of groupwork in Britain, the international dimension is very important and we hope to carry regular contributions from groupwork colleagues from other parts of the world. There are of course language difficulties, and as a small indication of our serious intent each issue will include brief summaries of article contents in both French and German.

We think it is essential that the journal gives the highest priority to values, continuously locating groupwork practice in the wider context of the kind of society to which group members and workers belong. The journal provides a focal point for groupworkers to identify and debate, both theoretically and in approaches to practice, those values which hitherto have not had the prominence they demand. In this issue there are two articles on race, anti-racism and groupwork, which we hope will raise consciousness on this topic, and lead to further contributions from readers.

There are three specifically 'practice-based' articles, drawn from the areas of mental health, transracial families, and adolescence, each sharing the authors' practice experience and drawing out learning points from which others can benefit. A continuing flow of practice articles like these is needed to provide the life-blood of the journal, and we urge all readers who have important groupwork experiences to share and/or who know of others with a contribution to make, to take the plunge and write. This journal exists as a medium for communicating all that effort and learning to others!

On this first occasion we have decided not to take reviews of individual publications, but instead to offer two articles which review some of the more recent UK groupwork literature. One of these analyses groupwork articles from the 'popular' social work press. The other reviews a range of groupwork books published in Britain during the period 1980-6. In future there will be reviews of new groupwork publications and videos, and we hope also to provide (and receive) information about groupwork literature appearing in other journals and sources.

What has struck us most forcibly during preparation of the journal has been the collective good wishes for its success from the many people who share a commitment to groupwork and it's development. The analogy with the very core of social groupwork is both close and significant: the group members share a common need or concern, and an essential ingredient for the effective mutual aid system they seek to generate is the richness, range and variety of the individual contributions to the whole. As editors we are very conscious that success depends on the collective efforts of contributors, subscribers, advisers, the publishers and the editorial board. One thing that has been particularly impressive and which augurs well for the future is the 'hidden' work of the assessors, whose considered and detailed feedback to authors is a quite crucial part of the whole process. Finally, the journal's association with the groupwork network based at the National Institute for Social Work is an important foundation, and information about the network and future events will be included regularly, either as an enclosure or in the journal itself.

Allan Brown and Andrew Kerslake

GROUPWORK (1988) 1, 5–16

GROUPWORK PRACTICE WITH HARD TO REACH CLIENTS: A MODALITY OF CHOICE

LAWRENCE SHULMAN

It is the central theme of this paper that groupwork practice has unique qualities which lends it to working with hard to reach populations as well as hard to handle issues. The two questions addressed are the following: What are the characteristics of these hard to reach populations with hard to handle issues?, and, what is it about groupwork which may make it a modality of choice with these clients?

Qualities of the hard to reach populations

In reflecting upon the qualities of these hard to reach populations I identified four factors which may be important. Even as I describe these I realise that they are characteristics which more or less can be used to portray any social work client population. Therefore, the difference with the hard to reach population may be one of degree and combination of qualities. The four I want to discuss are the following: powerlessness and hopelessness; shame and guilt; high levels of defensiveness, denial and resistance; and a strong need for acceptance, support and love from the social surround.

In the remainder of this paper I will discuss each of these, identifying the unique qualities of groupwork which may explain its particular usefulness in working with these populations. One of these is the 'strength in numbers' phenomenon which can increase client power and control over their behaviour, their environment and the helping process itself. A second is the healing powers released when clients find they are all in the same boat, powers which can help them overcome feelings of guilt and shame. Another is the group process which can be used by clients as a medium for communications in those situations where strong feelings of defensiveness, denial and resistance are present. And finally, the marvellous process in which the group itself becomes a laboratory for learning how to offer support, acceptance and love and for creating a significant mutual aid system in its own right. (For a complete description of the mutual aid process see Shulman, 1984,[a] Chapter 7; Schwartz, 1961; Social Welfare Forum, 1961).

Powerless and hopelessness

It is crucial for all of us to have a sense that we are in control of ourselves and our environment. Adversity can be faced and overcome if we believe we have even a small degree of influence over what happens to us. For many of the hard to reach populations, either internal or external factors have caused them to feel powerless in relation to their social surround. For example, senior citizens who enter a nursing home have lost their independence and after a lifetime of being able to take care of themselves must now depend upon others. In large institutions their feelings of apathy and hopelessness are compounded by institutional regimes which often serve to increase their sense of impotence in relation to their social surround.

For these group members and others like them, gaining control over their own actions and being able to influence their environment takes on added dimensions of importance. The mutual aid group may offer some unique helping qualities. For example, there is the 'strength in numbers' phenomenon which can help group members to find the strength to tackle difficult tasks. In one example, from a book examining the mutual aid process throughout the life-cycle, Toby Berman-Rossi describes work with the institutionalized aged in which she tries to help them deal with institution itself (Berman-Rossi, 1986). Her first efforts are directed at helping the group members overcome the 'You can't fight city hall' syndrome. Recognizing that loss of control over their environment and loss of independence is a crucial theme for them, she tries to mobilize them to use each other in a ward group to attempt to influence the institution. In one practice excerpt, she tackles the difficult task of defining her role as a third force, or mediator in the process. One group member, referring to her role in the middle between the residents and the nursing staff asks her: '*But aren't you on our side?*' She explains that if she is to be helpful she had to be '. . . *on the side of working out the troubles between them and nursing.*' The residents begin to understand this tricky role. However one winks at the worker and says: '*But you really know we are right*' (Berman-Rossi, *op. cit.*, p. 345). In the excerpt which follows, she tries to implement this role.

A central issue in this home for older Jewish people was related to food. After skilful groundwork was laid with both the residents and the dietary staff, the worker attempted to bring the two sides together thus increasing resident input to the system. As she helped them to negotiate the system she also helped them to face the underlying feelings associated with this dramatic change in status from an independent adult to one who must depend upon others. In some ways. no matter what the dietary department did it would not really help, for the residents were mourning the loss of their ability to cook for themselves. Berman-Rossi (*op. cit.*, pp. 346–347) describes the process.

> Residents were prepared for the meeting by discussions in the previous weeks about the particulars of their complaints. Whether they would speak or not remained to be seen. After we were assembled, I turned to the dieticians and said, 'I think it is important for you to know that many residents are feeling discouraged about the food problems getting solved, and I had to urge them to allow me to invite you.' Miss James said she could understand their discouragement, but she really did want to hear. Her department would continue to work on the problems and to do that, it was important to hear what residents had to say. I asked for someone to start us off.
>
> After a bit of sluggishness, the problems began to be mentioned. Mrs. Esman was hanging her head and speaking her complaints angrily to herself. I said that I knew Mrs. Esman felt especially bad about the food and I wondered if she would share some of her feelings. She just kept shaking her head and repeated 'no good, no good'. I asked 'What in particular?' She mentioned. 'Why no blintzes? I love them.' Then she hung her head and said, 'What's the use?' I said, 'Your discouragement is very strong.' 'Yes', she said, 'I've given up.' 'But it's not as if you don't care, you stay mad and I see you are bothered about the food all the time.' 'Yes' she answered quietly.
>
> There was a hush in the room. I turned to Miss James and Mrs. Hill and said that I thought they were hearing the kind of feeling from Mrs. Esman that many residents feel. Miss James said softly, 'I can understand that food is important, it's something to which you look forward. I bet you were a good cook Mrs. Esman, and preparing the table was important to you.' 'Yes' she said, and her mood began to soften. After her stroke she could no longer do it. Again the room was hushed. One sensed many recalled pleasures no longer possible. I said. 'And now that you can no longer prepare the table, you have to take what the home provides'. Mrs. Esman looked up but said nothing. I turned to the group and asked, 'Does not being able to do things as you did before make the problem worse?' There was a round of commiseration. When they came to the nursing home, they had to be grateful for what they got; they were sick and couldn't do it for themselves. Some of them felt they were glad they no longer had to cook for themselves.
>
> I returned to the particulars of the food problems. The complaints were exhausted and residents reaffirmed their desire for the traditional Friday night supper. Miss James said she had heard them last month and had made plans for some of their favourite foods to be returned. The menus were in the middle of being typed. Eyes picked up, smiles returned. I said I thought that was terrific. The mood felt hopeful and the tension had lessened.

The strength in numbers phenomenon not only helps group members to find the courage to tackle their systems, it also has a powerful influence on their ability to take control of the helping process itself.

In the next example, Dale Trimble (1986) describes his work in developing groups for men who batter women. Over an evolutionary process, he found it necessary to offer these groups to the men, as clients in their own rights, helping them to deal with their inability to control their anger. By combining mutual aid and a strong sense of accountability and responsibility for behaviour, he was able skillfully to blend support and understanding with confrontation. Recognizing that control was a central issue with these men, he directly faced the issue of control of the helping process in his first session as part of his contracting process.

> *Leader:* (After explaining attendance rules and expectations of participation on members, as well as the mandatory reporting role of the group leader). I'm sure it is possible to follow all these rules and not change, not open up to facing yourself or to the other men here. You can probably get through this group and not really change. That's up to you. The judge may order you to be here or your wife may be saying that she won't come back unless you get help. And as I have just said, we require your anger diary and regular attendance in order for you stay here, but no one can reach into your mind and heart and order a change. That's where you have complete control (Trimble, 1986, p. 234).

The anger diary mentioned by the leader was a behavioural technique designed to help the men to understand and keep track of the times they lost their temper and how they handled it. Trimble describes a group with a unique blend of mutual aid and behavioural approaches designed to help the men take control over their behaviour. At the start of each group, Trimble uses an exercise in which each man reports on which of four types of violence he had used the previous week. These included the following: physical, sexual, and psychological abuse or the destruction of property and pets. Somewhat concerned that this ritual might be a bit awkward or at times boring, he raised the question with the group members in the following manner.

> *Leader:* I always feel a bit awkard and artificial going around and asking each of you to report on the four kinds of violence even though I think it is really important to remember that is why we are here. What is it like for you?
>
> *Sam:* (speaking to Hank) When you were talking earlier about your wife I really knew what you meant. I felt that my wife had done similar things to yours. (The conversation went on between Sam and Hank in an animated manner, each of them sharing similar experiences. I asked my question again).
>
> *Bill:* (speaking to the leader) I think you got your answer. It really helped. I learn a lot listening to other guys and how they handle anger. It's not easy but I know it's what I need to do. (Many of the other group members

voice agreement). (Trimble, *op. cit.*, p. 236).

In a final example, Judith Lee (1986) described her work with homeless women in a New York City shelter. In her first session, as Lee explored a working contract with the potential members of her group, she invited them to discuss the feelings of hopelessness and powerlessness associated with being 'down and out' and trapped in the 'shelter system.' Lee pointed out that the existence of the group empowered them not only to deal with the administrators of the shelter, but also to provide support and help to each other. The following practice excerpt picks up at the point they are describing their feelings of lack of dignity and respect and their rage and hoplessness.

> . . . Carla said, there is frequent cursing at clients and hitting of residents has also been observed. 'We're all treated like we're crazy or in prison. It's hard enough to be down and out, but to be treated like dirt gets us desperate.' Then Jean said. 'This place is so tense, it's going to explode.' Everyone agreed. Iris said she felt really close to hurting someone and going to jail. I said I understood how angry they were. I asked Iris if she really wanted to go to jail. She said no. I asked the group what she could do. Jean suggested – 'Just what we're doing, talk about it here. I'm so glad you came. I don't explode but I am so depressed.' I said I heard her pain and asked her how the others felt. Everyone agreed to being very depressed. Carla said you need hope, you need to know your options, how you can get out of here or you don't know what you'd do in time. Sheryl said people who felt they were so angry they would hurt someone should get some help. Many would not hurt anyone and didn't want to be hurt. I said I heard her and understood, she didn't feel that way, and it was scary when others did. But everyone here is hurting in her own way. This brought forth more outpouring . . .
>
> Jean said she would sum it up for us. 'There is a lack of compassion here. Everything is hard and tough and soon you become hard and tough. You get treated like dirt, so you feel like dirt. To be treated like a criminal is the worst part of the pain. You already hate yourself for messing up and landing here. Where is the compassion?' It was a moving moment. I said I agreed and everyone nodded solemnly. I said I saw today that they cared about each other and that's why I brought them together as a group. Jean said. 'God bless you for coming here. This is the first time I talked my heart out and felt caring from anyone since I got here.' Everyone agreed. I thanked them for giving me a chance to hear them and work with them and share their pain and frustration. I suggested they could become a group here with me and we could worry about taking care of each other and I could help with that. Jean said, 'It's happening right here, right now. I'm so glad I spoke up this morning. Iris started joking and singing about everyone needing a little love' (Trimble, *op. cit.*, p. 252)

Shame and guilt

Populations described in this paper often experience strong feelings of shame and guilt. Even if the feelings are not rooted in reality, and intellectually one can understand why one shouldn't feel guilty or ashamed, the feelings are still there. It is possible in individual counselling to try to help a client deal with these feelings and to become less harsh and judgemental of themselves. However, in a mutual aid group, when clients can hear others, who are like themselves, reveal some of the same feelings which lead to the shame and the guilt, a powerful force for healing and acceptance can be released.

In the following example, Indelicato and Goldberg (1986) describe a dramatic moment in their group for parents of learning disabled children. In this excerpt, the worker reaches for the feelings of anger experienced by many parents in this situation – feelings which they believe they are not supposed to have. Just hearing these feelings expressed by others is a healing process as group members discover they are 'all in the same boat', and that their 'evil' feelings are quite understandable.

> Mrs. F. described how on Monday, her son would not get out of bed to go to school. She said: 'I kept reminding him to get up since I know he is very particular about his hair and he needs extra time to get ready. I knew he was pretending to be asleep so I smacked him in the face. He went into a rage, started kicking the covers and screaming. I ran out of the room crying. I sometimes want to hurt him . . .'
>
> I told Mrs. F. that I noticed when we talked earlier about the situation with her son, her hands were clenched, and her face was intense. I encouraged her to bring us on board about what she was experiencing. She responded: 'Yes, I get very angry, so angry I want to hit him'. I asked what do you get angry about the most? She replied: 'Wasting time! He has to go to school, has to learn, to get a job, raise a family. He can't stay dependent on me!'
>
> Mrs. M. spoke about her own fear of loss of control: 'I don't hit my children because I'm afraid I'll hurt them. It's just the frustration, the hurt, the anger, mostly the hurt. I look at my child, thinking, I have done everything I know, given you my time and look what you're doing. You're totally disrupting my life. Everything else is OK, but sometimes I get caught up in the feelings of how much he disrupts my schedule' (Indelicato and Goldbery, *op. cit.*, p. 203).

As members listen to others describing strong feelings, they may be put in touch with similar feelings within themselves which they have long denied. We can often easily see in other people those things which we have the most difficulty seeing and facing in ourselves.

In a second example, Margaret Jones (1986) illustrates how group members can use this process to modify their own harsh judgements of themselves and begin to take responsibility for what they can do about their problems. The group was for the non-offending parent of girls who have been sexually abused. Many of the group members turned out to have been abused themselves. In the following excerpt, one mother moved from discussing her self-blame to raising questions about her family.

Pat: This has happened in my family before. My father abused me. I should have been able to see it in my own family. It seems almost genetic . . . except it's not right? . . . but it's like it's in my blood.
Worker: You feel it might be related to your family?
Pat: Yes. I know that doesn't make sense.
Worker: Does anyone else have those feelings?
Ida: It is a family thing. My father abused me. My husband abused my daughter. So it's not genetic but maybe you learn it in your family.
Worker: What would you say your daughter learned in your family?
Ida: To be like me.
Worker: Can you say how she is like you?
Ida: Maybe not enough confidence? Maybe I never showed her how to stand up for herself. She's scared people won't like her. Like me. She takes care of people all the time. She's always taking care of her friends.
Worker: Is that like you too?
Ida: I always want to be the good Joe. I want everyone to like me. When she was little I was on drugs . . . I've changed a lot but maybe that's what I taught her.
Pat: Well isn't that what's expected of you? Like Mary said the other week . . . that's what women are taught . . . but then I guess we have all learned it to different degrees.
Worker: So when you two consider what you've each said, what do you feel?
Ida: Not guilty! (laughs). Some of me is responsible for what I taught my daughter. Some of me was just doing what I was taught.
Pat: I think it would have happened anyway . . . but my daughter needs to learn new attitudes . . . like how to say no . . . how to stand up, be more assertive (Jones, *op. cit.*, p. 221-222).

Defensiveness, denial and resistance

Every client experiences feelings of defensiveness, a desire to deny the existence of a problem, and points of resistance during the helping process. Since these feelings are strongest when we have the most to defend, deny and resist changing, it should not be surprising that clients in the categories discussed in this paper may have a greater stake in the *status quo*. The 'all in the same boat' phenomenon described in the previous section can be crucial in helping to create the conditions which allow such clients to begin to let down their defenses which are often the result of their own harsh judgements of themselves.

Another way in which groups may offer unique opportunities for dealing with these issues is that they can become a laboratory in which the process in the group is used as a medium through which a client may raise difficult concerns. If all clients are viewed as somewhat ambivalent about facing and dealing with painful feelings and issues, then group process can be one way in which clients send a message to the worker about the part of them that wants to grow and change.

In a poignant example from Vastola, Nierenburg and Graham's work (1986) with children who have had close relatives die, we see one child, Mark, playing the role of 'deviant member' by demonstrating how most of the children have learned to cope with the pain of the deaths – through denial and acting out behaviour. As the group leaders helped Mark to face the feelings, they were also helping their other client, the group, learn to tolerate and to talk about painful experiences.

> Eleven year old Mark was repeatedly writing Bob (his grandfather's name) on a sheet of paper in front of him.
> *Carl:* Mark, your grandfather died?
> *Mark:* I don't want any damn body talking about my grandfather or I'll kick their butt.
> *Leader:* You sound pretty angry.
> *Mark:* I'm not angry. I just don't want anybody talking about my grandfather.
> *Leader:* I guess it must be very difficult.
> *Mark:* It's not difficult: I just don't want anybody saying anything about him. (His anger was escalating and others in the group expressed similar feelings. 'Nobody wants to talk about nobody dying'.).
> *Dick:* Yes, we don't want to talk about that.
> *Leader:* (Exploring the resistance) Why?
> *Gloria:* (Insightfully noted) That's why he is running around. You can't force him if he doesn't want to.
> *Leader:* Are you saying that perhaps that's why you're running around, so you won't have to talk about something so upsetting?
> *Mark:* Nope.
> *Leader:* You may feel it's too hard to talk about.
> *Mark:* No, it's not hard for me to talk about anything . . . but that reminds you and you could be dreaming.
> *Carl:* Yup, you dream for about a week when you talk about your mother, then it takes about five days to try to get over it, but it comes back again and it stops and it comes back again . . . Nightmares I hate. I hate talking about my mother (Vastola *et al.*, *op. cit.*, p. 81).

In the example which follows, Schaefer and Pozzaglia (1986) describe their work with a group of Hispanic speaking parents of children with cancer. The excerpt demonstrates how they reach past the safe, opening conversation on housing and transportation, for the deeper theme of the session – the group members' fears for their children.

> *Mrs. J:* Oh, you're from Chile. So where are you living now?
> *Mr. P:* In a hotel.
> *Mrs. J:* (You live in a hotel and not an apartment?)
> *Mr. P:* Yes, because all of the apartments are either very far away from the

hospital or if they're close, they're too expensive. So, we are living on 32nd street, but it is still far and taxis are expensive.
Mrs. M: You can catch a bus right out front.
Mr. P: No. because of Gloria's disease she could get an infection being around so many other people on the bus.
Worker: It sounds as if it could be dangerous for her to get an infection. Why is that?
Mr. P: Gloria has extremely low blood counts since her bone marrow transplant. I worry about how unprotected she is so I try my best to keep her away from crowds.
Mrs. M: What does she have?
Mr. P: Leukemia.
Mrs. J: So does my son. (Period of silence).
Workers: (To the group) How did it affect you when you discovered that your children had leukemia?
Mrs. J: I was, like crazy. I couldn't believe that this could happen to my child. I kept asking. 'Why, why?' This disease is terrible. I was in a state of despair.
Mr P: (To Mrs. J.) When someone tells you something like that, it's terrible. I was sure my child was going to die, but thank God she's lived longer than the doctor originally thought: but we're still scared (Schaefer, *et. al.*, *op. cit.*, pp. 301–302).

The need for acceptance, love and support

While we all need and search for acceptance, love and support, the clients described in this paper are often cut off from meeting these basic human needs by the very problems for which they seek help. For example, changing societal patterns are increasing the number of parents who must raise their children alone. Not only are they cut off from support from a spouse, they also often find themselves losing their connections with their friends. A mutual aid group can become a place where clients can regain the intimacy they desperately need and relearn how to offer and take help from others.

In the following example from my own single parents group, one member described her frustration at trying to get her ex-spouse to be 'more of a Dad' for their five year old boy (Shulman, 1986). He appeared to reject this boy, while at the same time, caring for the youngest child. I put her feelings into words by articulating how hard it must be on her when the child questioned his rejection.

> I told Ginette I thought this must have put her in an awful bind with the child, when for example, he asked her 'When is Daddy going to visit me'? I wondered how she dealt with it. Ginette described her conversation which indicated she tried to cover up the problem, told 'white lies', and did what she could to avoid dealing with the child's feelings. I acknowledged to her, and the group, that I could appreciate the bind she felt.

> June, a new member who had been listening quietly all morning, began to speak. She spoke with a low, soft voice, and began to cry before she could complete her comments: 'I have been sitting here listening to Ginette thinking that what she is describing is my problem exactly. And now, I think I realize . . . (soft crying) . . . that I'm going to have to face my own rejection by my husband, who walked out on me, before the healing can start . . . and I can help my kids face their rejection'. (Shulman, *op. cit.*, pp. 188–189.

With deep emotions triggered by Ginette's comment, June moved the whole group into the underlying theme of rejection, beautifully stating the connection between their own need to resolve their feelings and their ability to help their children do the same. As is often the case, group members are moved and concerned by such a strong display of emotions. I tried to help the group members release that part of them which wanted to reach out to June, but might be embarrassed to do so. Note also, how much help is available from members in the group. This is a relief for the worker who does not have to provide all of the help but can concentrate, instead, on releasing the group's inherent potential for mutual aid.

> We all felt very moved by June's words. I could see the group members were upset. Marie was sitting next to June, and I could tell she was very agitated – looking around the room, looking at June, and literally moving in her seat. I said: "I think June's feelings have hit all of us very hard. I have a feeling you would like to reach out to June, wouldn't you Marie?' Marie said she really would. When I asked her: 'Why don't you', she said: 'Well I'm afraid to'. After a slight pause, she reached over and took June's hand, holding it tightly. June responded warmly to the gesture. I reassured June that it was OK to share her feelings with us and that her tears were an important part of how she felt. I told her that I felt she spoke for all of the group members, and they quickly assured her that I was correct.
>
> We then returned to Ginnette and her difficulty in being honest with her children and allowing them to express their feelings. She said: 'I want my son to share his feelings within certain guidelines'. I responded: 'You mean, you want him to share the feelings that are not too tough for you'. The group members, including Ginette laughed in recognition of the point. Ginette admitted she realized she had to be honest with him. The group members, at my suggestion, agreed to help her role play the conversation so she could find a supportive way of being honest (Shulman, 1986, p. 189)

Not only can group members find support from each other, they can also obtain it from a caring leader. In fact, an advantage of mutual aid groups, is that group members can watch as the leader models the very behaviours they need to develop in dealing with each other and significant others in their lives. In my final example, I draw upon my work with married couples who are trying to save their marriages. One of the members had come into the group alone, sat next to me, and shared a frightening problem she was facing. She cried during the presentation, and I and the other group members tried to comfort her.

> Fran said, 'I knew this was Jan's night to get help the minute she walked in the door'. When I inquired as to how she knew, she said, 'Because she sat in the crying chair'. She went on to point out that all of the people who had cried in sessions, four of the ten group members, had sat in that chair at the beginning of the session. Other members nodded in recognition. I inquired if they had any thought about why that was so. Rose said, 'Because that's the chair next to you, and we sit there to get some support when the going gets rough'. I encouraged them to elaborate on what they felt they got from me since that was also, what they probably wanted from each other.
>
> Louise said. 'It's because we can feel free to say anything to you, and you won't judge us. We can tell you our feelings'. Rose continued, 'And we know you really feel our hurt, it's not phoney – *you really care*'. Lou said, 'It's safe next to you. We can share our innermost feelings and know that you won't let us get hurt'. As I listened to the members, I felt myself deeply moved by the affect in their voices, and I shared that with them. 'You know, it means a great deal to me to have you feel that way – that you can sense my feelings for you. I have grown to care about you quite a bit. It's surprising to me, sometimes, just how hard things in this group hit me – just how important you have really become,' (Shulman, 1984[a], pp. 300–301).

It's important to recognize that the group members will also generate feelings in the worker. These feelings must also be understood and accepted.

Summary and conclusions

I have tried in this paper to reflect on my observation that social work with groups has increasingly moved into dealing with populations and themes of concern which are on the leading edge of the work of our profession. I have suggested that the general characterisitics of these populations include the following: strong feelings of powerlessness and hopelessness; guilt and shame; defensiveness, denial and resistance; and a strong need for acceptance, support and love.

I have also suggested that groupwork offers certain unique helping processes which may best meet some of the needs of these populations. These included the 'strength in numbers' and the 'all in the same boat' phenomenons, the use of group process by clients as a medium for communications, and the process in which the group itself becomes a significant mutual aid system in its own right.

If this trend continues, I believe we will see group workers moving to serve the most needy clients who are often overlooked by traditional social services. In a sense we may be coming full cycle, since our roots were in the neighbourhood houses and settlement houses which dealt with those clients who were most needy at that time – the many waves of immigrants attempting to become a healthy, functioning, part of the whole. Only this time, instead of immigrants we have new groups of clients on the outside who are seeking our help in integrating into our society. At a time when so much of social work energy appears to be directed towards private practice, third party payments, and the professional prestige building aspects of social work practice, it is with some pride that I see groupwork providing professional leadership in dealing with the social issues and problems which were the reasons most of us entered the profession.

This paper was presented at the Seventh Symposium on the Advancement of Social Work with Groups, October 1985, Rutgers University, New Brunswick, New Jersey.

References

Berman-Rossi, T. (1986) 'The fight against hopelessness and despair' in Gitterman, A. and Shulman, L. (eds.) *Mutual Aid Groups and the Life Cycle.* Itasca, Ill: F.E. Peacock, pp. 333-360.

Columbia University Press (1961) *The Social Welfare Forum.* New York: Columbia, pp. 146-77.

Indelicato, S. and Goldberg, P. (1986) 'Harassed and alone: parents of learning disabled children' in Gitterman, A. and Shulman, L. (eds.) *Mutual Aid Groups and the Life Cycle.* Itasca, Ill: F.E. Peacock, pp. 195-210.

Jones, M.J. (1986) 'Speaking the unspoken: parents of sexually abused children' in Gitterman, A. and Shulman, L. (eds.) *Mutual Aid Groups and the Life Cycle.* Itasca, Ill: F.E. Peacock pp. 211–228.

Lee, J.A.B. (1986) 'No place to go: homeless women' in Gitterman, A. and Shulman, L. (eds.) *Mutual Aid Groups and the Life Cycle.* Itasca, Ill: F.E. Peacock, pp. 245–262.

Schaefer, D.S. and Pozzaglia, D. (1986) 'Coping with a nightmare: Hispanic parents of children with cancer' in Gitterman, A. and Shulman, L. (eds.) *Mutual Aid Groups and the Life Cycle.* Itasca, Ill: F.E. Peacock, pp. 297–314.

Schwartz, W. (1961) 'The social worker in the group' in *New Perspectives on Services to Groups: Theory, Organization and Practice.* New York: National Association of Social Workers, pp. 7–34.

Shulman, L. (1984[a]) (ed.) *Skills of Helping Individuals and Groups,* 2nd Edition. Itasca, Ill: F.E. Peacock.

Shulman, L. (1984[b]) 'The group as a mutual aid system' in Shulman, L. (ed.) *The Skills of Helping Individuals and Groups,* 2nd Edition. Itasca, Ill: F.E. Peacock.

Shulman, L. (1986) 'Healing the hurts: single parents' in Gitterman, A. and Shulman, L. (eds.) *Mutual Aid Groups and The Life Cycle.* Itasca, Ill: F.E. Peacock, pp. 179–194.

Trimble, D. (1986) 'Confronting responsibility: men who batter their wives' in Gitterman, A. and Shulman, L. (eds.) *Mutual Aid Groups and the Life Cycle.* Itasca, Ill: F.E. Peacock, pp. 229–244.

Vastola, J. Nierenberg, A. and Graham. E.H. (1986) 'The lost and found group: group work with bereaved children' in Gitterman, A. and Shulman, L. (eds.) *Mutual Aid Groups and the Life Cycle.* Itasca, Ill: F.E. Peacock, pp. 75–90.

GROUPWORK (1988) 1, 17–29

THE WORKER AND THE GROUP PROCESS: A DILEMMA REVISITED

KEN HEAP

This article comments on the discrepancy between the wide acceptance of the principle of the 'use of the group' and the frequency with which practising groupworkers maintain an active, focal role. It is suggested that this is partly a residual confusion about the 'leadership' function. The author proposes that Redl's 'central person' role concept is applicable and points to both situational and emotional factors which place the groupworker in such a position. The worker may gradually abrogate this role but may also wish not to do so in order to achieve gains connected with modelling and ego-support. Gerontological groupwork is the main source of exemplification.

In contributing to the first issue of an important new journal it seems fitting to take up some issue of principle. I shall attempt to do so.

It is part of the challenge of professional development that we all find ourselves engrossed in some special concern – some elusive connection or some observation from practice – which we remain unable to clarify. For my part, though I have been much involved in groupwork development over the years, I remain embarrassingly confused about a very basic principle indeed. This concerns the concept of 'use of the group process' and its relation to the worker's role. I have earlier addressed this issue in ways which I found acceptable at the time (Heap 1968, 1979) but which I now find, at least in part, oversimplified and even dogmatic. I shall try again. The 'use of the group' and the 'use of self ' – how may they be reconciled?

The dilemma

It is a cardinal feature of groupwork that members' exchanges and relationships provide the major resource in achieving the aims of the group. It is a central principle and it is a cornerstone of method that the exchange of suggestion and experiences, the comparisons and abrasions of ideas and attitudes, the stimulus to experiment, to dare and to change which result from the mutual support and identification of members are all aspects of group behaviour which combine to provide the *raison d'être* of groupwork as a professional method. It is these phenomena, and not the insights or techniques of the worker, whose presence causes us to turn increasingly to the group as a vehicle for conveying relevant social and health services. The task of the worker is to facilitate, to stimulate and to mobilise the resources inherent in the group process.

This is all well described and documented in the professional literature. We have a well-accepted though diverse terminology referring to this. We are familiar with Vintner's (1974) term – *'the group as both context and means of treatment'*. Very early indeed, writers such as Wilson and Ryland (1945) and, later, Konopka (1960) were talking about 'use of the group' or 'use of the group process'. Whitaker and Lieberman (1965), Douglas (1979), Brown (1979) are among European writers who have further contributed to consolidating this principle.

As concept and as principle the primacy of the group process is, then, well-established. Putting it into practice, however, is less so. The occasional studies of groupworker functioning over the years have disclosed a curious disparity between our assertions of the primacy of group process as resource and the extent to which practising group workers in fact 'use the group process'. Saloshin (1954) early demonstrated that workers' use of group process *'fell far below the claims of the profession'*. Halleck (1963) showed that youth workers, far from using the group, imposed their own aims and evaluations on group members in concealed ways, thus manipulating the group and *'practising professional dishonesty'*. Parsloe (1971) conducted an empirical analysis of 'what social workers do in groups'. Only with a most generous and distorted interpretation of her categories of intervention would we be able to claim that use of group process figured at all in the material. My own supervision and consultation with colleagues also suggests similar conclusions, just as a critical appraisal of one's own practice reflects a continuing active use of oneself often in excess of that which would accord with the primacy of group process.

This is my dilemma. A strongly advocated principle is with frequency either abandoned or so modified in its application as to lose its claim to primacy.

Why does this occur? Explanations exist which continue to rest on the assumption that primacy of group process is desirable. The difficulty is in achieving it. For example, the worker may intend to work in this way but be encumbered by such long experience in casework that freeing oneself from the investment in the use of self which characterises the casework tradition remains too difficult. Or the worker may be anxious about the inherent power of the group or about members' perceptions of his or her competence, so that the worker both maintains control and demonstrates potency by being active in the face of real theoretical conviction. Or the group might be in a defensive mode and therefore manipulate the worker into inappropriately assuming responsibilities which negate the use of the group process.

Other explanations exist, however, which rest not on unintended deficiencies in applying the principle but on intended deviation from it where professional evaluation has indicated a need for greater emphasis on the worker's 'use of self' – either briefly and temporarily – as a more purposive feature of the dynamics of the group. One very important variable which underlies such evaluations is the varying interplay of group needs and resources at different stages of group functioning reflecting different emphases at different stages. Another important variable is the actual potential for autonomous behaviour present in different groups, a variable determined, of course, by their composition. I shall return to both of these questions.

Meanwhile, the dilemma remains. Is 'use of the group process' unconditionally and always the major resource and guiding principle in groupwork? If so, why do we deviate so frequently from it? Or have we expressed this principle in absolute and doctrinaire terms in order to convey its importance, while our own practice experiences indicate that it is by no means an inviolate principle and is to be tempered in accordance with other evaluations?

An approach to clarification

I suspect that this dilemma is partly semantically derived. Even in professionally sophisticated circles one still finds the worker being referred to as the 'group leader'. This practice is both historical and misleading. Groupwork's roots in the youth movement gave this term acceptance for many years, but with increased understanding of the power of the group process its inappropriateness as a general groupwork term became recognised. This gave rise to uneasy and ambiguous terms like the somewhat precious 'leading from behind' until finally the 'leader' concept was abandoned, in theory if not entirely in practice. It implied too authoritative and directive a role and bore many connotations difficult to reconcile with social work aims and principles. The less loaded 'worker' concept has gained acceptance but continues to need delineation, particularly in relation to how one 'works with' the group process while being oneself a secondary resource subsumed by the group process. If the 'worker' is not 'leader', what is he or she?

I have found the role concept of 'central person' to be useful here

The role of 'central person'

The concept of 'central person' is much less ambiguous and confining than that of leader. In a study of group formation and emotion, Redl (1942) found a variety of situations in which group formative processes had taken place around some person who had evoked common emotional responses in the members. On the basis of this shared feeling they *'developed group emotions towards each other'*, mutually identifying and thereby developing group cohesion. Redl called this individual the 'central person' and defined him or her as *'the one through emotional relationship to whom the group formative processes are evoked in the potential group members'.*

This concept is highly relevant to the social worker's role in groups. At times it will be a major feature of the relationship to the group, at others more recessive. This will vary in relation to the needs, setting, maturity and stage of development of the group.

Observations from practice suggest that two clusters of factors may place the worker in such a focal role. These are:

i. the professional situation and setting and
ii. the emotional needs and responses of the group members.

These factors are intimately related, but I shall now discuss them separately for the sake of clarity. I shall again refer to them respectively as 'situational factors' and 'emotional factors', as I have done in earlier attempts to clarify this issue.

Situational factors

The worker's role as central person is in large measure a product of the professional situation and setting. It is implicit in the worker's status and appointment by the agency that he or she is expected to possess knowledge and skills relevant to the group's needs. This involves a focus and, at least initially, some degree of dependence upon the worker, while the members explore the situation and discover its meaning for them. The worker and the agency have taken an initiative; the members reasonably look to him or her for help in clarifying the aims, the contract and perhaps the constraints on behaviour in the group. There is then an initial dependence arising in part from these expectations and from the feelings of uncertainty and usually of hope which the members also bring to the group. Failure of the worker to respond to this and to perceive this central role at this stage may well, as in the following example arouse the aggressive and resentful elements in the group's dependence.

EXAMPLE 1.

A group for mothers at risk was formed in a child guidance clinic as part of a program for prevention of child abuse and neglect. The group was built on the ideas of Walker and Irvine (1966), Breton (1979) and Wayne and Avery (1980). It was to be a supportive experience for isolated single mothers who were characterised by low self-esteem and by both social and economic poverty.

In earlier meetings, preparing the mothers for the group, the co-workers had been supportive and encouraging. In particular, they had been receptive and responsive to the potential members' anxiety and scepticism.

Both workers, however, had as their sole professional group experience, membership of confrontative therapy groups in their own training – where a demand for members' acceptance of responsibility for the group was a norm. Influenced as they were by this model, the workers provided neither introduction nor structure to the first meeting and adopted a passive and observing role. This disoriented the members and aroused frustration, anxiety and thus also anger. This painful situation was first relieved when one member left the room in tears saying that the silence frightened her and another member became able to demand of the workers that they accept some responsibility

> It is not easy for us to come here . . . you said that it would be nice . . . you are making fools of us . . . give us some help or there is no point in this.

We see here the group insisting that the workers recognise and accept the responsibilities of their role as central persons. It was entirely natural that this group should expect some sort of leadership from the workers who had brought them together. In not responding to this, the workers missed the opportunity of using the strengths implicit in the central person role at this early phase. In the formative phase, the worker may initially be the only person present who has previously met all members of the group and and has the contact with them all. In this sense alone he or she may provide both focus and security. The members are, further, aware of the worker's initiative in forming the group, of the worker's ready availability, and of the assurance during intake of the worker's involvement and periodic intervention in the later life of the group. The worker is a facilitator who may reasonably be expected to help them get started and later to be a point of reference in conflict, problem-solving and frustration. By his or her very existence and that of the agency the worker makes possible their activity as a group.

In the above example, the workers could have used this role in order to clarify the group's aims and help the members express and compare their expectations, to help the members locate common problems, thus increasing both interaction and identification with the group, and to demonstrate helpful and supportive attitudes, thereby modelling desirable norms, increasing motivation and reducing defences.

In addition to being the initiator, assembler and clarifier for the group, the worker is often focal to it for other situational reasons. He or she may be a source of particular knowledge or program skills relevant to the group's purpose, for example with young probationers learning rock-climbing in the group. Similarly a group of pensioners planning a protest against rent increases are perhaps initially somewhat dependent on the worker's special knowledge of the procedures and power structure of the municipal hierarchy as well as of use of media and contacts in the media. The worker's possession of the knowledge, understanding or skills needed by the group causes him or her to be its focus, at least until the members have acquired what they need and are equipped to meet their own needs adequately. Similarly, the worker may sometimes exercise considerable control over the facilities available to the group, or may in other ways be a valued and essential link with the surrounding agency or *milieu*. This is particularly the case in residential groupwork. While control of resources may of course also evoke hostility in some groups, it may often, used wisely, also have valuable treatment implications. The worker may use this situation as a useful means at the formative phase of providing focus for the group and as an initial stimulus to interaction.

Emotional factors

People offered groupwork service are in need of varying kinds and degrees of support and guidance, are all to some extent in conflict, and are experiencing some sort of disadvantage, impairment or inadequacy. In groups composed of clients with comparable problems and needs, the members may be helped to identify with and support each other and deal with these problems through their interactions. Some of this will occur spontaneously in successfully composed groups, but without the skilled guidance and intervention of the worker the group process may well develop in unhelpful directions.

In order to intervene in these processes and to guide them helpfully the worker uses certain interactional skills. Readers will have encountered diverse ways of designating these skills in the literature. A discussion of the nuances in these formulations lies outside the scope of the present paper, but one common feature is very germane indeed. Sanction for the excercise of skills by the worker is given not only by the agency but also of course by the group itself. The members usually seem to wish initially to place the worker either in some kind of 'leader' or 'resource person' role. This is often unclearly conceived, and may not be consistent with the role necessary for the exercise of helping skills such as the worker perceives them. Thus, in order to perform his professional function, the worker has to establish an appropriate relationship with the group members through which he can obtain their sanction. The worker is therefore active in clarifying the objectives of the group and in demonstrating understanding of the members' problems and feelings as well as attitudes of acceptance, respect, helpfulness and acknowledgement of members' resources and autonomy. Both the degree of the worker's own activity and the needs of the group members for support and resolution of conflict will then typically cause them to respond to the worker's understanding, attitudes and behaviour by focusing their interest upon him or her. The worker appears at that stage to be the source of help, support and possible insight into their difficulties, as well as the guide to behaviour in the group. This provides a common experience for the group members and the foundation of their relationship to the worker. Further, it places the latter in a position to aid the members in locating common needs, problems and interests as a first step towards developing the group itself into a viable instrument for support.

Redl (1942) speaks of *'the infectiousness of the unconflicted upon the conflicted personality'*. The worker's supportive attitudes, relative freedom from ambivalence, rational approach to problems, and ability to meet feelings are in a sense resources upon which the group members draw. In doing so they may identify with and perhaps invest feelings in him or her.

EXAMPLE 2.
A treatment group of teen-age drug abusers was held daily in a residential facility as a condition of a probation order. They were severely threatened by their own life-style and choices: they experienced heavy dependency both upon drugs and their network: they were both alienated from and diffusely angry with the 'straight' adult world. Their identification with each other was intense, so that group cohesion in their *milieu* in the community furthered their mutual self-devastation.

Members provoked the workers, testing them out with self-dramatising and colourful accounts of exploits and near fatal episodes. (Abusers seem commonly to enjoy success in manipulating workers into a *voyeur* position, so that the worker's therapeutic potential either dissolves in vicarious participation in the abusers' world or is made impotent by his anxious and protective response to the horror stories). The workers' unambivalent and unambiguous rejection of any positive facets of substance-misuse, their secure resistance to manipulation combined with their evident empathy and acceptance both changed and intensified members' relationships and use of the workers. There developed gradually an identification with certain of the workers' attitudes and with their ability to confront problems and conflicts and to express feelings. This was in marked contrast with the norms which were under development at the commencement of group life.

Clients in many groups experience certain needs which cannot be met solely by interaction with other members. They seem often to 'borrow' strengths and ways of behaving both in the group and outside it from the worker. This may be because of insecurity and identity problems, or of immaturity and lack of social experience, or because untenable norms and values have been integrated during the process of socialisation, or simply because they lack knowledge about the norms of the group or its cultural setting. The case illustrations given in this paper already imply that the worker has additional importance as a representative of certain values and forms of behaviour to which the members consciously or unconsciously aspire. Now the notion of purveying norms and values makes many of us uncomfortable. We hesitate to accept without further ado that such a role is consistent with social work principles of self-determination and non-judgementalism. Whatever view we take of this, it is an inescapable fact that many clients inevitably regard us as agents and symbols of the community. This leads to their focusing upon the worker the feelings they have about their situation and their aspirations, or resistances, to conformity. For example, a group of alcoholic clients may displace on to the worker the anger and resentment originally aroused by community disapproval. The underlying feelings of inadequacy and guilt may then be somewhat alleviated by the worker's understanding and acceptance. At the same time, the worker may help them towards a more realistic way of dealing with their feelings by questioning the reality of their attitude towards himself. (Such a response is in accord with Irvine's [1963] early clarification of the social work response to transference phenomena). The members of a refugee or immigrant group cannot meet all of their needs by interaction with each other. They are very preoccupied by the worker's attitudes and modes of behaviour because he or she is, among other roles, a representative of the host culture and as such the recipient and focus of many shared feelings on the part of the group.

Thus we see that the members' needs, the worker's function and the group setting often combine to create a situation where shared emotional responses to the worker are part of the group formative process. The worker thereby becomes a central person to the group and may thus have the functions described by Redl of providing an object of identification, an object of drives and an ego-support.

We will now look in more detail at the relevance of these ideas to group work in services for the elderly and aged. I have chosen to exemplify from this area of groupwork because of the urgency of developing methods in this field and because of my conviction that groupwork is the method of choice in much gerontological social work.

The worker as central person in gerontological groupwork

Groupwork in gerontological services is under rapid development, covering a spectrum from profoundly therapeutic work with the existential problems of frail and dying aged to the organisation of both self help groups and political action groups of active and resourceful elderly. Between these extremes are widely diverse interest oriented and discussion groups, reminiscence groups, carers' groups, groups working on present crises or unresolved grief, newcomers' groups in residential facilities, and many more.

In all of these, the guiding principle is use of the group process. The power generated by group bond facilitates support, problem-solving, increase in life quality and self-manifestation through collective activity. Relationships and exchange enrich us all, also when old... But the worker has taken the initiative to form the group. In gerontological service, groups are formed often in the face of resistance or apparent apathy, and the worker must often be very active in preparatory work. He or she is also representative of the welfare apparatus, usually also of a younger generation and therefore potentially is also a surrogate for the members' own adult children. For these reasons we usually see that elderly group members invest much attention in the worker, sharing feelings about him or her and in that way reinforcing their commonality. Again we see both situational and emotional factors underlying the worker's central role.

The danger exists that such a structure in the group may result in apparent confirmation and therefore reinforcement of the stereotype of old people as dependent and lacking in initiative. As recipients of social and health services, old people encounter many stereotypic and trivialising attitudes. They are, it is believed, passive, they withdraw, they cannot cope with expectations of autonomy. Life's *Stürm und Drang* is behind them, as are passion and protest. Intense affects and their connections with family life, sexuality and social and political involvement belong to the past. This combination of trivialisation and de-individualisation remains a prevailing theme in attitudes to the elderly and is a major threat to the self-esteem, personal autonomy and integrity of old people. Groupwork as a method is highly suited to counteract these tendencies because of its emphasis on recognition of members' values and priorities, on confidence in members' resources and skills, on the assumption of members' activity and responsibility for the group and on self-reinforcement through the give and take of response and acknowledgement in the group. The resources inherent in the group process are, however, neutralised unless the groupworker is able to handle the relationship with members in appropriate ways – particularly where the use of the focal role is concerned.

The worker is again placed in the role of central person and as such is subject to members' curiosity and testing, dependence and ambivalence. He or she becomes, in Redl's terms, *'an object of drives, an object of identification and an ego-support'*. Members perceive the worker as a source of help in finding ways to use and behave in the group. But a markedly ambivalent attitude is often present with regard to responsibility for the group. At one level is the wish for recognition and autonomy. At another level is both expectation of and a partial wish for freedom from the demands inherent in self-direction. We frequently meet self-fulfilling prophecies here, since many such groups invite and manipulate the worker into the position of directive leader. This is partly an expression of the real energy-loss which many old people necessarily experience, partly of learned helplessness and partly of an anxious and ambivalent testing of the worker who is offered power in the hope that he or she will not accept it.

In the light of such emotional investment in the worker we may readily see how important it is that he or she consistently demonstrates realistic confidence in members' abilities and respect for their priorities and solutions.

Further, it is vital that the worker – who is a model – legitimises and normalises the expression of feelings, particularly in regard to the inescapable losses and crises of old age. This latter point is important, because one of our means of simplifying services for the aged is to repress them by denying, minimising or ignoring their often over controlled emotional reactions and their often desperate silent battle with unresolved crisis and loss. The elderly members' ego-resources in the sense of ability to mobilise rational thought, appropriate feelings and ability to confront problems and decisions is strengthened or weakened in relation to the way in which the worker uses the role of central person (see Heap, 1985).

Conclusion: Change in the role of central person.

Much of the foregoing has implied that the worker's role as central person may be particularly relevant to the early stages of the worker/group relationship, but that both the group's changing needs and the worker's conscious use of self often lead, perhaps ideally, to a diminution of its importance in the group process. I wish, finally, to elaborate this observation a little further.

Time and shared experiences bring about developments in group life which involve change in the group's structure, culture and pattern of communication. A feature of such group development is that the members are likely to adopt other, more mature, cohesive devices instead of identification with or dependence upon the worker as central person. Indeed, I have earlier suggested that it is normally appropriate for the worker to help the group to give him or her up as central person by consciously and gradually abrogating this role, (Heap 1968, 1979). In doing this the worker will try to keep in step with the group's increasing capacity, through their relationships with each other, for mature and purposive use of the group situation. The need to do this is indicated by observations from practice, but is also implicit in certain theoretical formulations.

Well regarded method models which build on group development theory commonly advocate change from a high level of use of self at early stages to a maximisation of use of the group process. For example, Sarri and Galinsky (1975) move from their early injunction to *'institute, support and stimulate group norms in line with (the worker's) objectives'* to a later rejection of *'major responsibilities for aiding the group in coping with internal or external pressure to change.'*

The worker enables the group gradually to give him or her up as a focus for cohesion at a stage in their development where interpersonal relationships between the members provide alternative support and control, and where the group's own interaction has in other ways developed into a viable means of problem-solving or of attaining other objectives of the group.

This was somewhat differently stated by Wilson and Ryland (1945) who demonstrated graphically that the worker's direct involvement in leadership (control, decision-taking, problem-solving) decreases in inverse ratio to the 'social health' of the group members. These factors are seen to vary not only from group to group but also within a given group over a period of time.

It is here, however, that I wish to make the most important amendment to my earlier formulations on this theme. I now believe that the notion of abrogating the role of the central person is not a generally applicable strategy but is to be understood in a partial and differentiated way. It is now my contention that the *situational* and the *emotional* components of the role are to be handled differently.

Situationally determined features of the role should indeed gradually become more recessive as members become familiar with and secure in the operations of the group. A highest possible level of self-direction in the group's instrumental activity should be aimed at in all group work. *Emotionally* determined features, however, may well have quite a different place in the ongoing life of the group. Certainly, some of these features are also of transient importance to members, such as use of the worker as a model of group behaviour and as a shield against early insecurity and disorientation. Testing out of the worker may also cease to be necessary with time. But other emotional components of the central person role may have continuing importance *throughout the life of the group* and they continue to represent therapeutic or growth potential. It is these aspects of the workers' self which presents difficulty in achieving their balance with use of the group.

These continuing aspects of the central person role concern the worker as a model of values, as a model of a rational problem-solver and as a symbolic representative of absent entities or persons which are important features of members' life situations. As surrogate for parents, authority, or whatever, the worker remains focal to the group and in his or her performance in this symbolic role provides an object which members may test out and in relation to which they may experiment with new attitudes and perceptions.

This latter point may well be exemplified by co-leadership by men and women workers. As I have pointed out elsewhere (Heap, 1985), man/woman co-leadership carries with it considerable potential for the modelling of a relationship. This is of continuing value in any group, whether of adults, youth or children, whose presenting problems wholly or in part concern family or sexual relationships. Groupwork with incest survivors is a case in point. An earlier paper by Gottlieb and Dean (1978) draws attention to this, but it is strongly highlighted in Deighton and McPeek (1985) and in a paper now in press by Furniss, Bingley-Miller and van Elburg (1987). Furniss *et al.* concerns long term groupwork with late puberty/early adult incest survivors, the group being led jointly by a woman social worker and male psychotherapist. Both workers' surrogate roles and their relationships to each other were subject to continuing curiosity, challenge and attitudinal experimentation throughout the life of the group. Their ability to avoid confirmation of the members' stereotype expectations, to avoid manipulation, provocation and seduction and to demonstrate a respectful, caring, non-sexual, egalitarian man/woman relationship may well have been one of the most valuable therapeutic factors in the entire project. The group's members brought with them very different models indeed. The question of what the workers *were*, how they would behave and respond, kept them in a central position throughout the life of the group though not to the detriment of facilitating members' relationships with and use of each other. They remained objects of identification and supporters of ego-striving, central persons, in Redl's terminology. I believe that analogous situations are quite common and that they represent a both defensible and purposive explanation of workers' continuing 'use-of-self ', even if this at times competes with or indeed reduces for a time emphasis on the use of the group.

We will no doubt continue to clarify the worker's role in both *using* the group and *being* in the group, and I hope that these reflections may be a contribution to such clarification.

References

Breton, Margot (1979) 'Nurturing abused and abusive mothers – the Hairdressing Group', *Social Work with Groups*, Vol. 2, No. 2, pp.161-164.

Brown, Allan (1979) *Groupwork*. London: Heinemann.

Deighton, Joan and McPeek, Phil (1985) 'Group treatment': adult victims of child sexual abuse', *Social Casework*, Sept. 1985, pp.403-410.

Douglas, Tom (1976) *Groupwork Practice*. London: Tavistock Press.

Furniss, Tilman, Bindley-Miller, Liza and van Elburg, Annemarie (1987) 'Goal-oriented group treatment for sexually abused adolescent girls", *British Journal of Psychiatry*, (in press).

Gottlieb, Bruce and Dean, Janet (1981) 'The co-therapy relationship in group treatment of sexually mistreated adolescent girls', in Mrazek, P.B. and Kempe, C.H. (eds.) *Sexually Abused Children and their Families*. Oxford: Pergamon.

Halleck, Sydney (1963) 'The impact of professional dishonesty on the behaviour of disturbed adolescents', *Social Work*, Vol. 8, No. 2, pp.48-56.

Heap, Ken (1968) 'The social group worker as central person', *Social Work*, Vol. 26, No. 1.

Heap, Ken (1979) *Process and Action in Work with Groups – The Preconditions for Treatment and Growth*. London: Pergamon.

Heap, Ken (1985) *The Practice of Social Work with Groups – A Systematic Approach*. London: Geo. Allen and Unwin (now Hyman Unwin).

Irvine, Elisabeth E. (1963) 'Transference and reality in the casework relationship' in *Relationship in Casework*. London: Association of Psychiatric Social Workers.

Konopa, Gisela (1960) 'Social group work: A social work method', *Social Work*, Oct.

Parsloe, Phyllida (1969) 'What social workers say in groups of clients', *British Journal of Social Work*, Vol. 10, No. 7.

Redl, Fritz (1942) 'Group emotion and leadership', *Psychiatry*, Vol. 5, No. 4. Also in Hare, Borgotta and Bales (eds.) (1955) *Small Groups: Studies in Social Integration.* New York: Knopf, pp.71-87.

Saloshin, H. Etta (1954) *Development of an Instrument for the Analysis of the Social Group Work Method in Therapeutic Settings*, PhD Thesis. Minneapolis: University of Minnesota. (Available as microfilm 8486 Mic. A 54-2159, University Microfilms, Michigan.)

Saloshin, H. Etta (1962) 'Five capital C's: Conceptualisation through classification-confusing, confining or clarifying?', in *Educational Developments in Social Group Work.* New York: Council on Social Work Education, pp.37-52.

Sarri, Rosemary and Galinsky, Maeda (1975), 'A conceptual framework for group development', in Glasser, P., Sarri, R. and Vinter, R. (eds.), *Individual Change through Small Groups.* New York: Free Press, pp.71-80.

Vinter, Robert D. (1974) 'The essential components of social group work practice', in Vinter, R.D., Sarri, R.C. and Glasser, P. (eds.) *Individual Change through Small Groups.* New York: Free Press, s.9-33.

Walker, Lorna and Irvine, Elisabeth E. (1966) *Groupwork with the Inarticulate – the Bradford F.S.U. Mothers' Group.* FSU Paper No. 1.

Wayne, Julianne L. and Avery, Nancy C. (1980) *'Child Abuse: Prevention and Treatment Through Social Group Work.* Boston: Charles River Books.

Whitaker, Dorothy S. and Lieberman, Morton A. (1965) *Psycotherapy Through the Group Process.* London: Tavistock Press.

Wilson, Gertrude, and Ryland, Gladys (1949) *Social Group Work Practice.* Cambridge, Mass.: Houghton Miffin Co., Chap. III, pp.60-101.

GROUPWORK (1988) 1, 30–40

RACE AND GROUPWORK: SOME EXPERIENCES IN PRACTICE AND TRAINING

ROS MUSTON and JEREMY WEINSTEIN

The paper starts from our concern that many groupworkers adopt a 'colour blind' approach in their work. This ignores the needs and experiences of the various black communities in Britain, and denies the fact that we live in a racist society which impacts upon the institutions within which we work and the daily lives of us all, white or black, professionals or clients.

Groupwork needs to find ways of acknowledging and then confronting racism, otherwise we are in danger of attracting neither black practitioners nor clients, leading to a position where groupwork is marginalised, professionally and politically, within social work as a whole.

To begin the process we draw on the experiences of specially convened workshops, held at the National Institute for Social Work (NISW) as part of the groupwork 'network', to help us examine ways of dealing with race and racism in groups and encouraging black participation in groups. Training issues are also analysed and suggestions made, including the use of trigger role-play scenes, to help exploration of the personal and professional dimensions.

Introduction

A story is told of a number of white groupworkers meeting in a training session. One describes a black person in his therapy group who is difficult to understand but seems to be talking incessantly of '*babbling on*'. One of the more aware members suddenly realises that the phrase intended is 'Babylon' and then has to explain to the still uncomprehending colleagues the importance of that word and concept to many Afro-Caribbeans.

At another gathering, where people are meeting together specifically to look at 'race and groupwork', one individual complains of all the emphasis '*on black people and white people, why can't we just talk about people?*'

These two stories are not just picked at random. They represent a certain naivety within groupwork which means that whilst in social services departments and training courses, issues about race and equal opportunities are continually being raised, the subject does not even seem to be on the groupwork agenda. This lack of a perspective should be a concern to us on at least two counts.

Firstly, many of us were originally drawn to groupwork because we saw it as a radical element within social work, raising issues and demands and awkward questions about how we perceived 'clients' and 'service delivery'. In the eighties, within a profession in danger of closing in on itself under the pressures of cuts and child care scandals, that challenging and critical role is coming from black colleagues, often working in sections once seen as traditional and conservative, such as adoption and fostering. Among groupworkers the prevailing mood is cautious and confused. Many practitioners espouse a professionalism which they see as synonymous with political neutrality: when focussed on race this means that groupwork should be 'colour blind'.

Secondly, if groupwork is not attracting black practitioners or offering an effective, culturally sensitive service to clients from the various minority ethnic groups, then it is in danger of becoming quite marginalised, both professionally and politically.

Many groupworkers are inevitably caught up in the racial dimension of their work and are trying to develop a practice that is, at the very least, transcultural and, at its most ambitious, actually anti-racist. It is easy, however, to get discouraged and come to doubt either the validity or effectiveness of that work. There is, also, a lack of writing which can be drawn on to help develop an analysis. One source is *Ethnicity in Social Groupwork Practice* (Davis, 1984), a special issue of the American journal, *Social Work With Groups*, which although relatively inaccessible in the UK (except in some libraries) is nonetheless welcome. There is a short but useful chapter about an Asian mothers' self-help group (Sheik, in Ahmed *et al.*, 1986), and some related material from David Thomas' study of community work, *White Bolts, Black Locks* (1986), which we discuss below.

In an attempt to frame the beginnings of an analysis and to provide a forum for practitioners and trainers concerned about 'race and groupwork', there have been a series of workshops based on the NISW groupwork 'network'. This began with some very tentative ideas put forward in September 1986 followed by a session in February 1987, both of which were part of the regular two day NISW network meetings. In May and July 1987, there were follow up days inviting people quite specifically to look at the issues of 'race and groupwork'.

This paper draws on the experience of those workshops to examine two separate but related issues. The first concerns itself with ways of dealing with race and racism in groups and encouraging black participation in groups. The second issue, also based on the lessons of the NISW sessions, is that of training, and the problems involved when groupworkers meet together to tackle the issues of race and groupwork.

Black participation in groups

Thomas (*op. cit.*) provides us with a starting point in his discussion of the various factors that inhibit or stop black people from becoming involved in community organisations. Thomas defines 'black people' to include primarily Afro-Caribbean and Asian people, a definition adopted in this paper, although our analysis applies also to other 'non-white' minority ethnic groups.

RACIAL HOSTILITY AND HARASSMENT

With good reason black people in Britain expect, at best, a racist response from white society and agencies and, at worst, anticipate a degree of harassment and violence from individual white people. Workers from the statutory services need, therefore, to be aware of how much caution black people might show before readily involving themselves in outside and unknown groups. The leaders have the responsibility '*to signal that they offer a different experience*'. (Thomas, *op. cit.*, p.143)

This means:–

i. advertising and other material must be translated into the relevant languages;
ii. meetings are not held at inappropriate times or unwelcoming venues;
iii. that just as group rules ban violence, so they must also include a bar on racist language;
iv. that there is an understanding of the various cultural aspects of black peoples' lives. This could, for example, include expectations within some Asian communities about gender roles which, in turn, could preclude mixed groups.

THE IMPORTANCE OF CULTURE

This is an issue important in itself but it cannot be seen as separate from that of racism. As Thomas (*op. cit.*, p. 144) puts it:

> If people feel threatened in society, and if they feel that important cultural values are at risk, then the amount of personal risk they are prepared to take will be minimal. Involvement in community groups with white people assumes a confidence about one's self, values and culture, as well as an openness to change and challenge. In a hostile society, such confidence and openness are at a premium, not least because one way of surviving such an environment is to hold on to traditional values and ways of doing things.

Another aspect of this issue is that, for all the differences around class or gender, there is still, at core, a shared culture and set of expectations, an anglo-conformity, shared by the white majority of group members. An important part of any group is not the formal agenda but the relaxed periods of the coffee breaks or when people wander off at the end. The feel of this, the banter, etc., '*often define . . . togetherness and convey to the newcomer that there is a history of which they have no part.'* (Thomas, *op. cit.*, p. 156).

A CASE EXAMPLE; A GROUP FOR THE BLACK ELDERLY

One response to these dilemmas is to aim for all-black groups. This also has its problems as was illustrated by a black student who established a black pensioners' group while on placement in a social work team (Eytle 1985). Although this was a team based on an estate and committed to developing a patch based service, she faced a number of challenges from the social workers who could see no need for such a group. They raised three basic points:

i. *Social services did not believe there was any significant number of black pensioners on the estate who could be recruited to such a group.* The student had to approach a doctor who took less than five minutes to identify 15 elderly black pensioners. Few of these were familiar with the workings of the local council or aware of their rights and so did not present themselves to the social services. They thus remained isolated and officially invisible.

ii. *Social services did not believe the black elderly people would need a group.* It was assumed that they would be cared for by the extended family or by various minority ethnic organisations. The student had to point out that these networks were very strained, where they existed at all, weakened by council housing policies, the pressures of unemployment and other factors.

iii. *Social services did not see the need for a specifically black group.* There were already several existing pensioners' clubs on the estate that they should join. The student argued that black pensioners faced particular problems:

> Integration and assimilation are frequently seen as one of the ways to overcome racism, but they often operate as a form of racism. When black people have an equal status and power relationship with the white population then integration and assimilation may be desirable. (Eytle, 1985).

This is a powerful picture of one person's efforts and a strong argument for same race groups. Whether or not a group should be a single race or mixed is, however, a very complex and controversial area and we need to suggest some pointers towards clarifying the various choices.

SINGLE OR MIXED RACE GROUPS?

In the example described above the worker was clear. She sought to provide a service for a group, the black elderly, whose needs had been ignored and who had a range of experiences which were best shared with those of similar background. Another example, which was brought to the NISW workshop, was one where workers were trying to attract Bangladeshi mothers to a family unit. Here again the shared experiences, culture and language demanded a single race group. Another group known to us was one for the families of children suffering from sickle cell where the members were, given the nature of the illness, all Afro-Caribbean.

There are other situations where individuals are already involved in some service or agency but need to meet in single race groups to make space for their own particular perspective, to oppose racism or to organise for change within the agency. Examples from our experience include a group for black children in care; one for users of a mental health day centre; and a community based group for the parents of children with special needs. In this last example black parents had, one by one, joined the group only to be frozen out. They were then brought together as a separate group to get to know each other and gain collective strength, before rejoining the mainstream group.

There are, however, many other examples where it seems less easy to recognise a specific racial or cultural factor, e.g. groups for sexually abused girls or the bereaved. One NISW workshop member had found a model, originally intended for psychotherapy in the United States, which can help groupworkers identify the race dimension in certain areas of work and so be clearer when mixed or single race groups are appropriate. Arthur Jones (1985) uses an interactive model which consists of four classes of variables which he argues influence individual black clients. These are:

i. reactions to racial oppression;
ii. influence of the majority culture;
iii influence of the traditional Afro-American culture;
iv. individual and family experiences and endowments.

Jones uses a diagram (Figure 1) to show how each class has its own separate influence while also overlapping with the others.

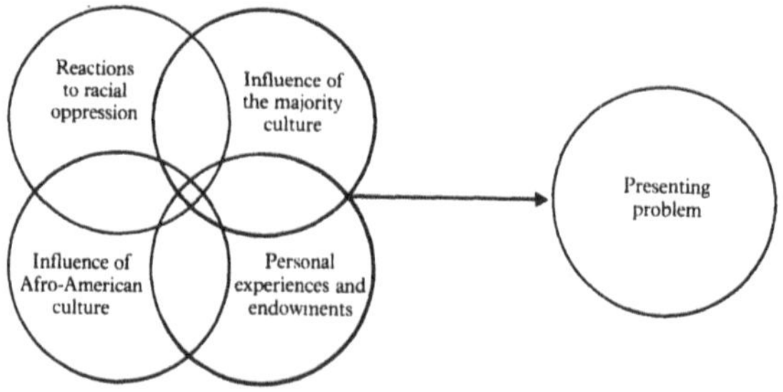

Figure 1. The interaction of the four sets of factors in the model.

He then goes on to illustrate how the variables differ from individual to individual (Figure 2) but will also shift, as in our context, according to the nature or task of the group. For example, on an estate in the inner-city, if members of a womens' group are discussing police treatment of youths the factors concerning 'reactions to racial oppression' and 'influence of Afro-Caribbean culture' would be paramount, whereas a session on the lack of nursery places will be just as keenly felt but with an emphasis on 'influence of the majority culture'.

Some Afro-Caribbean workshop members described the influence of the historical perspective (an aspect of variables i, ii and iv). They argued strongly that many black women in particular are taught culturally that it is safer not to show emotions to whites for fear of being misunderstood, and to present an (often smiling) mask to whites, reserving the true expression of feelings for their home ground. This would seem to be an indicator for race specific groups.

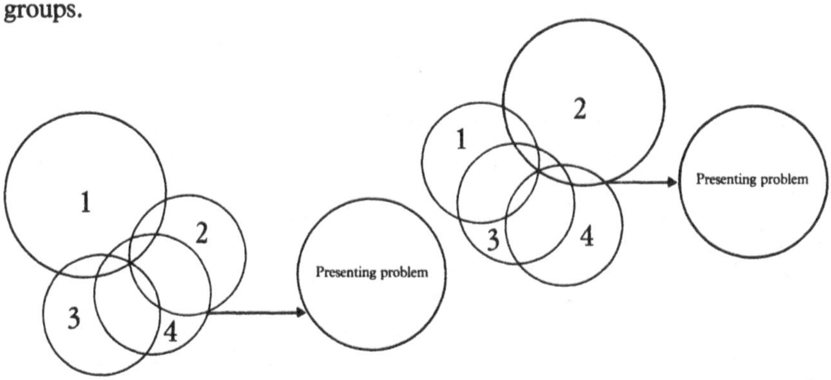

Figure 2. Relative influence of different factors in two patients.

WORKING IN MIXED RACE GROUPS

As has been seen, same race groups have advantages in many circumstances and only experience (and our mistakes) can help build the confidence to know when and how to set up such groups. There will, however, also be times when we *do* work within mixed groups and then leaders have a number of strategies to consider:–

When choosing leaders

i. Co-leaders should be black and white and should share fully, and be seen to be sharing, responsibility for the group.

ii It may be more important for a co-leader to have relevant life experiences and attitudes than a social work qualification.

iii If there is only one, white, leader then s/he should have access to a black consultant who is tuned into the possible tensions.

When setting up a group

i There should be a significant core of black members to make it less easy for them to be isolated, silenced or scapegoated.

ii. If there is no black input from within the agency then some indication of the range of black perspectives and attitudes could be included by involving black people from the community.

iii All practice should be reconsidered to evaluate its level of eurocentricity, e.g. the tendency to select group members according to age structure.

Many black communities, for example, do not share the notion of adolescence or old age as a discrete developmental stage. We are told that the Vietnamese view the family as the most significant grouping, bringing similar pressure to that of a European adolescent peer group.

iv Discuss individually with each black member how s/he views the subject of race being raised.

When conducting the group

i. The onus is on the leader to acknowledge the racial mix and the need to point out possible overt/covert racism, varying experiences of reality and so on.

ii. White members must not be allowed to deny the importance of race.

iii. Leaders should do all this very openly and in the early stages of the group.

iv. Leaders need to be aware that because of racism black members can bring with them considerable distrust of the white worker(s), other white group members and the sponsoring agency.

v. Both black and white group members might have stereotyped and unreal expectations of a black group leader.

vi. Looking at race and racism is a difficult and painful area, and when considered in depth the feelings engendered are normally very sad. The group leaders need to be very careful in making space for that work and introducing it when the group is performing well.

vii. The leaders should have clear goals and boundaries but, in recognition of the anger and distress that can be aroused by the subject, they should be prepared to respond and confront those moods rather than just staying with the pre-planned programme.

Training issues

Much of what we have said so far arises from the specific circumstances of three separate training days based on the NISW groupwork network, a London based meeting of practitioners and teachers scattered amongst many different agencies. Over the three sessions 50 people attended, 14 to more than one session, a core of eight attending all three. Some work places sent a couple of workers to a session, or different people to a series of sessions, others were colleagues, friends even, because of other networks within the claustrophobic world of social work. On the whole, however, members did not know each other, or each others' practice. This has a different feel to 'in-house' training within an agency where there can be a degree of continuity, a shared set of strategies around equal opportunity policies, and accountability for what is learned and then put into practice. We feel it important, nonetheless, to describe some of the training issues that came up and which may help others, whatever their circumstances, to set up similar training exercises. These issues are set out separately below but, as should be clear, the points are interrelated and not listed in any order of importance.

SHARED COMMITTMENT IF NOT SHARED VIEWS

In any discussion about race and groupwork, there must clearly be room for disagreement whether about techniques or more fundamental issues about how and when to confront racism. Yet too wide a range of attitudes seems to be immobilising. At the February meeting one participant made it clear that he was present because it was part of the two day NISW 'network' meeting, not because he had any specific interest in race. It was at the same session that a member made the comment already referred to, namely that she was confused about why we were referring to specifically black or white responses in groups, *'why can't we just talk about people?'*. We are not sure these individuals could have gained very much from the day and certainly the comments left other members feeling very angry. What members need to have, if not shared views, is at least a shared commitment to seeing race as important in groupwork, and a wish to work on the issue.

A SIGNIFICANT CORE OF BLACK PARTICIPANTS

Only at one session, the middle one in May, did we have a significant core of black members. At our first session this meant that, especially in the large and rather unstructured group, the few black people present tended to be silenced or turned into 'representatives' of the black experience as a whole, explaining and elaborating the impact of race to white members, without room to speak to their own issues and emotions. In May there seemed to be a far more equal and honest sharing of views which we suspect was to do with the racial balance, a point made in the earlier part of this paper when we discussed the racial mix in client based groups. It may help to quote some members' responses:

> (The session was) a wonderful opening up and beginning to share half-expressed sadness, guilt, expectation and so on.
>
> For the first time I saw clearly what 'sharing the other's reality' really involved, and how extremely important this is. Many sessions of discussion at a cognitive rather than feeling level had not had the impact that this one produced.
>
> We've never previously had the opportunity to look at these issues. I've never before seen white people really working on the issue of black/white relations and finding it so difficult.

A STRUCTURE THAT ACKNOWLEDGED THE IMPACT OF FEELINGS BUT ROOTED IT IN PRACTICE

Any teaching around race and groupwork must be more than a listing of tips and techniques: race and racism is a political issue and a deeply charged one emotionally. The structure of any study day needs to acknowledge this while finding ways of relating the strength of feeling back to groupwork practice. Unless we do this we can echo the most uniformly criticised aspects of racism awareness training, the moralising and guilt trips where participants can learn to use the 'right' words but are never then tested out as to what they actually do.

It is also very important not to have groups larger than 10 or 12 members, otherwise there are opportunities for attack and polarisation of attitudes with little space for the silences which enable the thinking through and the sharing of deep feelings so important to this subject.

In the February session we started with an exercise which asked people to think about two incidents – the first time they personally encountered racism and the first time they encountered it within a group setting. They then shared the memories with a partner. This was an attempt to link the personal with the professional and worked well, unfortunately the impetus was then lost in the session that followed, an unstructured, open ended experience in the large group.

In subsequent sessions, in May and July, we shifted gear and had a very definite programme. The initial exercises were short and focussed with the bulk of the day then given over to self-selected small groups and a plenary session which could be used to share ideas from those groups but which also respected the right of people not to feedback. In May, role plays (see appendix) were distributed with the promise of time to explore what came out of the exercise. The role plays were very effective both in touching the raw nerves of how race and racism emerges in groupwork settings (including teams), and in taking people immediately but safely into the feelings. In July, members chose their own programme, which was to group around set themes, one to do with developing a different model of anti-racist training, one focussing on practice issues and the third, with no fixed agenda but discovering that it was all white, decided to consider what it is that stops individuals from relating easily to black colleagues and/or clients.

Conclusions

In conclusion we must acknowledge how limited and fragmented is our knowledge. The NISW network meetings did involve a number of black practitioners and we have drawn on their, and others, experiences. Nonetheless we, the authors of this article and the initiators of the NISW workshops, are white: for all our social work empathy, this still means an inevitable limitation to our full understanding of the issues of race. Certainly we are cushioned from the impact of racism. The starting point for our interest, and from which the workshops emanated, was that we had many questions but no satisfactory answers. After the NISW sessions we still would hesitate to give more than tentative answers; our only certainty is that the subject arouses strong feelings, and much confusion and pain. When grappled with, however, in an atmosphere of mutual acceptance and trust, the rewards in terms of both knowledge gained and feelings shared are immense.

But we must also return to the theme of our introduction. Something else we have discovered is that any examination of 'race' and 'groupwork' is part of a process which helps groupwork reclaim its radical traditions and address the questions central to social work as a whole. Some hint of this lies in the comments of the contributors to the special issue of *Social Work with Groups* (Vol. 7, No. 3, 1984) as they think through the impact of theory. Davis (1984) takes a wide focus because:

> . . . blacks, more so than whites, perceive a great deal of what happens to them as being outside of their personal control and a function of environmental forces (p.106).

Brown (1984) reinforces the point, arguing that the emphasis on the individual (remedial model) needs to give way to the reciprocal approach with the group being seen as a way of achieving mutual aid: *'the groupworker assumes a mediating, enabling role as he/she attempts to address systematic stress'* (p.115).

In the NISW workshops and in the teaching at our colleges it is often black students whose sharp and honest analysis reveals what careful phrases like 'environmental forces' and 'systematic stress' actually mean. In dealing with race in groups we are, of course, confronting racism in society, and given the opportunity to respond as anti-racists. The SWG editorial (Davis, 1984) talks rather breathlessly about our profession's *'societal mission'* as regards race. It seems the impact is the other way round and that groupwork is still coming to terms, all too slowly, with the implications.

References

Ahmed, S. *et al.* (1984) *Social Work with Black Children and their Families.* London: Batsford.

Brown, J.A. (1984) 'Groupwork with low income black youths' in Davis, L.E. (ed.) *Ethnicity in Social Groupwork Practice, Social Work with Groups,* Special Issue, 7(3).

Davis, L.E. (ed). (1984) *Ethnicity in Social Groupwork Practice, Social Work with Groups,* Special Issue, 7(3).

Eytle, J. (1985) 'Setting up a Black Pensioners Group' (unpublished).

Jones, A. (1985) 'Psychological functioning in black Americans: A conceptual guide for use in psychotherapy' *Psychotherapy*, Vol. 22.

Thomas, D. (1986) *White Bolts, Black Locks. Participation in the Inner City.* London: Allen & Unwin.

Appendix

Role plays for race and groupwork training

Two white social workers are planning to set up an estate based group for single parents. The area has many young Afro-Caribbean women/mothers and the workers assume the group will reflect that racial mix.

The first home visit to a potential member is going well, she is white and interested in trying the group out. Then she suddenly says: *'there won't be any blacks will there? I can't stand the blacks . . .'*

A new black worker has joined a patch team of a social services department. All her colleagues are white. S/he is keen to get a group going and knows from a discussion with a black health visitor that there is an increasing and isolated population of black elderly in the area.

Today is the team meeting and the worker raises the idea of such a group. The other team members argue that, in turn, there isn't a significant number of black elderly in the patch, that any way, they would be supported by their extended family networks and, even if they weren't, what's wrong with the already existing pensioners' groups?

This is a first meeting of a group for parents of children with special needs. All the parents have turned up as couples, apart from a Bengali man who is thought not to be the main carer of the child but states that he doesn't want his wife coming out in the evening to a group with other men.

This is a childrens' home and the newest member of staff is black, s/he is unqualified and from a nursing background.

At a staff meeting this worker complains that the children are calling him/her a 'black bastard', that s/he wouldn't put up with that sort of racist shit in the outside world and s/he has no intention of putting up with it here! The other workers suggest that the kids are testing out the new worker, the words are just expressions and not meant as racial taunts, the worker should be more understanding of how disturbed the kids are.

Both sides turn to the officer-in-charge to sort it out.

This is a group for the parents of youngsters with learning difficulties. It is an all-white group in a racially mixed area.

The white worker wants to prepare the group for a new member who has been referred and is black. In the past black members have never stayed more than a few sessions before dropping out, the worker feels that this is because the existing members have not been prepared to accept or welcome black members. This time the worker is determined that it will be different!

A black social worker is running a group for black foster parents. In this session one of the parents, who is generally well liked and respected, complains of a white social worker who she sees as discounting her views about a black child's needs and is racist. The black groupworker is challenged as to her/his views.

A black worker and a white worker are co-leading a racially mixed group. An incident has occurred which has brought to a head the black worker's feelings that s/he is being put into a secondary role within the group. The white worker denies this and they take it to their consultant.

In the role play the consultant should be played first as white, then as black.

This is a group for young unsupported mothers. It is mixed white and Afro-Caribbean and is co-led by a white and black worker.

In the session one of the white women refers to the corner 'Paki shop' which the black worker immediately challenges as racist. The white worker considers it as just a harmless comment and thinks her colleague has gone well over the top.

GROUPWORK (1988) 1, 41–47

A GROUP FOR WHITE WOMEN WITH BLACK CHILDREN

CLARE RHULE

This group was set up by two workers, a white woman and a black woman, to look at issues of racism and anti-racist parenting. The group, which ran for 18 months, provided a forum for women to share their experiences of having a relationship with a black man and bringing up a black child in a white ethnocentric society. Using various groupwork methods, the workers attempted to raise group members' awareness of both personal and institutional racism and how they affect both black and white people.

The initial idea of a group for white women with black children came from Marcia Marriott, a youth worker. She wished to do some work on racism with young white women, but needed a point of entry. She realised that a section of young white women who might have a vested interest would be those who have black children. Marcia herself is a white woman with a black child.

She felt it important to have a black woman co-worker and so contacted me, Clare Rhule. I have been in youth and community work, part and full-time, for several years. For the past four I have been working for the South London Family Service Unit and I work with women who have children under five on an estate in North Brixton.

I was interested in Marcia's idea because I wanted a change from running 'drop-in' type groups and welcomed something more structured and challenging. I had no particular desire to work on a group aimed exclusively at white women but the reasons for doing so seemed worthwhile.

Little work is done with children who have both black and white parents or with parents who have children from a black/white relationship. Given the nature of a white ethnocentric society it is hardly surprising that these children can suffer problems of identity. This is especially so if the child/ren are brought up by a sole white parent and the people they have most contact with are white. Their attitudes and behaviour will deeply affect and influence the development of the child.

Group aims

i. To work with a group of young white women under 25 (the youth work age limit) with black children on issues of racism, in order that they should have a greater understanding of the way racism operates and discover ways of challenging it.
ii. To look at ways of anti-racist parenting and encourage a black identity in their children.
iii. To help group members build a support group.
iv. To provide space for their children to meet with other children from similar backgrounds and provide appropriate anti-racist child care.
v. To enable the women to build up their confidence and self esteem by participating in a group and various group activities.

Why have a group particularly for white women when racism affects both black and white people? We felt a same colour group would be a far more effective way to learn about racism because the effects of racism on black and white people are so different.

We did not choose to use any particular models or approaches but decided on a combination of methods drawn from our past experiences. We thought it best to vary the sessions by using games, discussion, outside speakers, films, cultural trips, *etc.*, as far as our limited budgets would allow. Luckily, transport was not a problem as both of us had access to minibuses.

We decided upon active leadership, sometimes directive, at times non-directive depending on the task in hand, because of our assumptions that the group members would probably have a simplified understanding of racism. To this end we tried to create a reasonably de-jargonised definition of racism, not an easy task, and finally decided on: 'the oppression black people suffer by white people, who hold beliefs and opinions that black people are an inferior race, and, from a position of power, have created and maintained a society which discriminates against black people in all aspects of their lives.' Explanations would follow!

Given the nature of the group it was important that there was no hierarchy between Marcia and myself. We needed to ensure a shared leadership practice, not allowing Marcia to be more active or to assume a more prominent role, thus recreating what is happening in society – the white person being in a more dominant, powerful position. It was also important for me not to take on a more dominant leadership role as there was a danger of me being seen as the expert on all black people everywhere. Neither did I want to take on too much responsibility for something that was not my problem. It was vital that we co-operate closely, as it was inevitable that racism would manifest itself in group sessions. In fact we found this occurred several times during the group's life.

As we were unsure how long it would take to achieve our aims we decided to have an ongoing group that was continually assessed and evaluated. To help with this and issues around group dynamics, co-working and programming we needed to find a supervisor or consultant. Marcia and myself were supervised individually in our own employment agencies, both by white women. We felt it necessary to be supervised together on this group by a black woman, preferably one who had had experience of running a similar group or one whose own life experiences would be of value to us. We found the ideal person, a black woman who had a great deal of groupwork/social work/consultancy experience, was politically astute, worked locally and who had a white mother and black father. Ideally we would have wished to meet fortnightly but due to time constraints we arranged to meet every three weeks.

We contacted health visitors, community workers and social workers in the area for referrals. The first health visitor we saw was quite hostile to the idea. She thought we were stirring up trouble and 'making a fuss'. She made some racist comments, seemed to be threatened by the word 'racism' and was very patronising and condescending particularly toward me. However she did refer some women to us. Angry and discouraged we continued. A black health visitor questioned us about working only with white women when there were so many black children who have white fathers, but nonetheless referred some women.

We needed some publicity to attract women who didn't have contact with our referral agencies. We were afraid of frightening women off if we advertised the group as being about challenging personal and institutional racism and so played safe and publicised the group as looking at issues such as hair and skin care, multi-racial books and toys, coping with parents' reactions, experiences of racism towards their child/ren and helping their child/ren find a positive identity. We wanted to illustrate the leaflet showing a white woman with a black child but this proved difficult so we had to join two separate pictures.

We finally got a list of 18 women, whom we visited. Some were over the age limit, some were not interested, but about nine agreed to come. We decided on nine as the maximum number and once a core group of between five and nine was established the group would be a closed one, so some intensive work could be done.

We needed at least two *crêche* workers, one of whom had to be black, and both to be aware and committed to anti-racist, anti-sexist child care. We found a black woman and a white woman, and we involved them both closely in the group process.

The group ran one afternoon per week at the local nursery which had a large room with a dividing wall and was an ideal place for groupwork with women with children, especially as it had access to an equipped toy garden.

We devised a tentative programme for the first six weeks, which we left flexible, not wanting to be tied down to something inappropriate yet having some ideas so we would not be stuck. In the initial weeks we covered some of the topics advertised on the leaflet and left time to work out a programme with the group members.

The first week two young women turned up. They were friends who came together. We talked about the aims of the group and tried to set the tone without launching in too much. They were quite responsive. Obviously we were disappointed but not surprised at the low turnout having experienced this before in other groups. We revisited and the second week two more came. We reverted to three in the third week but the following week five women turned up. Marcia and I were quite relieved; we felt we had sufficient numbers to begin a programme of work.

We spent the fifth session discussing all our names and the names of the children, where they came from and what they meant to us. This exercise was useful for setting the scene. It was also useful in giving people the opportunity to talk about something personal but not private and it gave Marcia and myself a taste of the thinking of the individuals within the group. One little boy was named after an African country whilst other women gave their children names because they liked them.

During the session the women were all very talkative, some had never attended a group before and seemed to welcome the opportunity to talk with other women.

The next session was equally well attended. We invited an outside speaker to talk about and demonstrate good black skin and hair care. This went down very well. The women expressed difficulties particularly to do with hair care. Some of the women became adept at cane-rowing hair and we were to see some elaborate styles over the next year and a half.

Numerous issues began to arise, many of which are commonly heard, for example: 'everyone is the same'; 'colour is no big thing, I don't even see it'; 'black people are just as racist' etc. But the most discussed and problematic to Marcia and myself was the issue of black men. All the stereotypes of the 'black super stud' came out. One of the most expressed sayings was: 'once you've had a black man you would never want a white one'. We really floundered with this subject. Some of the stereotypes I let myself get drawn into, even though at the time I realised I was doing so.

Many times we let racist remarks go unchallenged because we felt the timing inappropriate. Our consultant was excellent in helping us sort out some of these issues, giving us encouragement and suggesting we log everything mentally and deal with them on another more opportune occasion. She advised us to point out the contradiction to do with black men, *i.e.* the women saying they did not see colour and that everyone was the same, and yet when it came to men, colour was of the utmost importance. Why didn't we think of this! She gave me the inspiration to keep going.

As leaders Marcia and myself were on the receiving end of a great deal of anger. The women felt threatened by the word racism, acknowledging its existence in others but not in themselves. They claimed that black people were just as racist. Without denying them their experiences, we attempted to discuss the nature and structure of society and how it affected both black and white people. We looked at the definitions of racism and prejudice and the use of language.

In one session we were discussing transracial fostering and adoption after watching a documentary which tried to show both sides, but still implied that the practice was not in the best interests of black children. I agreed with this and voiced that agreement. The women took personal affront, believing what was being said was tantamount to saying they were incapable of looking after their own children, being white mothers of black children. One woman normally quite placid and amicable spoke out fervently, quite rightly questioning her position if her partner died and she wanted a brother or sister for her daughter – could she not adopt a black child? It was a very difficult discussion with many angry statements being made and a refusal to hear the points Marcia and I were making. For the next few weeks a strained relationship developed between this young woman and myself, and although I tried to approach her she kept her distance. Finally a few weeks later she came to me and said she understood and agreed with my comments. She had talked about it with her partner and was able to get an overall perspective. We discussed it and I was relieved to find the strain lifting from our relationship.

In retrospect this issue was introduced far too early in the group's life, before members realised that challenging racism could directly affect themselves. More preparation and probing about attitudes and feelings should have been done before such a documentary was shown.

Each week we asked for ideas and suggestions on what they would like to do so we could make up future programmes. They were always quite happy to do external activities rather than look at themselves. They began to take on some of the responsibilities for organising activities and we had some productive sessions on Caribbean cooking, black history, examining books and toys for racist material, and some cultural outings, one memorable one being a visit to 'Aklowa', the African (Ghanaian) village, in Hertfordshire.

In the later stages of the group relationships between group members grew solid. The women visited each other at home, they had video nights and nights out. Consequently the group sessions became much more an informal chat group.

Whilst the group had been willing to understand and challenge racism I was prepared to continue. This was now not happening, and so after an assessment and evaluation meeting with our consultant we decided to close the group. We agreed to end by having a residential holiday. We went to a place in the Kent countryside called Lower Rawlings and stayed in a lovely cottage for five days. It was a good note on which to end.

Evaluation

Some progress was made on racism. The women began to look more closely at issues relating to race, noticing television programmes, noticing and challenging racist comments, and looking at the toys and books they bought for their child/ren ensuring there were black images their child/ren could relate to. One woman had even written a letter to the *Sun* newspaper after reading a racist article; this same woman in the initial stages of the group had bought her child a golliwog, so real progress was made.

They now understood how important language was and why words such as 'coloured' and 'half-caste' were derogatory terms. They understood the difference between racism and prejudice and why black people cannot be racist. There was an overall heightened sense of awareness of external factors but little recognition of their own racism *e.g.* not being able to realise they could have a black partner and a black child and still be racist.

Our biggest failure was not affecting their stereotypes of black men. Societal images of black men are very potent and reinforced everywhere. The women were entrenched in the image of the black, sultry, physical, rhythmic, super stud who could give a woman a good time especially as his white counterpart was a 'slob with two left feet whose idea of a good time was getting drunk down the local boozer'. In my opinion, it seemed as though they needed this image to protect themselves from the way a racist society would view their involvement with black men, and to convince themselves they were doing the right thing. This glorification of black men continued until the end of the group. I felt an acute sense of inadequacy in this area.

Marcia felt the group helped her to think clearly about racism and to learn about herself as a white woman with a black child. I found the experience of this group frustrating. I was forever in conflict and turmoil wondering how much racism I should tolerate in order to fulfill the purposes of the group. I felt I sold myself out at times, not sure where to draw the line between being a 'professional' and being a black woman although clearly the two are not mutually exclusive.

Many times I had a festering anger that I would not allow to show until the group session ended, and even talking about it with Marcia afterwards did not help, as after all she was another white face, no matter how supportive she was. I need to stress here that white professionals would not get remotely the level of tolerance from me that these white women received, as I would expect white professionals to take on the responsibility of increasing their awareness of the way British society operates and to be actively committed to challenging the inequalities in the system in which they live and work.

Overall because of the movement made by the group members I felt that the group was worth spending some time on. I found it to be a 'learning' experience and would make some changes if I decided to do a similar group.

As the only black woman in the group I felt isolated. My position in the group changed to suit the needs of the members whilst Marcia's position remained fairly stable. If they wanted information on any issue to do with black people irrespective of nationality, culture or tradition, I was expected to know; if I made a statement about the black experience, they would accept it if I had personally been through that experience; if I was challenging and they felt uncomfortable, then I had a chip on my shoulder.

There is a definite need for black workers to protect themselves. Our consultant had suggested that we enlist another black woman worker to give me support. At that time we felt this would change the dynamics of the group as it was already formed and also the member/worker ratio would have been far too high. Two black workers involved from the outset with one white worker and a larger group membership, perhaps eight women would be one way of dealing with this. I would also recommend that supervision be regular, at least fortnightly, and that the black workers have some supervision without the white worker, for additional personal support. Some separate sessions could also be beneficial for the white worker, in addition to meetings when all three workers would meet with the consultant together. Eighteen months was much too long to run a group looking at racism. From a worker's point of view it would have been far better to have a 'time expired' group that was more directive and with a tighter programme incorporating both members' and workers' needs.

Black workers also must be aware of using too much of our own experiences which can make us defensive and protective or, alternatively, defenceless, open and vulnerable. Time must be allocated after group sessions to get out of role and for workers to unwind. Racism is a highly emotive subject, and therefore emotions are to be expected to run high, not least for the black worker. To run a community group on racism is a very ambitious project. It requires a lot of forethought and equivalent amounts of emotional and practical preparation.

GROUPWORK (1988) 1, 48–59

STRUCTURED ACTIVITIES WITH ADOLESCENT BOYS

ROD CRAIG

This article describes and evaluates an activity group. The idea for a group using work and play to achieve treatment goals came from a wide variety of sources. The guiding principle is that being in a group should be fun, active and high in participation and interest. As Rose and Edelson (1987) note, these features make the group more attractive to members. They also maximise the effectiveness of certain elements of cognitive-behavioural groupwork – cognitive restructuring, group discussion, problem-solving, exercises, modelling, rehearsal, feedback and setting and reviewing homework assignments (Rose and Edelson, 1987; Rose, 1981).

The context

This groupwork was undertaken at a school run by a local education authority. It is a single sex school for boarders and day-boys of secondary school age with behavioural, emotional and educational difficulties.

The group was intended to be a short-term exercise in helping adolescents look at and deal with disruptive, aggressive and angry feelings and behaviour which, in the past, had led them into trouble. The aim was to increase their ability to control angry and violent behaviour by providing appropriate options and methods of expression and by examining the positive and negative consequences of different behaviours.

General planning

The group was co-led, allowing more accurate observation and evaluation. My role was task-centred; my co-leader's focused on group processes (Douglas, 1978). Considering the age, characteristics and ability of adolescents at the school we decided that the style adopted would, of necessity, be active and directive – especially in the introduction of activities. However, this did not prevent group members from expressing their own thoughts and ideas. We attempted to be appropriately directive, but reinforced the sharing of personal thoughts and experiences in a genuine and warm way. We aimed to be models, prompters and interpreters in the group; and set firm limits on behaviour that impeded task achievement and/or prevented the group from operating together (Douglas, 1978).

Potential group members were chosen after discussion with staff and parents; observation around the school; and an examination of the log-book which records such behaviour as aggression, bullying and temper tantrums. They were of similar age (12-14 years) and in one unit at the school. This was an easier starting point as these adolescents knew each other reasonably well. The literature suggests that the optimum group size is between five and eight (eg. Douglas, 1978; Brown, 1979). We chose five as this was to be our first experience of leadership. The group was then closed with a fixed membership. We decided that it should meet in school time rather than in free time as it would have a greater chance of maintaining interest. The group was planned to consist of nine sessions, each lasting between one and one and a half hours. We found a room that was big enough to accommodate warm-up games and away from classrooms and other distractions in the school.

Although there was a general overall plan of activities for the nine sessions, specific activities for each were finalised after the previous session. Therefore, some activities that were originally part of the overall plan were dropped completely. We planned to use a video to maximise the effectiveness of modelling and rehearsal in role-plays. However it took two sessions for group members to become comfortable with role-playing, and we felt that getting used to the camera would take up too much valuable time. Activities were also dropped or included in response to items that went well or badly, or took longer than anticipated and needed to be completed at the following session. Flexibility of approach was the key to planning before the group started and before and during each session.

We approached the five adolescents individually and explained the principles, aims and objectives of the group; and how it might benefit them at home and in the school. This was in the context of a conversation about behaviour and its consequences. The general planning, methods and considerations of time and place were explained; and that attendance at the first session would not commit them to continuing. All five decided to 'suck-it-and-see'. In the event there was a great sense of group identity and loyalty. So much so that when one group member did drop-out (Kevin had grown increasingly disaffected with me as a result of factors outside the group) the others said they would have refused to have him back if he had returned. This highlights two things. It is logistically easier to set up a committed group in a residential setting, but it is easier for external factors to play a role.

Group activities

Group activities can be split into six main categories:

i. simple activities where the purpose was to warm-up and introduce or close each session, or the group as a whole;
ii. activities that set boundaries and made sure all members had the chance to express their feelings;

iii. activities that introduced skills (e.g. role-play) needed later in the group;
iv. activities that allowed information to be gathered to facilitate the planning of further sessions, and promoted insight through discussion;
v. activities that drew attention to group processes;
vi. activities that were most directly related to achieving the stated goals of the group ('work').

A theoretical base helps in gaining an understanding of which aspects or components of an activity are useful in achieving the aims of a group and maximising their potential. Rose and Edelson (1987) provide such a base and their work is used in describing and evaluating this group.

Rose and Edelson (1987) analyse group activities according to the three components which make up the 'setting'.

i. '*Physical field*' – each activity requires a minimum of time, space and resources. Analysis of a group includes what these are and their effect on the group or individual.
ii. '*Constituent behaviours*' – the actions that are necessarily required to take part in an activity.
iii. '*Informal behaviours*' – these are not essential but are often associated with the activity (e.g. cheering) and widen learning opportunities.

The authors go on to develop this theme, discussing the following dimensions:

i. '*Level of prescriptiveness*' – the extent to which rules regulate activities. The most difficult to control are those with lower levels of prescription.
ii. '*External vs. internal controls*' – with adolescents activities with external rules are more likely to lead to co-operation than rules originating in the group. Group rules are better than the instruction of an adult leader, reducing conflict and power struggles.
iii. '*Participant interactiveness*' – high levels of participation are correlated with outcome.
iv. '*Competence required for performance*' – this should not be too high or too low if motivation is to be maintained.
v. '*Provision for physical movement*' – desirability and purpose must be questioned.
vi. '*Reward structure*' – this is best achieved if rewards are not just for winning but also for taking part, trying, helping others etc.

Warm-up and introductory activities

Their purpose is to introduce people to the group, increase cohesion and co-operation, warm-up for a particular session, end on a high note of pure fun, etc. In this group they generally required few resources, didn't take long or use too much space. Their advantages were that the rules were given by the game and not by the leaders, which meant that they had external controls, and so, once introduced, there were no conflicts or power struggles over them. However there was a conflict in session 2, two group members (Kevin and John) wanted to carry-on 'playing games' for the whole session. The leaders had to point out that there was much more to the group than this type of activity. Another member, Bill, was very quick to see this and wanted to see what else was on offer. It was agreed that once a repertoire of these games were established the group would decide which 'game' was to open and close each session. At the end of session 6 John suggested a memory game that his family often played. These activities were easy to control as the rules were prescribed by the game, interaction and levels of participation were high, and many levels of competence were involved. According to the theory above this makes for an effective group.

Examples of the games used include 'How do you like your neighbour?' chosen to engage in controlled physical movement to help with anxiety; 'Pig, wolf and farmer', 'Famous people'; 'Tick tock'; 'Killer'; chosen to enhance concentration and co-operation. These games are described in Brandes and Phillips (1977) and Brandes (1982).

Group guidance and individual evaluation

Having welcomed everybody to the first session and introduced a little of what groupwork was all about, two activities were explained that would occur throughout the sessions. Firstly the 'Waiting game' (Brandes and Phillips, 1977). The purpose of the game is for any member or leader to gain attention or quiet. A group member simply states 'I'm playing the waiting game'. It is then up to the other group members to take responsibility for their attention. The member waits quietly (with what these authors describe as a 'quality of nothingness'). If applied patiently and consistently it is highly effective in keeping the group on task. This has the advantage of moving control away from the strictures of the leaders to the rules of a group game. With time we found that individuals could control themselves in staying on task. Rose and Edelson (1987) argue that this helps to maximise group effectiveness.

Secondly 'Rounds' (Brandes and Phillips, 1977). Each person, in a safe environment (i.e. without negative comment), can have the space to complete a statement which gives an indication of feeling or learning. Anyone could 'pass' if they wanted to. Examples include completion of sentences such as: 'I learnt/liked/discovered/found difficult…'. Though the rounds were difficult for members with frequent passes at first, with praise and reinforcement they led to useful discussion and allowed activities to be rounded off. Such indicators allow greater participation and help group planning.

'Brainstorming' was also introduced at the first session as a useful tool for other activities. However it was approached as an enjoyable activity in its own right – brainstorming a list of football teams.

Activities with a serious introductory purpose

The most important activity of the first session was the game 'What am I doing here?' (Brandes, 1982). The purpose of this was to explore individual and group aims. These aims, with rules and methods arrived at through discussion, would form the basis for a group contract. This process of making a contract is high in participation, and this led, we felt, to more committed members because they had explored their reasons for coming.

The group brainstormed answers to the question 'What am I doing here?' in the same way as before. Each of the 35 reasons was copied on to two different cards. These 70 cards were shuffled and dealt to all members of the group (ten each). Members then traded cards (if they wished) until everybody had their three favourite. These reasons were discussed, bringing in the methods and rules that were to apply. The contract drawn up by this method was signed at the beginning of session 2 (see Appendix). This was a group contract but individual strategies and goals were negotiated verbally as the group unfolded. In choosing the three most favoured options it was pleasing to see silly reasons (e.g. 'Beat up Rodney' or 'Watch Rodney work'), and negative reasons (e.g. 'Better fun than reading groups' or 'Get out of class') dropped in favour of more positive reasons (e.g. 'Stop name calling', 'Have fun' or 'Less fighting').

Another activity in this category was 'Adverb' (Brandes and Phillips, 1977). This was intended to introduce role-play through acting adverbs e.g. quickly or grumpily. All members felt uncomfortable, embarrassed and intimidated by role-plays later on, but 'Adverb' showed how competent they could be in a more relaxed atmosphere. It was useful to remind group members of the fact later on.

Information gathering activities

The aim of these activities was to gather information that could be used to assess the type of situation group members found led to anger, aggression or lack of assertion. This information was extremely useful in planning future sessions, role-play and homework. These activities also led to interesting discussions.

One activity was simply to brainstorm, 'This makes me angry...'. The things that seemed to induce anger at the school were bullying, name calling, not getting your own way, people taking no notice, frustration etc. The group was able to discuss different ways of dealing with such situations but our impression was that the members thought that hitting out or abusing people/ property was a justifiable response to many situations.

Two instruments adapted from McGuire and Priestley (1985) were also used. In 'Anger sentence completion' members completed a series of 22 sentences: e.g. 'I lose my temper when...'. 'Anyone who stares at me is...'.

'My pet hate is...'. In the 'Assertion situation survey' the members rated on a scale of 1-5 how confident they felt about a list of 20 situations e.g. 'Being told off by a teacher'. 'Leaving an activity early'. 'Asking a question in class'. In carrying out these tasks it was extremely important to take into account levels of competence, considering the difficulties some of the group had with following instructions and reading/writing. We gave appropriate help that did not interfere with task completion. Good discussions arose in which all members of the group were able to follow on, present ideas and contradict each other. The group discussed why it was easier to break-up from a girl rather than ask her out – the consensus being that you could put on an act and weren't likely to be hurt when splitting-up. Secondly the rights and wrongs of grassing were discussed – and when it was important.

Activities that draw attention to group processes

When the group began role-playing different incidents in order to model and rehearse solutions, it was quite difficult on occasion, as has been mentioned, to get people to volunteer. A way of getting the group to see and discuss this problem was to play the 'Chairs' game (Brandes, 1982). At the beginning of session 5, I asked for two volunteers – Bill and Tom, the two group members who were the most self-confident, eventually agreed. One volunteer left the room and the other was asked to tell the rest of the group what went on in his head between the voices that said:

i. 'You should volunteer' (whilst sitting on one chair) and
ii. You shouldn't (whilst sitting on the other).

The other volunteer did exactly the same. The group discussed which voice was stronger. This made the point that volunteering is hard for everybody, but we all needed people to relax and take part in the role-plays. The group seemed much more comfortable with role-play after that. Perhaps this was because the situations used from then on were real rather than 'made-up' ones. Perhaps the group also felt a relief of pressure after Kevin had left after session 4.

The other activity in this category was 'Guess who said it'! (Brandes, 1982). The aim of this activity was to improve the giving and receiving of positive feedback through practise.

'Work'

The theory guiding our work on aggression was that aggression is due in part to a lack of options. Therefore the relationship between assertion, aggression and lack of assertion needed to be explained by discussing the consequences of behaviours in certain situations. This was carried out using the 'Assertion game' (Brandes, 1982). The group brainstorms descriptions of the following types of behaviour:

i. non-assertive,
ii. assertive,
iii. aggressive,

being careful to define what is meant by assertion. The description is as behavioural as possible, describing posture, hand movement, eye contact, tone of voice, what is said, proximity, facial expression. Then the group discusses the type of situation where a person might act in these ways and why. Situations such as 'dealing with a queue jumper' or 'complaining about my chips' (taken from the 'Assertion situation survey') were role-played with each of the characters being in turn shy, assertive or aggressive using the brainstormed material as a model. The others in the group reinforced, prompted and modelled the behaviour until the most appropriate solution was found. David found the role-play very difficult, and although Bill and Tom had the right idea the role-plays were quite stilted and self-conscious. John was good at criticising and prompting others but at this stage refused to role-play.

This exercise was extended during the next sessions to situations that the group members brought. These included arguments about which channel to watch on TV, how to deal with people picking on you at school or brothers and sisters at home, a fight that occurred between Bill and Tom, and so on. These incidents were looked at and alternatives modelled and rehearsed; and cues were examined that would help thought-stopping, self-prompting and self-instruction. Homework was then worked out where such strategies could be put into action. Tom, Bill and David all succeeded in using what they had learnt in situations outside the group.

Towards the end of the sessions all these threads were drawn together by the use of a 'Change matrix' (McGuire and Priestley, 1985). The members filled in the matrix imagining how to avoid trouble, or to prevent situations from escalating by writing down things they should or should not think, say or do. Bill asked if he could put this over his bed at school so that he could look at it - the others followed suit.

The other activity that took up a whole session was a 'Contingency algorithm' (McGuire and Priestley, 1985) – see Figure 2. This was presented as a 'What I say matters game', whose aim is to look at the consequences of what people say and do. The group split into two sub-groups and imagined a situation in which someone (a stranger) comes up and calls aggressively 'Hey you!'. In this activity there are three types of reply:

Conciliatory	examples being	'Yes?'
Neutral		'You talking to me?'
Provocative		'Get stuffed!'

The third reply obviously leads to confrontation. The sub-groups think of a further aggressive retort for the stranger (only to the conciliatory and neutral replies); and then three further options according to the above plan (and so on). The growing tree of possible conversations is recorded on a large sheet of paper. This chart is then swopped between sub-groups, and members attempt to categorise the different types of reply the other sub-group has written.

The leaders observe that as the group progressed, and the type and content of activities changed in emphasis (roughly in parallel with the progression through this article) towards those activities most directly concerned with reaching the stated goals, so the levels of control and prescription decreased and passed into the hands of the group. The pace and type of activity was determined more by the group, whereas at the beginning it was the leaders. Concomitant with this was an increase in the degree of interaction, participation, competence and reward that the members displayed. The best criterion of success is when individuals retain their improvement in these areas after the group has finished.

Assessment and evaluation

This could best have been carried out by baselining and monitoring particular behaviours and their triggers and consequences for each of the five adolescents over a period. We lacked the resources for this. School staff were briefed to reinforce group members finding options for dealing with anger and aggression, and several such instances were reported back to us. However, assessment of the group had to take the form of subjective ratings of the group's effectiveness.

The leaders evaluated each session using as a framework a self-monitoring schedule for group leaders to be found in Priestley and McGuire's *Learning to Help* (1983), covering areas of preparation, recruitment, group composition, starting and ending sessions, who spoke, what people said, atmosphere, problems and outcomes. Some of the most salient points have been made earlier in the article.

The assertion abilities of the group were measured by repeating the 'Assertion situation survey' (the rationale being that an ability to be more appropriately assertive would make a person less likely to use aggression). Only three members of the group repeated this activity (due to illness and one member leaving the group). The survey was scored in a rough and ready manner by scoring the increase or decrease in confidence since the beginning of the group. All three showed slight increases in their scores, perhaps showing some success for the group on this criterion.

These three group members also filled in a 'Group evaluation sheet'. In response to a question about the aims of the group, the members indicated that the aims were clear and coincided with those of the contract made in sessions 1 and 2. All three agreed that the aims had not been completely achieved but that the level of achievement was better than halfway towards full achievement. The members were asked to select from a series of adjectives the ones that best described the group. The group was described as relaxed, friendly and pleasant (3× each); alright, active, productive, frustrating (because of an inability to totally express themselves in what they said and role-plays) and amusing (2× each); and warm (×1). None of the three described the group as boring, tense, anxious, average, timewasting or businesslike. This seems to indicate that the group had been enjoyed, and found to be stimulating if not challenging. The members variously described the leaders as 60 per cent, 80 per cent and 90 per cent prepared.

The members then scored the activities according to how much they were found to be difficult, enjoyable or helpful, giving a score out of 12. The paper and pen exercises and discussions were the most difficult scoring 9, (perhaps because they were the most directly challenging and asked individuals to look at and talk about their own behaviour). The change matrix scored 8, and the brainstorms, role-plays and algorithm were the easiest, scoring 7. All the scores were above the half-way mark. Again, perhaps this indicates that the group was quite challenging.

The algorithm, change matrix and brainstorms were regarded as very enjoyable, all scoring a maximum 12. The role-plays and discussions came next with 10 and 9 respectively; and the paper and pen exercises were the least enjoyed with a score of 5 out of 12, suggesting an inverse relation between enjoyment and difficulty.

The most helpful exercises were the role-plays, brainstorms and change matrix all scoring 10 out of 12 – perhaps the generation of ideas, trying them out and selecting the most useful is the best way of giving such children options in angry or aggressive situations. The discussion and algorithm were the next most useful, scoring 9; and the least useful were the paper and pen exercises scoring 6 (though they were of great use to the leaders for group preparation). In general the games were enjoyed and mentioned as liked – the role-play was disliked, probably because it was hard.

The reaction to the group seemed to be that it was enjoyable, fairly difficult, challenging and in some ways useful. I feel that it has offered options to deal with situations that often escalate, for these adolescents, into temper and aggression. But whether these options are taken is a moot point. Tom had almost constantly been in a temper for the two days before the last session – completely unable to put what he had practised into effect. We agreed that David had put a lot in and got a great deal from the group, probably the most in terms of confidence and attempting to use strategies. Bill and John worked hard, and showed the most 'group cohesion' skills; they tried out some of the strategies talked about in the group, with some success.

The group could best be improved by careful baselining and monitoring of behaviour to compare before and after; and by extending the number of sessions so that video could be used, and to allow further exploration of situations by getting into a more settled sequence of role-play, rehearsal in the group and homework assignment outside. This approach has much to offer this client group, and has potential for repetition and expansion.

Acknowledgements
The author would like to acknowledge the patience, help and advice of Barbara L. Hudson, Esther Duras, Lesley Ribbens and David Allen.

References

Brandes, D. (1982) *Gamesters' Handbook Two.* London: Hutchinson.
Brandes, D. and Phillips, H. (1977) *Gamesters' Handbook.* London: Hutchinson.
Brown, A. (1979) *Groupwork.* London; Heinemann.
Douglas, T. (1978) Basic Groupwork. London: Tavistock.
McGuire, J. and Priestley, P. (1985) *Offending Behaviour.* London: Batsford.
Priestley, P. and McGuire, J. (1983) *Learning to Help.* London: Tavistock.
Rose, S. D. (1981) 'How group attributes relate to outcome in behaviour group therapy'. *Social Work Research and Abstracts,* **17**, pp 25-29.
Rose, S. D. and Edelson, J. L. (1987) *Working with Children and Adolescents in Groups.* San Francisco: Jossey-Bass.

Figure 1 – Agenda of activities

Session 1
Introduction – explaining 'Rounds' and the 'Waiting game'.
'How do you like your neighbour?'
'Pig, wolf and farmer'.
'Brainstorm: football teams'.
'What am I doing here?' – discussion.
Closing Round.

Session 2
Signed contract.
'How do you like your neighbour?'
'Adverb'
Brainstorm 'This makes me angry'.
Closing Round.

Session 3
'Famous people'.
'Assertion situation survey' – discussion.
'Killer'.
Anger sentence completion – discussion.
'Pig, wolf and farmer'.

Session 4
'Tick, tock'.
Round.
'Assertion game'.
'Famous people'.

Session 5
'How do you like your neighbour?'.
'Chairs game'.
Round.
'Assertion game' – role-play of 'real' situations and homework.
'Tick, tock'.

Session 6
'Guess who said it'.
Discussion of homework.
Role-play, modelling, rehearsal, etc.
John's memory game.

Session 7
'How do you like your neighbour?'
Role-play, modelling, rehearsal etc.
'Contingency algorithm' – discussion.
John's memory game.

Session 8
'Killer'.
'Assertion situation survey'.
Discussion about group activities – Change matrix.
Round.
'Pig, wolf and farmer'.

Session 9
Finished change matrix.
Group evaluation sheet.
Round.
'Tick, tock'.
Closing game.

Appendix

Contract between the members of the Tuesday and Friday group

1. The aims of the group are to:
   i. Have fun, get on with and help other people through teamwork and making friends.
   ii. Think about, explore and find ways of trying to keep out of trouble by less swearing, losing temper, messing about, damaging things, name calling or fighting.
   iii. Practise these ways both inside and outside the group.
   iv. For the co-leaders to learn how to run a group.

2. There will be nine sessions of approximately one hour. The sessions will be held in the snooker room of Old Block. Planning and materials will be appropriately provided by the co-leaders, though the members may have tasks to complete between sessions if agreed.

3. The methods of achieving these aims will be by playing games, brainstorming, role-play and discussion.

4. The rules of the group are as follows:
   i. Taking part in each session or activity is voluntary.
   ii. Members should attempt to reach the group aims to the best of their ability.
   iii. Members should attempt to help each other reach aims.
   iv. There will be no violence or personal abuse.
   v. Everyone should be given the opportunity to speak and be heard – one person is to speak at a time.
   vi. Personal information will not be divulged without that person's permission outside the group.
   vii. Further rules or problems will be discussed by the group.
   viii. If rules are broken then the group will decide on the appropriate action or sanction.

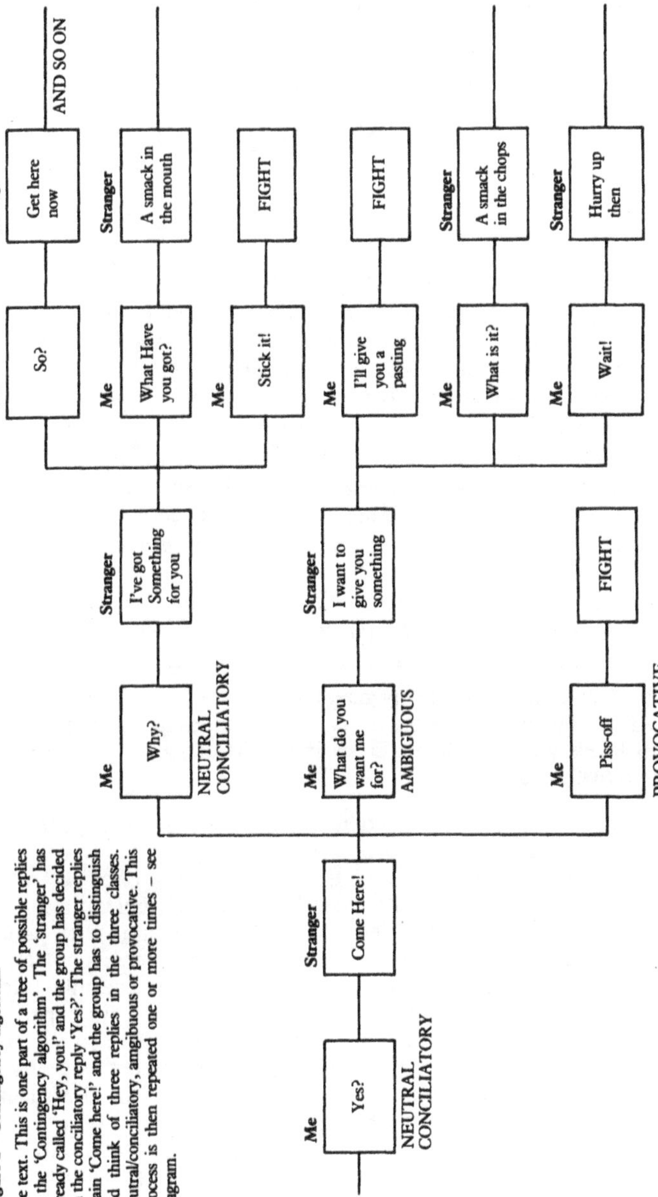

Figure 2 – Contingency algorithm

See text. This is one part of a tree of possible replies in the 'Contingency algorithm'. The 'stranger' has already called 'Hey, you!' and the group has decided on the conciliatory reply 'Yes?'. The stranger replies again 'Come here!' and the group has to distinguish and think of three replies in the three classes. neutral/conciliatory, amgibuous or provocative. This process is then repeated one or more times – see diagram.

GROUPWORK (1988) 1, 60–66

SUPPORTING VOICES

Groupwork with People Suffering from Schizophrenia

LYNDA RANDALL and WENDY WALKER

This is an account of a group for schizophrenic people in an acute psychiatric unit attached to a general hospital. Workers in the unit had identified a number of (predominantly) young schizophrenic patients who were thought to be particularly vulnerable to suicide and who needed more help than had hitherto been provided in coming to terms with their illness. These patients possessed a good deal of insight into their condition and their symptoms were well controlled by medication, but they mourned the loss of previous life-styles and were saddened by their diminishing prospects. The authors describe the setting up of a task-centred, problem-solving group that also sought to develop and maintain communication skills; the choosing of an appropriate therapeutic approach; and the importance of multi-disciplinary communication in a hospital.

The group highlighted the feelings of loss and the need to regain control of their lives, experienced by people who are diagnosed as schizophrenic.

> The voices in my head hate my guts, they give me no rest and spurn all I love best. The voices tear my dreams apart and ravage my heart. They strangle every hope. The me in my head kills the child in me and the person that would be.

This brief self-description by a patient provides a graphic picture of what it feels like to be suffering from schizophrenia.

We work in a modern psychiatric unit attached to a large district general hospital. A substantial number of recently diagnosed schizophrenic patients pass through the unit. Most attention, time and help given to such patients had been on a one-to-one basis, usually by the doctors or nurses. The day hospital sometimes worked with a specific problem area, for example offering an anxiety management programme, social skills training or work experience. An informal 'drop-in' was also available for patients who wanted social contact rather than formal therapy. The social work department was involved in dealing with practical and emotional issues arising from the diagnosis of schizophrenia but again this was on an individual or family basis.

Whilst for some patients what was on offer was sufficient, there was concern in the multi-disciplinary teams that a number of patients needed more help in developing skills to cope with their illness if they were to have a reasonable quality of life. These patients had a good deal of insight into their condition and their symptoms were well controlled by medication, but they were fearful of deteriorating. They mourned the loss of their previous lifestyles and were saddened by their diminishing life prospects, for example in relation to employment, friendships and marriage. They often expressed suicidal ideas and a number of deaths by suicide in this group of patients encouraged our desire to provide more help.

We felt that groupwork would offer an effective method of helping such patients come to terms with and develop strategies for dealing with their illness. Literature and practice suggest that groupwork may offer a greater opportunity to share experiences, reduce feelings of isolation and enhance problem-solving skills than individual work is able to do.

Much has been written in recent years on working with the families of patients described as schizophrenic (Falloon and Pederson, 1985; Doane *et al.*, 1986; Tarrier and Barrowclough, 1986). Such writings have helped to inform our own work. There was in the hospital a relatives' support group in which issues of family interaction were already being addressed. What we wanted to do (and what we felt this literature also encouraged us to think about) was to consider another important issue – the need for *patients* to develop their abilities to cope with their illness, the problems arising from it, and the role of stress in relation to the recurrence of schizophrenia.

The available literature on groupwork with schizophrenic patients can be somewhat disconcerting with its warnings about the dangers of insight oriented approaches perhaps provoking a psychotic episode; or alternatively under stimulating patients and thus encouraging apathy and withdrawal (Kanas, 1985). Informal discussions in the multi-disciplinary teams disclosed similiar anxieties, and colleagues needed reassurance that we would not employ psychodynamic methods which used 'uncovering' techniques and excessive self-disclosure. We decided that group therapy using a task-centred, problem-solving approach which also maintained and developed communication skills would be of most value to our patient group. This approach has been shown to be useful with schizophrenic patients and some studies have shown this type of groupwork to be more effective in preventing relapse than medication coupled with individual work (Malm, 1982; Walker and Mcleod, 1982; Scott and Griffith, 1982).

After the informal discussions, we wrote up our ideas on the aims, objectives and composition of the group and our roles within it. The notes were circulated to the multi-disciplinary teams with an invitation to provide referrals. The criteria we established for group membership were that members should have been diagnosed as schizophrenic, that their symptoms were controlled by medication and that they should positively wish to join the group. We decided also on equal numbers of men and women, between six and eight of each. Because of the type of person being sought (insightful and with a relatively intact personality), members were likely to be in their twenties or thirties but we also considered people who had become schizophrenic in later life and who had had one or two recent episodes.

The purpose of the group was to provide support by recognising shared experiences, strengths and abilities which existed in spite of illness; to provide information and suggest strategies for coping with schizophrenia. (We likened the patients' position to the situation of a recently diagnosed person with diabetes being encouraged to work out how best to live with their illness.) It was intended that the group should also provide enjoyment and fun, and strengthen the members' orientation in the present by the use of games and communication exercises. We also hoped to explore the possibility of a self-help group growing out of the support group (as it came to be called).

We also gave the planning notes to prospective group members as we wanted to involve them in generating ideas for the group. Four issues in particular emerged in preliminary interviews with prospective members. First, most people felt they wanted the group membership to be 'closed' as soon as possible, perhaps after the first two meetings when a stable group had been established. It was felt that having a closed group would enable a trusting, friendly atmosphere to be established more readily. We also discussed the time-span of the group and the consensus seemed to be that 12 one hour meetings at weekly intervals would be sufficient and a manageable commitment for both staff and group members. Secondly, there was a strong demand for information about schizophrenia, its possible causes, treatment and outcome. Thirdly, as most people were anxious about being in a group, the idea of using games to break the ice was welcomed and, in fact, suggested spontaneously by some people who had been in groups before. Last but not least was the issue of confidentiality and feedback to the multi-disciplinary teams. It was agreed at the first group meeting that feedback could be given but that nothing would be disclosed without members' consent. Feedback was in two parts: first, a general report on the group, outlining subjects discussed so as to give some idea of what was important for this group of patients; and secondly, a short report about each individual, their experience in the group and what further assistance (if any) they wanted.

We have now run two groups involving 18 people and are planning to run similar groups on a regular basis in the unit. It seems helpful in reviewing our work to examine three separate but interdependent aspects of these groups: *co-working and planning, group processes* and *outcome*.

Co-working can be difficult as well as fruitful and we resolved to put a good deal of effort into learning how to work together in the pre-group planning stage. We chose to operate in this manner partly so as to provide a role model of co-operative interaction for all the group members. Early sessions were quite closely structured to help everyone to feel safe. However, after a couple of meetings this degree of structuring proved unnecessary –as we had hoped it would – and group members worked out how they wished to see the meetings structured. Figure 1 gives an example of the plan for a meeting, typical of the outline of the first two meetings.

Our desire to structure the group was, we think, partly a measure of our own anxiety about the group process. How would group members interact? Would they interact at all?

Figure 1

SUPPORT GROUP MEETING

TIME	WORKER	TASK	
5 mins	Lynda Randall Wendy Walker	**Introduction:** talk about last week's meeting; state the agenda for this week's meeting; introduce new members; give positive feedback for the hard work they engaged in last week.	
		Exercises	**Aims**
5 mins	Wendy	Name volley with softball	Remind people of names, introduce new people, relax people.
5 mins	Wendy	Name and action to identify self, to be copied by the whole group.	
5 mins	Lynda	Trust exercise – every member closes their eyes and names the person on their right and left, go round the circle twice.	Orientation exercise, make people aware of the here and now. Trust group.
40 mins	Lynda & Wendy	Group discussion of last week's brain storming and the ideas produced.	Prioritize areas they identify; encourage group to work together. Group cohesiveness.
5 mins	Wendy	Pass the squeeze.	Fun, group trust.

Feedback
All exercises went well, discussed relaxation exercise and it was agreed that those group members who wanted it, could stay and the rest could go for a coffee.

In the first meeting we used a 'brainstorm' (a title greeted with some hilarity!) to generate ideas from members as to what they wanted from the group. This exercise generated sufficient material to plan subsequent meetings. The areas selected were information and discussion about schizophrenia; coping with friendships and making new friends; managing family relationships; and dealing with employment, unemployment and re-training for different, sometimes sheltered, work situations. There was an overall concern that the group would become a warm, caring setting within which members could talk openly and honestly about themselves. Group members felt isolated by their illness and wanted to talk about their experiences of schizophrenia with others who 'knew' their experience.

The groups became 'closed' after two meetings and it is interesting to look at the various reasons why people dropped out. Twelve people were invited to each group initially. Of the first group of six men and six women, one man left to return to his employment; and one woman decided after the first meeting that the group would be too 'intrusive' for her – she did not want to talk about herself or her illness. This view was shared by one of the men in the second group, which eventually continued with four men and four women. One man and one woman did not attend as they had returned to work. Another man left because, although interested in the group, he could not motivate himself sufficiently to attend – *'I know I'd enjoy it if I got there but I can't get out of bed in the morning'*.

The feedback after covering all the topics suggested made it clear that the most valued aspects of the group experience were the information gained about their illness, its origins, treatment and prognosis; and the opportunity to share with other sufferers their experiences of the illness and its impact on their lives. Joan*, for example, said:

> I feel so guilty about the voices telling me to hurt the children. I know it's not me but it makes me feel bad . . . it's such a struggle not to hear the voices. It helps me to know that other people have the same experience, that it's an illness and that it's possible to cope.

Or Pat, who said:

> If I meet someone who I think might be a friend, I always tell them I am schizophrenic – then I lose them – I feel I should be honest.

To which Dave responded:

> I establish a friendship and when I'm sure it's OK I might say I have a problem with my nerves but I don't say I'm a schizophrenic until I think they can take it – after all, when we're well we're the same as other people – there's no need to look for trouble.

Some group members decided to set up a self-help group, which will help to fill an unmet need in the locality, providing a valuable community resource. We agreed to introduce a community worker who had expertise in facilitating self-help groups and we are now involved only as somewhat distant contacts for this group.

We conclude this paper with a few points which we feel it is important to bear in mind in groupwork with people described as schizophrenic. First, it is important to be sensitive to the amount of emotional disturbance which they may be able to tolerate. Some members, for example, were adamant that they would not talk about their families as this would be too upsetting. Some did not want to get too close to people as they felt too threatened, and we felt it was important to respect their wishes.

*names have been changed in the interests of confidentiality

In seeking to achieve an appropriate level of stimulation it is helpful to use physical exercises. Many schizophrenic patients are 'slowed down' emotionally and physically and a variety of activities can release latent energy and relax tensions.

It is also necessary to consider how to manage difficulties which may arise from two particular symptoms of schizophrenia, thought disorder and flattening of affect. In relation to thought disorder, some members found it difficult to concentrate and would apparently wander off the subject under discussion. One example was Andrew, a very withdrawn young man, who commented in several meetings:

> My uncle wants me to buy a house. I've been living out in the field next door to him and now he's going to buy me a house.

Attempts made to decode Andrew's comment (sometimes the only remark he made in the meeting) met with little success until the group decided to devote an entire meeting to housing and family problems. It then became clear that although Andrew's comment was based on a delusion – he was in fact living at home with his parents – he did need to find somewhere to live as his family home was overcrowded. It is probably significant that those who showed most signs of thought disorder did not become involved in the self-help group.

Flattening of affect was movingly described by Caroline, as follows:

> I can remember the day when my feelings stopped. I know that I love my children but I cannot feel what that means any more. I have to go through the motions and it's an act. On a bad day I cannot do that: I am unresponsive, I cannot be happy or sad – just flat.

Some people did not have her insight and were flat most of the time. This could be disconcerting. For example, if a group member disclosed something that upset them, some group members seemed offhand and uninterested, which was hurtful. Caroline's comment touched people and enabled them to respond to others more sensitively.

It is important to appreciate the significance of the patient role. There is something about 'being a patient' that seems disabling from the point of view of coming to terms with and understanding illness. It was clear that although a fair amount of information had been given to group members by their doctors, it had not been absorbed. The passivity of the 'patient patient' who expects to be acted upon rather than being an actor inhibits the gaining of knowledge and therefore some control over the impact and meaning of the diagnosis of schizophrenia. Those who had been out of hospital for more than two months seemed more able to be 'actors' than those more recently discharged.

Finally, related to the wish for information, is the importance of repetition and sharing of experience and knowledge in coming to terms with their illness. All the group members wanted to recapitulate their experience of illness in a way that seemed to be an attempt to own their illness and thus themselves. Before joining the group, they had tended to see themselves as having 'split' personalities, a healthy self and a sick self that is 'out there' and dependent on others for its care – this perception of being split reflecting the popular view of schizophrenia. Being in the group – with its supporting voices – seemed to enable members to begin to heal the split in themselves, both emotionally and cognitively.

References

Doane, J.A., Goldstein, M.J., Miklowitz, D.J. and Falloon, I.R.H. (1986) 'The impact of individual and family treatment on the affective climate of families of schizophrenics', *British Journal of Psychiatry*, 148, pp.279-287.

Falloon, I.R.H. and Pederson (1985) 'Family management in the prevention of morbidity of schizophrenia: the adjustment of the family', *British Journal of Psychiatry*, 147, pp.156-163.

Kanas, N. (1985) 'In-patient and out-patient group therapy for schizophrenic patients', *American Journal of Psychotherapy*, 39 (3), pp.431-439.

Malm, U. (1982) 'The influence of group therapy on schizophrenia' *Acta Psychiatrica Scandinavica*, 65 (Supplement 297).

Scott, D. and Griffith, M. (1982) 'The evaluation of group therapy in the treatment of schizophrenia', *Small Group Behaviour*, 13 (3), pp.415-422.

Tarrier, N. and Barrowclough, C. (1986) 'Providing information to relatives about schizophrenia: some comments', *British Journal of Psychiatry*, 149, pp.458-463.

Walker, J.I. and McLeod, G. (1982) 'Group therapy with schizophrenics', *Social Work*, 27 (4), pp.364-367.

GROUPWORK (1988) 1, 67–76

GROUPWORK BOOKS PUBLISHED IN BRITAIN 1980–86

HAROLD MARCHANT

The article reviews 13 books on groups and groupwork by European writers published in Britain during the years 1980–1986. It ranges from 'self-help' and growth-group approaches, through mainstream social groupwork, and applications to specialist settings. It provides a brief outline of the main concerns of each writer, and offers a lightly critical look at 'homegrown groupwork literature' during a particularly flourishing period.

Those trying to use social groupwork methods in the 1950s and early 1960s drew much of their theoretical underpinning and practical inspiration from the United States of America. The writings of Wilson and Rylands, Grace Coyle, Lewin, Homans, Trecker and the Sherifs certainly helped this practitioner to move towards a greater understanding of what was going on in groups, and how I could intervene sensitively and teach usefully. However, the examples in the books often seemed remote from the day-to-day groups I was involved with, and a good deal of cultural translation had to go on in my head. Literature on groupwork on this side of the Atlantic was sparse and, in my studies, depended heavily on *Social Group Work in Great Britain* (1955) edited by Peter Kuenstler, Josephine Klein's *Study of Groups* (1956), W.J.H. Sprott's *Human Groups* (1958) and *Experiences in Groups* (1961) by W.R. Bion. The situation began to improve in the seventies, with Tom Douglas, Bernard Davies, Nano McCaughan and Ken Heap publishing work. In the eighties a flurry of groupwork books in English has emanated from European sources: it is the part of the flurry that appeared between 1980 and 1986 that I intend to reflect upon in this article.

How to approach the task

There are 13 volumes on my list. Is it possible to use a *Which* approach and come up with a 'best buy'? Does it help to know that the most expensive volume costs 5.7 pence a page, as against the least expensive volume's page cost of 5.9 pence? Or who has the most references, and the most diagrams? Would it, for example, be possible to do the job without actually *reading* any of the books – a kind of review by feel, by weight, or by aesthetic response to the cover design? Will it lie flat on the table when opened? Is the contents page clear? Who quotes from whom and, more significantly, who doesn't quote from whom. All these seemed interesting and certainly original approaches to an overview. Tempting though it was – and a temptation not entirely resisted – I eventually concluded that reading and re-reading was unavoidable if I was to comment on the usefulness of these tools when in the hands of practising groupworkers.

Where to begin?

I shall follow the advice given to Alice in Wonderland – '*begin at the beginning*'. For me, that is with Peter B. Smith's *Group Processes and Personal Change* (1980) because it emphasises the centrality of 'change'. The groupwork method is one that enables change to occur, and the place of sensitivity training, which is Peter Smith's particular focus for the use of groups, is an important one for all groupworkers. The reader is reminded that individuals are in charge of their own change, and that groups do not 'change people' unless there is a willingness to embrace some personal change as a result of the insights obtained through group membership. The book is a scholarly, thorough and comprehensive account of sensitivity training groups. The author wants to '*encourage a more research-minded approach among practitioners of sensitivity training*'. His book reflects this and is heavily referenced, and although some of the reported research is not overly rigorous, a critical stance is taken on various forms of experiential groups. There is a particularly good outline of the diversification of experiential approaches, with sections on T-groups, interpretative groups (e.g. transactional analysis), encounter groups (e.g. Gestalt) and self-help groups (e.g. Synanon). For those who seek to create 'the cultural island' in working with people in groups, there is much of value in the book. For those who wish to learn about the different emphases, or to clarify particular methods, it is clear. For example, the essence of the T-group approach is that it is here-and-now, consists of self-disclosure and feedback, requires voluntary participation, and seeks to reduce the differential between the members and those who lead it. There are sections describing various encounter approaches, using Gestalt and psychodrama as elements of the method. There is also a chapter on the application of T-group training in organizational development.

There have been many worries expressed about introducing the T-group approach, but Peter Smith tackles these directly. Overall, the author is clearly committed to the value of 'growth groups' yet he is able to provide academic backing for – and a critique of – a form of groupwork that many groupworkers are fearful of, and the majority curious about. This volume will go a long way to satisfy the curiosity and reduce the fear, and indicate ways of incorporating sensitivity work into other, perhaps more prosaic and certainly more common, ways of running groups. Peter Smith is not surprised that '*some people get worse after groups, while others get better*' saying the same is true of the older forms of group psychotherapy. The advocates of the newer forms of experiential groups see them as safer, but with a quotation from I.D. Yalom (1975) the author reminds us of the proviso:

> ... if the leader is well-trained (both clinically and in group dynamics), is responsible, screens his members either before or during the group, provides sufficient information for applicants to de-select themselves, and permits members to proceed at their own pace, the group experience is quite likely to be a safe and rewarding one.

Following such guidelines, who among us will feel able to offer an experiential group? Such strictures may at least prevent an enthusiastic if naive entry into providing any of these forms of 'new group therapy' while recognising the insights and self-awareness that can accrue from such approaches.

These matters are also explored in a useful reader *Small Groups and Personal Change* (1980) which is edited by Peter B. Smith and contains one of his chapters from the previous book, and a good deal of new material. Part of the problem of this kind of publication is, for me, the difficulty of remembering each writer's contribution. It may be useful to outline the contributions relevant to this review. Peter Smith provides a succinct overview of the emergence of groupwork as a means of bringing about change, and he combines with Gerald Smale and Heather Wood in a chapter on 'The usefulness of groups in clinical settings'; David Robinson contributes a piece on 'Self-help health groups', and Keith Oatley one on 'Theories of personal learning in groups'. Nano McCaughan provides some useful categorisation in her chapter on 'Purposes of groupwork in social work'.

The theme of personal growth and self-awareness is evident in two 'self-help' books. The first is *In Our Own Hands – A Book of Self-Help Therapy* (Sheila Ernst and Lucy Goodman, 1981) and written primarily from a feminist perspective, and a belief that '*each of us has the ability to heal ourselves and help others*'. The book indicates how to start and carry through a self-help group, offering guidelines and many examples across a broad spectrum of 'growth' approaches, including Gestalt, co-counselling, encounter, dreams, meditation, psychodrama, Reichian therapy, bodywork, bio-energetics, psycho-synthensis, TA and primal therapy. A regular gamut of self-realisation by means of self-help. The authors write from an overt political position, and while the main direction of their work is towards, with and for women, there is much in the book for any student of groups. They face the dangers of the self-help approach squarely, but in general follow Boadella's view – which they quote – that the '*neurosis is the crucifixion, not therapy*'. A view which would probably be shared by the author of the other self-help book *The Relative-Sized Red Book of Gestalt* (Gaie Houston, 1982). The book offers a step-by-step guide to running a Gestalt group. With some amusing cartoons to ease the way, group members are invited to do something about '*the internal clutter which comes between me in the world and stops me responding*' (a double-echo here of Fritz Perls' book *In and Out of the Garbage Pail*). It makes crystal clear such intellectual concepts as projection, introjection and retroflection, while at the same time offering the simple directive that '*there is no one right way to work with anyone in Gestalt, beyond the principle of staying as close to "now" as you have skill to*'. In an easy and clear way, Gaie Houston's book will enhance the skill of many people.

I now move to what I will call 'mainstream' books. This encompasses *The Red Books of Groups* (Gaie Houston, 1984); *The Practice of Social Work in Groups* (Ken Heap, 1985); *Using Groups to Help People* (Dorothy Stock Whitaker, 1985); and *Groupwork* (Allan Brown, 1986).

Gaie Houston's book is a delight to me. The matchstick illustrations break up the text and bring a smile to what are basically serious matters. There is a lightness of touch that is often missing from books about groupwork – Gaie Houston makes it an enjoyable while challenging experience. Her approach is Rogerian and also draws upon the Gestalt tradition. She aims at providing help in running small informal groups, and bases her approach on the belief that a degree of self-knowledge is a pre-requisite of effective performance in a group – a clear link with Peter Smith here. It is practical and provides many examples and exercises for the group. She thinks the groupworker's job is '*to enable, not disable*'. I agree, and this book helps me to do it. I also agree with her encouragement to workers to separate out intellectual reactions from emotional ones. So often 'I feel' is used as synonymous to 'I think'. Helping group members to identify a thought and identify a feeling, and not confuse the two, can help in the sorting out process that goes on in all groups, not only those focusing on interpersonal concerns. She also encourages workers to share in the group themselves (reducing the differential, in Peter Smith's terms) since '*I have never yet found a group incapable of commenting on my work in a way I could learn from*'.

Ken Heap and Allan Brown are more solid, traditional texts, and cover a wider range of groupwork issues and practices. I found Allan Brown's the most economical yet comprehensive introductory text (which is what it is advertised as being) and an excellent guide to would-be groupworkers. It also provides a number of pegs for more experienced workers to hang their thoughts and develop their ideas. The focus of the book is primarily on formed groups, as those most likely to occur in social work practice. Allan Brown does not think that the 'sensitivity group' is a useful social work model, and concentrates on task and social goals models. He demystifies the groupwork method without demeaning it, and breathes encouragement into practitioners by his systematic and forthright approach. I found few substantial differences in the second edition, though there is an enriching of various bits of text and a longer piece on the need for groupworkers to be sensitive to issues of race and gender. Inexplicably, a useful piece on responses to scapegoating in the first edition (published by Heinemann, 1979) cannot be found by this reader in the second. There are practical references and quotes from Konopka and from Stock Whitaker – unlike the Houston book which is devoid of references. I found *Groupwork* a useful textbook.

Ken Heap takes workers a step further along the road, with detailed examples to illustrate the points he makes about the practice of social work with groups. He incorporates both formed and informal or 'natural' groups. It is systematic in a sequential way, taking the reader through what happens in groups and the workers' roles in what he describes as each '*working phase*'. It is pragmatic and while there are many references, it does not lean on any one theory. What seems important is that 'it works' and the 39 examples are very useful in showing possible worker interventions of an 'enabling' kind. The author's enthusiasm for groups comes through and the book is highly readable, although at times rather wordy and set rather densely on the page. There is little if any attention given to the race dimension in groupwork, but this may reflect the make-up of groups worked with by the author in Scandinavia. I particularly valued the sections on silence and on co-working. There is also an emphasis on the pressures exerted upon individuals by the societal system in which they are located, and the importance of groupworker recognition of this systemic aspect which may hamper or prevent change at individual or group level.

Tom Douglas has written about groups from a different perspective. In *Groups* he is more concerned with the identification and exploration of elements common to all groups. It is about groups, not groupwork, though the one informs the other. He distinguishes between natural groups and created or 'designed' groups, and by demonstrating '*the ubiquitous nature...of group processes in human assemblies*' urges the reader to apply what is known about natural groups to inform approaches to the design of special groups. It is a theoretical underpinning of groups, illustrating the common factors within family, friendship, work, team and committee groupings that come together naturally, and the effect that experience in such groups has on behaviour in groups that are 'designed' by workers. I found the book hard going – it has a philosophical perspective complicated by long sentences and a use of language not normally part of this groupworker's vocabulary. I do not think often about the '*non-orthogonous nature of group processes*' nor do I often see groups as '*a kaleidoscope of dyadic communications*', though I am sure both are true. Overcoming my prejudice there is value in the book, and I found the chapters on teams and on committees useful reminders of the particular phenomena affecting such groupings. Tom Douglas is somewhat pessimistic, seeing that '*our efforts at design are seldom good; they are always imbalanced, and our understanding of the elements of design and their function is poor*'. In concluding that '*we have a long long way to go to master the art of Gathering Together*' he does little to foster the confidence that groupworkers need if they are to learn from his analysis, and to know '*what the processes of group design are and how they might best be used*'. This is a book for the more experienced groupworker, wishing to grapple with Tom Douglas' ideas.

I now come to what in film terms is a 'blockbuster'. Dorothy Stock Whitaker has written a mammoth book. It deserves and I hope will get a more substantial review. Like Brown and Heap, it takes a sequential view of the groupwork process. Unlike the others, Stock Whitaker prefers the term 'conductor' rather than facilitator, leader, central person or groupworker, so there will continue to be a wide variation in the title given to whoever is seen as being 'in charge' by the agency. The writer aims to convey '*common sense plainly expressed*' and does so in an interesting and, at times, absorbing way. There is a large bibliography but little name-dropping in the text, apart from a strong reference to the works of Kurt Lewin and Thomas French as central to the 'group focal conflict model' used as a framework for the book. Dipping into this book is stimulating – for example, looking at 'high risk' and 'low risk' interventions (Chapter 10), exploring the dangers of 'plunging interpretations' (Chapter 11), and in the following chapter, pages and pages on scapegoating, the many stances taken by the conductor and the management of attacks by group members. There is a helpful section on self-disclosure. Many sections have excellent examples, though often from psychotherapeutic settings. In dealing with problems in the 'established phase' of groups the author argues for seeing every problem as an opportunity – a good example of what Balgopal and Vassil (1983) in an American blockbuster call 'cognitive re-structuring' – of crucial value in helping groups (and groupworkers it seems) think afresh around issues that baffle them. The writer defines terms clearly, and she gives a lucid exposition of complex phenomena. Despite its therapeutic focus, it is down to earth in that the bottom line of the 'conductors' task is to try to '*avoid the irredeemable collapse of the structure*'. The issues of race and gender get little attention apart from a mention in relation to the dangers of isolation when selecting the group. There is a need for publications addressing these issues head-on, as many workers are now centrally involved in multi-racial groupings. But there are many good things in the volume, and while it is the most expensive hardback at £25, there is now a paperback version at £6.95, and the reader will get added interest from every page. It will be around for a long time, and I shall certainly be using it when enmeshed in leading – I mean conducting – a group in future.

I now turn to a book that is, in my view, much more than its title suggests. It is Daphne Lennox's book on *Residential Group Therapy for Children* (1982). I read this expecting it to be of particular applicability to work with a particular clientele in particular locations. I was surprised to find a book that had a lot of general application. It gives a clear outline of three major personality theories and the forms of therapy that derive from them. It defines 'therapy' broadly, and outlines transactional analysis, behavioural and encounter approaches to work with groups, gives many examples in work with children and a vast number of exercises that would be useable in a wide range of groupings outside institutions. In the encounter group practice chapter alone there are some 80 exercises. The book also has a fascinating section on the behaviourist approach, which is barely touched on in the other publications mentioned in this article. In short, a book sadly mistitled, and one that would have received wider readership if it could have been shown as relevant to the wider population of groupworkers.

Now I will look at a cluster of books and booklets which seek to apply groupwork methods to specific services and which, unlike the Lennox book, do have an applicability to practitioners in a relatively narrow field of groupwork activity.

Tom Douglas' book *Group Living* (1986) applies major groupwork concepts like 'leadership' and 'structure' to residential settings. The book devotes a lot of space to general group phenomena, and the application to group living is given rather less attention that I would have expected from the title. The book is heavily referenced, and some pretty high-sounding quotations from the literature may not be well received by workers grappling with the need to work simply and directly with people, some of whom are unwilling members of groups. I very much wanted some examples of actual groupwork practice in residential settings, to illustrate the theoretical material. It added up to a difficult and rather unsatisfying read for me, though in looking at membership of groups Tom Douglas gives several interesting pages to the issue of race in relation to the composition of groups, and comments on the sparsity of the literature in this area.

The Probation Service's involvement in the use of groupwork is well presented in *Intake Groups for Clients (1983)* edited by Allan Brown and Bruce Seymour. The presentation is particularly strong on the preparation stage, and on ways in which the group can be used to make assessments in such a way as to enable participants to 'own' the assessment. Distinctions are made (not always clearly) between orientation, intake, reception, induction and assessment groups. Many of these groups are formed in order to increase motivation to use the wider services provided by probation officers, and to achieve a measure of personal awareness and change. It is a straight and detailed account, and excellent for comparison with services other than probation who do (or could) use groupwork during the intake period. Brian Caddick provides a chapter on intake group evaluation that could also be applied to evaluating groupwork in other settings.

In another part of the social work forest, Lucy Ball and Theo Sowa have assembled a *Practical Handbook on Groupwork and I.T. (1985)*. This is not the upstart information technology, but the social work IT of 'intermediate treatment'. It is short and to the point, and emphasises the importance of workers clarifying their own values in relation to law and order issues. It is sharply focused and very practical, with many exercises to help young people explore attitudes to the police, their own offences, the courts and to rights and rules. The authors express a clear view that '*group work entails working in a structured way with clear aims and objectives and specific methods with a specified group*'. This is a very long way from the emergent possibilities of the experimental T-group and encounter approaches. Truly groupwork is a broad church!

Last, but as is said in the pulpit, by no means least, comes a booklet by John Hodge titled *Planning for Co-Leadership* (1985). No references, but a handy guide, setting out 13 advantages of co-working and 13 possible causes of disturbances in the worker relationship. A useful schedule, with an application primarily to social work. While I hold no particular brief for Dorothy Stock Whitaker's use of 'conductor', it would be preferred by me to John Hodge's use of 'leader'. Styling the worker as leader may make it difficult to 'give up the power' inherent in the 'leader' role, or result in strong competitiveness. I prefer to keep the concept of 'leader' as a group phenomena. The use of the 'worker' or 'groupworker' title, in my view, leaves the way clear for others to take the leader position or perform leadership acts, and may therefore be more 'enabling' and go some way towards 'reducing the differential'. But this is nit-picking criticism: the concluding seven '*conditions necessary for effective co-leadership*' are a valuable *aide memoire* for would-be co-workers.

This article has covered 13 publications in all. There may well be others, but as it stands it is already a good crop of titles. There is little truly original thinking – but with many workers trying to get to grips with what is, it is perhaps unfair to burden the reader with sets of sparkling new ideas. Most of the material is a re-working of thinking and writing about groups and groupwork, but its major value is that it is 'homegrown' and relates very appropriately to the groupwork scene in Britain. The emphasis is on the task and social goals models, though the advocates of personal awareness as a goal are still a strong voice. There is little attachment to doctrinaire theory, and pragmatism rules more or less OK. The theories are not always clearly presented, and the emphasis is on practical guidelines. All the publications are relatively easy to obtain locally, and are not beyond the reach of the most junior of groupwork practitioners or the most strapped of training departments. There is a strong argument for a copy of each to be available in every training department and social work library.

To be critical, books in this period make only fleeting reference to issues of race and how this affects the groupworkers thought and actions. There are books and monographs yet to be written focusing more sharply on multi-racial groupwork practice and rationale at every stage or phase of the groupwork process. There is also a need for more attention to be paid to the effect of the external environment, and the addressing of system issues in groupwork. This will require an increasing recognition that groupwork is not only about change in the individual or group, but is also a means of bringing about change in the wider elements of the system in which the group and the individual find themselves enmeshed. If much of the emphasis of these publications is around remedial and reciprocal models of groupwork, there is also a place for further exploration and development of social action models of groupwork practice. As Nano McCaughan writes in her chapter: '*The field of social groupwork contains the potential for addressing both private sorrows and social issues*'. In conclusion, and returning to the *Which* analogy with which I began this article, can I move towards recommending a 'best buy'?

As a general and readable introduction to groupwork I choose Allan Brown's *Groupwork* – a volume that is also a useful reminder for more experienced workers. In order to remind us all that groupwork is meant to be an enjoyable as well as a serious approach to growth and change, I choose Gaie Houston's *Red Book of Groups*. As a permanent enricher to thought about every aspect of the groupwork process I choose Dorothy Stock Whitaker's *Using Groups to Help People*.

Of the specialist volumes, none shine out as a best buy. There is so little specialist literature that almost anything is welcome in the field to which it relates. There is a real need for more volumes applying groupwork understanding to particular areas of work.

Finally, no one involved in co-working should be without John Hodge's 33 pages of practical wisdom in *Planning for Co-Leadership*.

There are still many gaps. But progress is being made on this side of the Atlantic now, and I echo Peter Smith's concluding line in the first book discussed, that while '*our search for perfection breeds a spirit of scepticism and critique*...(it)...*should not be allowed to blind us to what has already been achieved*'. This reminds me of the need for all groupworkers to sustain optimism about the human propensity for change, and the important part groups play in facilitating change. The groupworkers task is to '*enable, not disable*' and the growing body of knowledge has a contribution to make to the enabling process.

The Publications

Ball, L. and Sowa, T. (1985) *Groupwork and I.T.* London Intermediate Treatment Association, Junction Project, 37 Royal Street, London SE1.
Brown, A. (1986) *Groupwork*. Aldershot: Gower Publishing Co.
Brown, A. and Seymour, B. (eds.) (1983) *Intake Groups for Clients*. School for Advanced Urban Studies, University of Bristol.
Douglas, T. (1983) *Groups*. London: Tavistock Publications.
Douglas, T. (1986) *Group Living*. London: Tavistock Publications
Ernst, S. and Goodman, L. *In Our Own Hands*. London: The Women's Press Ltd.
Heap, K. (1985) *The Practice of Social Work with Groups*. London: Allen and Unwin.
Hodge, J. (1985) *Planning for Co-Leadership*. Groupvine, 43 Fern Avenue, Newcastle upon Tyne NE2 2QU.
Houston, G. (1984) *The Red Book of Groups*. Rochester Foundation, 8 Rochester Terrace, London NW1.
Houston, G. (1982) *The Relative-Sized Red Book of Gestalt*. London: Rochester Foundation.
Lennox, D. (1982) *Residential Group Therapy for Children*. London: Tavistock Publications.
Smith, Peter B. (ed.) (1980) *Small Groups and Personal Change*. London: Methuen.
Smith, Peter B. (1980) *Group Processes and Personal Change*. London: Harper & Row.
Whitaker, D.S. (1985) *Using Groups to Help People*. London: Routledge and Kegan Paul.

References

Balgopal, P.R. and Vassil, T.V. (1983) *Groups in Social Work*. London: Macmillan.
Bion, W.R. (1961) *Experiences in Groups*. London: Tavistock.
Klein, J. (1956) *The Study of Groups*. London: Routledge and Kegan Paul.
Kuenstler, P. (ed.) (1955) *Social Group Work in Great Britain*. London: Faber and Faber.
Sprott, W.J.H. (1958) *Human Groups*. Harmondsworth: Penguin.
Yalom, I.D. (1975) *The Theory and Practice of Group Psychotherapy*. New York: Basic Books.

GROUPWORK (1988) 1, 77–89

SWIMMING UPSTREAM
A Survey of Articles on Groupwork in Social Work Journals 1986–87

NANO McCAUGHAN

This is a literature review of articles appearing in weekly social work journals 1986–1987, describing groupwork projects and developments. The articles were classified into the following categories groupwork methods; groups used in child abuse; women's groups; ethnic issues; parents groups; work with offenders; groups for elderly and physically handicapped people and self-help groups. The paper gives a brief description of the groupwork, and discusses the implications of this work for service delivery particularly in local authority social work departments.

Introduction

One way of speculating on the state of the art of social group work as practised in UK social work agencies is to study the relevant publications in contemporary social work journals. For the purpose of this review, 44 short articles, published within the previous 18 months, were collated. They appeared mainly in *Social Work Today* or *Community Care*, with two contributions from the *Probation Journal* and one from *Practice*. The variety of client groups worked with, and the range of settings involved, demonstrated the wide generalist remit of UK groupwork. There are also significant gaps, so any subsequent analysis must be regarded with caution. The gaps may indicate not so much that certain types of project do not exist, but that no one has happened to write about them recently. For example, the frequency of articles describing groupwork with women or with offending young people is very marked compared to the dearth of groupwork reported with men clients, or with disabled people.

As a criterion for inclusion, the author has designated a 'project' as the formation of a small group – five to fifteen or so members – by social workers or similar professionals, to achieve objectives falling within the recognised current remit of the social work profession. These include – emotional support; help with practical problems of living; assessment for service; welfare rights information or other social education objectives; initiating mutual aid in various kinds of stressful situations; and rehabilitation.

Groupwork methods

Under the general theme of 'methods', there were four papers. Only one of these dealt with a description of using a particular theoretical approach – transactional analysis – with some description of the theoretical underpinnings (Hodgson, 1987). This method was used successfully with a group of adults with some degree of mental handicap, as the author felt that the usual behavioural techniques used to change behaviour could be de-humanising. The other articles comprised descriptive accounts of using art therapy for women attending a community centre (Otway and Ellis, 1987); and games and drama for children in care to enable them to express feelings and to work on them with sympathetic adults and peer support (Crawley *et al.*, 1986). Most groupworkers nowadays use action methods rather than straight discussion methods in problem solving, but the description of methods used in these articles were unusual in that they were used consistently by workers with some specialised training. Thus (as Hodgson remarked) they made available to people from other than the middle classes, therapies that must have been an unusual experience for the members concerned. The accounts indicate that nonetheless these methods were adapted to, and enjoyed by, the group members.

The final article in this section was concerned with the marginalisation of groupwork in social services departments and an analysis of the probable reasons for this (Preston Shoot, 1987). He states:

> Groupwork, in common with all social work, must hold a balance between the social and the personal... In this respect group work must include community development skills and techniques drawn from structural and systemic family therapy alongside the more familiar discussion, role play, art and games orientated programme.

The very small proportion of the articles indicating a consistent use of theory to inform practice must concern us as it detracts from the possibility of evaluating work accurately, and deprives workers of good consistent analytical and interpretive tools. Without these, it is difficult to find concepts to pass on to members which enable them to have more understanding of collective behaviour in general, and to function more adeptly in normal social groups. This last is usually one of the objectives stated by groupworkers in planning the group. The lack of theory is probably due to the marginalisation of teaching about social and collective behaviour on qualifying courses. There are a number of quite useful models around, and some opportunity to learn about groups experientially, even though most theory building has been developed outside the UK.

Groups used in child abuse

Moving to practice accounts, one of the most mentioned types of groups were those around the theme of child abuse, and groups for parents and for victims were described. Brayne and Chandler (1986) describe a group set up for children who had been sexually abused within the family. It was clear from the experience that both the feelings about the abuse and the consequences of telling about it needed to be worked on. In this group of adolescent girls, guilt and powerlessness were the predominant feelings around. All were concerned about future intimate relationships they might make and how or who to tell what had happened to them. The workers used expressive techniques – art and role play – to bring out the inner feelings, and assertion training to enable the children to take control over their bodies and their lives.

A group project with parents of physically abused children (Rogowski and McGrath, 1986) set out to help the parents improve their living situations. The authors' hypothesis, shared by the parents, was that abuse (mainly over-chastisement) stemmed from the tensions and frustrations of poor housing, unemployment and poverty. These led to feelings of isolation. The main complaint of the parents was the secrecy of case conferences and reviews. Another group project with sexually abused girls (Paley and Cox, 1985) had similar findings to that mentioned above. The girls were feeling ashamed and guilty, blaming themselves for the abuse. The workers found it important to help the children place the blame on the adult concerned. The powerlessness and pain about meeting parents again was handled by assertion training – helping them to distinguish what they wanted, and to learn to say 'No'.

Another article describes the efficacy of live supervision of social workers working with families referred to a child protection team. The supervisor was easily accepted by the families. This was family therapy rather than groupwork, but the paper raises the interesting possibility of having similar 'extravision' during the sessions of groupwork with some tense and difficult clients. These articles indicate that groupwork can be employed creatively in the core interactions of statutory social work. It can be a major method in its own right, perhaps used as a preventive measure with parents of children 'at risk' or used as an additional therapeutic tool in work with parents and children where separation has had to be legally enforced. Parents frequently complain that once a child or children have been removed, no one seems to be interested in them, the parents. It is no wonder that rehabilitation plans often fail to succeed. Parents also suffer the isolation and shame consequent upon breaking the social norms of childcare. The support engendered by being helped to discuss tensions and problems alongside other parents in a similar situation must at least diminish the feelings of painful uniqueness in this 'badness'.

Women's groups

Seven of the articles had a focus on groups for women or girls, or in one case a forum for women professionals to enable them to share experiences of work with girls, and help to promote developments locally. This type of groupwork appears to be a consequence of the women's movement, and its consciousness raising influence on women social workers. It was an important ingredient of most of these groups that they were run by women. The work had a feminist flavour for the most part, although for some groups the motive appeared to be mixed, especially when the groups are organised by social workers who may have concerns about the childcare skills of some of the clients.

In one group, the workers believed it was important to have a male co-worker. This was a group for women who had been involved in abusive relationships (Clark and Huckle, 1986). The results were not evaluated in the descriptive paper, but the presence of a male prepared to handle projections of anger and guilt may have helped surface some mutual or reciprocal behaviour between the violent partners. This work had a strong problem solving and information giving focus. One aim was to help facilitate a new start or a better parting. Legal, housing and benefit experts were invited as visitors to the group when the time seemed right.

Two of the projects had a focus on normalisation, or an opportunity to work on health issues that may cause difficulties for a wide variety of women, not just clients of social workers. Starr (1986) describes a support group for women in middle age. Her thesis was that the impact of physical changes over a short period of time, coupled with changes in roles and family relationships required major adjustments as did the transitions in adolescence although the former were not acknowledged. The group was recruited by advertising in the local press, and started off with 17 members. An initial programme of ten fortnightly meetings was succeeded by a 'self-help' phase, which has lasted three years to date and which has attracted some older women to join. Another community resource project is described by Dawson (1985) in which a women's group was formed as a result of attracting local residents to a community centre by first offering a keep-fit class. It was hoped that this would enable a move away from the stigmatising effect often experienced by those on the receiving end of welfare services. The women were encouraged to see themselves as resources rather than problems. The actions they took towards developing services such as a toy library seemed to indicate it was successful. Another similar goup is described by Cree and MacDonald (1985) in discussing their work in developing a single parents' centre in Edinburgh. In both instances the groupwork was varied and included relaxation or keep-fit classes, provision and preparation of food, help with childcare, and talks from appropriate specialists. The main difference from the similar aims and practice of the Settlements seems to be an emphasis on validating womanhood and every effort is made to reinforce the consumers' view of themselves as positive important contributors to society and not just 'parents'.

Randall (1986) writes of a group she set up among psychiatric in-patients, women who were suffering from depression, probably as a consequence of unsatisfactory relationships with a male partner. Randall comments that it became apparent over the life-time of the group that they were living in quite intolerable oppressive relationships, and their careers as patients had oppressed them still further. A feminist approach was explicitly used in the therapy. The women were encouraged to examine society's expectations of women generally and the implications of these for the individuals. They were encouraged to feel and express appropriate anger at some of the demands made on them as wives and mothers. The members clearly felt safe and more supported in this women's group and therefore more able to talk about painful issues like sexual assualt and marital violence.

Schaffer describes a different women's group with a therapeutic intent (1986). This was a group for mothers and adolescent daughters whose behaviour had been causing concern at home, and who were truanting from school. This seems a novel approach and seemed to pay dividends. The first group ran for six months, a total of 17 sessions. The format was to have separate groups for mothers and daughters, and to have joint meetings periodically. The adults were encouraged to look back at their own childhoods and relationships with their mothers through a technique of making a 'life map'.

Finally, Williment and Shearer (1986) share an account of a group set up in a social services department area team, to assess, monitor and support women parents of children on the abuse register, as an alternative to casework.

The group presented a challenge to customary working practices and procedures in the department, and guidelines had to be agreed by the divisional management team to fit in with the local area review committee's policy. There was some evidence that the groupwork was more efficacious than individual work with these clients. Some of the ex-members, two years later have set up a well attended community crèche, and see themselves in a different light from the women with low self esteem and full of tension who had joined the group (Shearer and Williment, 1987).

Social workers with feminist sympathies find themselves in a difficult position with regard to women clients who are depressed, unhappy and burdened with the care of under-fives. The organisational panic created by the potential exposure to national media if a case of child abuse occurs, creates pressure on the front-line workers to monitor, intrude and to take few risks themselves. However, the paradox is that parent child interactions are not going to be enhanced under these conditions. Feelings of isolation and rejection by neighbours and relatives seem to be associated with most abusing families, coupled with the presence of a step-parent or the fact that both adults are young and inexperienced.

Very little is offered to men in these families – there were no groups reported as intentionally set up for men only. It could be that attempts are made and failed. However, a more probable reason is the gender of most front-line workers. Males are a small minority in social services department staff until one reaches a higher grade. Women obviously cannot run men's groups. The resulting situation reinforces the myth that women are totally responsible for the welfare and organisation of the family and for all family problems. If violence between partners is an issue in a women's group, and assertiveness training methods are used, it is obviously important to sensitise the consumers to possible added risks to them at home if they begin to change their behaviour. Clearly, for many women who attend women's groups because the aim is support and changing low self image, groupwork is experienced as therapeutic (even if 'therapeutic' as a concept may be distasteful to the organisers!).

Ethnic issues

Another cluster of articles describe projects which were aimed at women from ethnic minority communities. Jervis (1986[a]) describes work in Brent Council and other local authorities by voluntary pressure groups, to facilitate a more sympathetic and sensitive approach to Asian women who have been victims of violence at home but who because of cultural reasons, are reluctant to use the women's refuges. A few Asian women who have been battered have been offered support groups led by workers who understand their needs. Jervis also describes (1986[b]) the Coventry Asian Mothers with Handicapped Children's Group. Asian women living in extended families but still relatively isolated were under great pressure. They were frequently blamed for the handicap and often at home unable to speak directly to the social worker. '*Husbands and mothers-in-law do the talking for them*'. Similar groups are being set up in other parts of the country as a result of the success of the first.

Parents' groups

Some projects are described which are specifically designed for parents of both sexes. One of these (Hagan, 1986) stemmed from the initiatives of a bereavement 'core group', and an inter-disciplinary staff group which aimed to improve and sensitise the service to parents. Through the support it has offered, various small groups have been organised. A deliberate effort is made to attract men '*to reduce the temptation to dismiss the group setting as women's business*'. A number of parents who attend have said the second year after the death is more difficult to cope with. A similar group run at Enfield Social Services Department (Kerr Wood, 1986) provided an equally valued space for parents. Kerr Wood discusses in more detail obstacles to fathers attending such a group. The death of a child is such a traumatic experience that it may lead to a split between the partners because of different needs in grieving.

Two other projects were offered to parents to support in the child rearing tasks when life becomes difficult. Rogers *et al.* (1986) describe how they harness parents' skills in self-help groups to complement the work of intermediate treatment groups. The approach led the parents to establish some local community self-help groups. It was also seen as an important factor in the successful rehabilitation of children who had been in care. Boyd Tonkin (1986) reports on the work of SPAN, a support group for stressed parents of pre-school children. The group is linked with a volunteer scheme – experienced parents visit weekly or more often and help in practical and emotional ways if asked. Training is given to the volunteers to sensitise them to problems of possible dependent relationships that might be set up, and to enable them to leave the family when the time is right.

Work with offenders

Mark (1986) described a group for offenders run at a day treatment centre, with a major difference to other group projects mentioned so far in that it was a compulsory group. Male offenders were required to attend a group lasting for 12 weeks for 2½ hour sessions per day. The aim of the work was to *'confront the human needs behind criminal behaviour'*. The consumers had a record of convictions and presented as institutionalised. A nine month follow-up survey showed a 70 per cent non re-offending rate. This is a positive, if short term outcome compared with the re-offending rate following other types of sentencing. The group was psychodynamic in its theoretical underpinning and used the 'here and now' experience to focus attention on both the behaviour of individuals towards one another and significantly towards the authority figures involved.

Caddick (1987) reviews the development of an induction group for probationers set up in Bristol ten years ago. Having interviewed the ex-attenders the officers were able to suggest some alterations to the programme used.

One development in intermediate treatment type programmes seems to be a wish to involve parents more closely in the work of professionals, and an educational welfare officer (Wilson, 1986) ran groups for truants as a preventive measure in cases of Care Orders for non-school attendance. Care Orders dropped from eight to two as a result. If the proceedings came to Court a parents' support group was also offered, which influenced magistrates in the direction of using lower 'tariff' alternatives. The more community based approach is described briefly by Miller *et al.* (1986). As part of a campaign against juvenile incarceration the 'patch team' set up an alternative programme, the Saturday group. By an inspired but simple device the social workers hit upon an activity which fulfilled varied objectives for the persistent offenders who were directed to the group. They were helped to make good quality garden seats and donate them to charities or community agencies. The group thus acquired useful and respectable skills, and received praise from their local community for their work – the results of which were highly visible. As a result, the project has been fully accepted by the Court, and its catchment area extended from the 'patch' to two areas of Nottingham Social Services Department. Francis (1985) tells us of a group set up by group workers from Dr. Barnardos Society for young boys addicted to solvents. The work involves both a child centred discussion of experiences caused by the addiction as well as a meaning of the addiction itself to the young people. A reward system (cigarettes) was devised for those who managed to avoid the habit. Fortunately, the group developed anti-abuse norms, with the peer pressure seeming to the workers to be the most important ingredient.

A different group of adolescents also appeared to benefit from groupwork. The After-care Support Team in Bradford Social Services Department offers group sessions to young people leaving Care. It was crucial to have a proper physical base as most were in lodgings or flats. The project required a room in a former children's home. Groups are only part of a programme designed to offer support during those first crucial and often lonely years of adulthood without parental support. (Hempsley, 1985).

Elderly and physically handicapped

Surprisingly the last targetted group, the elderly and physically handicapped did not attract many papers. Perhaps groupwork in day centres and homes for elderly people is taken for granted and is not recognised for the tremendously important influence it has – we refer typically to the ordinary exchanges of group living and remedial work or craft programmes. Only two papers referred to work with handicapped clients.

Gendall (1986) writes about a blind mothers' group formed to convey practical and helpful information about handling young children when the mother is blind. The paper describes a mental handicap liaison group – comprising both parents and professionals, set up to acquire and share information about services and to draw attention to needs for service development. Two papers describe carers' groups set up to support relatives of the elderly, frail or mentally ill. Rowlings and Peacock (1986) facilitated the group for ten sessions, and the members who wish to continue now meet in each other's homes. Green (1986) provides a useful analysis of why some carers' support schemes may be unacceptable to the consumers. The Birley

Moor Project she describes, importantly included the development of a supported volunteer service to provide care relief. With this support they were able to help carers in a variety of ways and not just the way that was preferable to the providers.

Self help group work

The four or five articles on self-help were remarkable for the difference of the views expressed and no doubt the experiences on which the reviews were based. Wilson (1987) comments: '*constructive partnership? uneasy bed-fellows? subtle colonisation? what is the relationship between Social Workers and other professional workers and self help groups?*' This article provides an attractive check list for professionals who wish to 'help groups to grow'. It emphasizes the skills needed to hand over 'ownership' from the initiating steps. For example, introducing people to one another as individuals; organising a series of information giving meetings, and allowing potential members to meet one another naturally; and creating opportunities for past and present clients to be useful to one another.

Cannon (1986) reports on visits to different family centres ranging from those offering a treatment programme to a small children's group, to a much more open community resource type, where local residents can wander in and have a say in what programmes are offered. She states:

> . . . a regular criticism of Social Services planning is that there is a failure to discover the views of the consumer. It could be that one of the shortcomings in Family Centre work is a tendency to gloss over the difference between 'problem families' and 'normal' poor families.

Hatch (1986) analyses the state of most self-help groups – they start off with enthusiasm and reciprocity, making an impact, but tail off to leave the burden to be carried by just a few. He describes an antidote to that decline in the work of Contact a Family, a developing project for families with a handicapped child. His research appears in a monograph *Self Help in Practice* (1987).

The final article (Houlihan, 1986) is a sensitive description of the effective help offered to a client who had been the victim of incest. This support and advice enabled the client to set up a self-help group and telephone counselling service for other victims.

Conclusions

Planned work with various client groups has been part of the tradition of social work in the UK since its professionalisation began in the late 19th century. Theoretical development and model building has taken place mainly in the USA with the possible exception of the 'learning by experience' movement developed by the Tavistock Institute of Human Relations. (Miller and Rice, 1967). As a result, groupwork has not been seriously offered as a specialism on

UK social work courses, and is viewed with suspicion or at least ambivalence by many social work managers.

The Barclay Report (1982) makes one direct reference to the method. However, understanding of and skill in working with small face to face groups must be a basic requisite of the agencies if they are to promote and develop community social work, as the report proposes. There exists uncomfortable boundary disputes between groupwork and case work, and between community work and groupwork. Both the latter activities tend to be marginalised in social services departments and hospitals. Perhaps this is not so much the case in the Probation Service.

This collection of articles is unbalanced in terms of the work carried out by the minority of social workers who struggle in their organisations to obtain the opportunity to learn about and to practice goupwork, both as an alternative, and in addition to, one to one casework. However, perhaps they do represent the current concerns about social control in our communities; the suspected incompetence in childcare practices of many parents, not to say the increasing awareness about cases of cruelty and exploitation; and the fear that the alienation of some of our young people will turn increasingly to violent crime. The groupwork projects described demonstrate enthusiasm and hope in the face of these concerns. It would appear that this is the result of the good experiences of workers and consumers in taking the risks required in joining together in a group to work at these difficult problems.

For the professionals, the paradox is that it requires a challenge to the increasing pre-occupation with roles and specialisation of tasks in local authority social services, in order to give an opportunity for creativity in human relations.

Social workers and others who are prepared to risk their roles in a group, by refusing to stand outside it, by using participative methods, by remaining open and by listening to anger and dispair, can demonstrate that they can be truly helpful. These articles indicate that they can sometimes empower oppressed or depressed people to take positive action on their own behalf and perhaps on behalf of others with similar problems. The actions are sometimes to create informal support networks to help people through transitional periods of difficulty and sometimes they can also work together to succeed in changing the context in which the problems arise.

The papers seem to spell out that groupwork is still in the repertoire of service position in local authority departments and while it is alive and kicking it is clear that forces are operating to reduce and minimise its impact and to marginalise it. Preston Shoot (1987) details the reasons for this which could be chanted in unison by every groupwork trainer, developer or manager.

Primarily, as he states:

> The organisation and focus of many social work organisations mitigates

against integrating groupwork into agency responses since these are reactive rather than pro-active and channelled through individual workers with individual caseloads and clients.

Personal obstacles can include: the lack of preparation training on most qualifying or in-service courses; fears that one will not be seen as competent in this more public activity; fears that the group might present problems of control and chaos, or that some members may push ahead too quickly for others and thus make things worse.

Social workers and others who set up groups on the whole require different capacities than are called for normally in one to one work. For example, in the pre-group phase, marketing skills in order to sell the group to the potential consumers and mobilising the network to release resources such as suitable premises, finances and referrals. On the evidence of the groups described, the social workers tend to have need of a participative and collaborative style in working with clients, to be interested in the potential of mutual aid rather than reliance on an expert, to be skilled at handling dependency appropriately and have a capacity to identify and bring together helping networks. These qualities imply a type of management skill – the management of resources in the interests of people – which requires organisation, experience and usually some training or supervision.

Group workers have the opportunity to learn more about the exercise of power and authority (defining 'authority' as being the legitimate and sanctioned role behaviour in this situation). The hierarchical systems of management which they experience in their own institutions provide an interesting contrast and a tension to the collaborative way most wish to work in groups.

It is possible that groupwork survives at its current level particularly in social services departments because some social workers find their statutory powers alienate them from people they wish to befriend and prevent creative interaction. The lessons from these studies demonstrate that group methods can be used to good effect in tackling deep seated problems, such as those experienced by the victims of child sexual abuse, or the loss of a child.

One important lesson from these studies seems to be that rather than tackling organisational resistance to the development of groupwork directly, it is probably more constructive to form support networks of staff concerned about particular issues in order to enable them to learn from and support one another. It is from the seed bed of these 'mini-communities of interest' that groupwork seems to grow naturally in the supportive and creative context. (Whittle, 1987; Hagen, 1986). Thus those situations which cause institutional anxieties, for example, handling bereavement in a hospital setting, child abuse panics and stress to workers, and racism in social work agencies, may be diffused sufficiently to enable more constructive approaches and responses to happen if the effect on the front line staff is openly faced up to and discussed, preferably in inter-disciplinary groups.

Acknowledgements

I would like to thank Suzanne Williment who kindly collated the articles from *Social Work Today* and *Community Care*.

Barclays Report (1982) *Social Workers, Their Roles and Tasks*. Bedford Square Press.

Blakely, C. *et al.* (1986) 'The one way screen', *Community Care*, 25 Sept.

Brayne, E. and Chandler, T. (1986) 'Overcoming guilt loss and difficulty of telling', *Social Work Today*, 4 August.

Caddick, B. (1987) 'Induction group; means and ends', *Probation Journal*, Vol. 34 No. 1.

Cannon, C. (1986) 'Sanctuary or stigma', *Community Care*, 22 May.

Clark, P. and Huckle, L. (1986) 'Four point plan to help abused women', *Social Work Today*, 1 Sept.

Crawley, J. *et al.* (1986) 'Playing Apollo', *Community Care*, 30 Oct.

Cree, V. and MacDonald, M. (1985) *Social Work Today*, 29 August

Dawson, J. (1985) 'Keep fit to volunteer', *Community Care*, 29 August.

Francis, W. (1985) 'Old skills applied, new lessons learned', *Community Care*, 5 Sept.

Gendall, G. (1986) 'What's the matter, can't you see?', *Community Care*, 27 March.

Green, J. (1986) 'A break or a breakdown', *Community Care*, 15 May.

Hagan, C. (1986) 'A chance for parents to share their sad experience', *Social Work Today*, 24 Nov.

Hatch, S. (1987) *Self Help in Practice*. Community Care/JUSSR.

Hatch, S. (1986) 'Families in contact', *Community care*, 9 Oct.

Helmsley, J. (1986) 'Stepping out into unknown territory', *Community Care*, 21 Nov.

Hodgson, C. (1987) 'Rewarding experiences which helped clients make gains in self esteem', *Social Work Today*, 9 March.

Houlihan, J. (1986) 'Permission to tell', *Community Care*, 23 Oct.

Jervis, M. (1986[a]) 'Asian mums fight back', *Social Work Today*, 7 April.

Jervis, M. (1986[b]) 'Why Asian women need a helping hand', *Social Work Today*, 18 Aug.

Kerr Wood, J. (1986) 'When a child dies . . .' *Community Care*, 8 May.

Mark, P. December (1986) 'Offending behaviour or better adjusted criminals?', *Probation Journal*, Vol. 33 No. 4.

Miller, E. and Rice, K. (1967) *Systems of Organisation*. London: Tavistock.

Miller *et al.* (1987) 'Working with the Saturday group', *Social Work Today*, 20 Oct.

Otway, O. and Ellis, M.L. (1987) 'Painting their way out of the blues', *Community Care*, 9 April.

Paley, C. and Cox, K. (1985) 'Breaking the wall of silence' *Social Work Today*, 3 Oct.

Preston-Shoot, M. (1987) 'Group work presents its challenges and its rewards – for those with the right initiatives', *Social Work Today*, 9 March.

Randall, L. (1986) 'Some women I know; group work in a psychiatric setting', *Social Work Today*, 18 August.

Rogers, S.B. (1986) 'Helping parents solve their children's problems', *Community Care*, 30 Jan.

Rogowski, S. and McGrath, M. (1986) 'United we stand up to pressures that lead to abuse', *Social Work Today*, 26 May.
Rowlings, C. and Peacock, B. (1986) 'Its nice to know that someone takes an interest in me', *Community Care*, 9 Jan.
Shearer, P. and Williment, S. (1987) 'Taking a risk', *Practice*, Vol. 1 No. 1.
Starr, I. (1986) 'Tackling the problems of adjusting to middle age', *Social Work Today*, 18 August.
Tonkin, B. (1986) 'We span a part of life', *Community Care*, 16 Oct.
Whittle, J. (1987) 'Making care a positive experience', *Social Work Today*, 9 March.
Wilson, J. 'Dealing with disruptive pupils'. *Community Care*.
Wilson, J. (1987) 'Helping groups to grow', *Community Care*, 2 July.

FRENCH SUMMARIES

Groupwork Practice with Hard-to-Reach Clients

LAWRENCE SHULMAN

Schulmann considère quatre des facteurs qui rendent difficile le travail social avec certains clients: le sentiment d'impuissance; la honte et la culpabilité; une attitude défensive; le refus de reconnaître l'existence d'un problème, accompagné d'une résistance a l'aide offerte. Il discute aussi comment le travail de groupe peut être la meilleure méthode d'intervention avec les clients présentants de telles caracteristiques.

Structured Activities with Adolescent Boys

ROD CRAIG

Se fondant sur son propre travail, l'auteur discute de l'utilisation du travail et du jeu comme moyen d'atteindre les objectifs de traitement chez les adolescents mâles. L'auteur présente et discute les principes et techniques permettant de faire fonctionner adequatement ce type de travail de groupe.

Groupwork with People Suffering from Schizophrenia

LYNDA RANDALL AND WENDY WALKER

Il s'agit de la description d'un groupe de personnes souffrant de schizophrénie, à l'unité psychiatrique d'un hopital général. L'article est base sur le travail fait aupres de patients à tendance suicidaire qui requièrent plus qu'une simple médication pour surmonter leurs problèmes.

The Worker and the Group Process

KEN HEAP

Heap examine de nouveau le concept, proposé tout d'abord par Redl, relatif aux conséquences découlant du fait que le travailleur de groupe soit une personne centrale a ce groupe. L'article se base sur des compte-rendus d'expériences de travail avec des personnes agées.

Race and Groupwork

ROS MUSTON AND JEREMY WEINSTEIN

Cet article soutient que les travailleurs de groupe ignorent trop souvent les besoins et le vécu des diverses communautés noires de Grande-Bretagne. Il y est affirmé qu'il faut reconnaître et attaquer de front le racisme, sous peine d'être dans l'impossibilité d'attirer praticiens et clients noirs.

A Group for White Women with Black Children

CLARE RHULE

Rhule décrit un groupe visant à offrir aux femmes un forum où elles puissent partager leur expérience de la vie avec un homme noir et de l'éducation d'un enfant noir dans une société majoritairement blanche.

Groupwork Books Published in Britain 1980-86

HAROLD MARCHANT

Cet article fait le compte-rendu de 13 livres portant sur les groupes et le travail de groupe, publiés en Grande-Bretagne, par des auteurs européens, entre 1980 et 1986.

Articles on Groupwork in Social Work Journals 1986-87

NANO McCAUGHAN

Il s'agit d'une revue de littérature portant sur les articles parus dans les publications hebdomadaires specialisées en travail social, durant les deux années ci-haut mentionnées.

Hélène Laverdière

GERMAN SUMMARIES

Groupwork Practice with Hard-to-Reach Clients

LAWRENCE SHULMAN

Schulmann betrachtet die vier Faktoren, die Sozialarbeit mit bestimmten Klienten erschweren, namlich: Gefühle der Machtosigkeit und Hoffnungslosigkeit, Scham und Schuldgefühle, Defensivsein, und Verneinung das Probleme bestehen, wahrend Hilfe Widerstand geleistet wird. Er untersucht, wie Gruppenarbeit die beste Interventionsmethode mit solchen Klienten sein kann.

Structured Activities with Adolescent Boys

ROD CRAIG

Dieser Artikel baut auf die Arbeit des Authors auf, und beschäftigt sich mit Arbeit und Spiel als Methoden, therapeutische Ziele mit Jungen zu erreichen. Bestimmte Prinzipien werden vertreten, und Praxismethoden diskutiert, die diese Art von Gruppenarbeit geeignet machen.

Groupwork with People Suffering from Schizophrenia
LYNDA RANDALL AND WENDY WALKER

Dies ist eine Darstellung einer Gruppe in der psychiatrischen Abteilung eines Krankenhauses für Patienten die an Schizophrenie leiden. Der Artikel bezieht sich auf Arbeit mit potentiell selbsmörderischen Patienten die mehr als medizinische Behandlung brauchten um ihre Probleme zu bewältigen.

The Worker and the Group Process
KEN HEAP

Heap untersucht die Konsequenzen des Gruppenarbeiters als die "Zentral person" der Gruppe, ein Konzept das ursprünglich von Redl vorgebracht wurde. Der Artikel baut auf Praxisbeschreibungen von Arbeit mit älteren Leuten auf.

Race and Groupwork
ROS MUSTON AND JEREMY WEINSTEIN

Hier wird dargelegt, dass Gruppenarbeiter oft die Bedurfnisse und Erfahrungen der verschiedenen schwarzen Gemeinschaften in Grossbritannien ignorieren. Die Authoren stellen fest das Rasismus eingestanden und konfrontiert werden muss, weil es anders nicht möglich wird, schwarze Praktiker oder schwarze Klienten anzuziehen.

A Group for White Women with Black Children
CLARE RHULE

Rhule beschreibt eine Gruppe, die ein Forum für Frauen bot um Erfahrungen auszutauschen was Beziehungen mit schwarzen Mannern und das Erziehen von schwarzen Kindern in einer uberwiegend weissen Gesellschaft betraf.

Groupwork Books Published in Britain 1980-86
HAROLD MARCHANT

Dieser Artikel bespricht 13 Bücher uber Gruppen und Gruppenarbeit von europaischen Authoren, die in England in dem obengenannten Zeitspann veröffentlicht wurden.

Articles on Groupwork in Social Work Journals 1986-87
NANO McCAUGHAN

Dies ist ein Literaturüberblick von Artikeln, die in wöchentlichen Sozialarbeit Journalen in 86/87 erschienen sind.

Sigrid Engelen

NOTES ON CONTRIBUTORS

Rod Craig is currently studying for an MSc/CQSW in Applied Social Studies at Oxford University and has a BSc in Psychology and Philosophy from Bristol University. He spent three years as a residential worker in a children's home and has also worked with people with a mental handicap.

Ken Heap is a British social worker who has been resident in Scandinavia since the early 1960s. He trained at the University of Nottingham, Tavistock Clinic and University of Bradford and has experience of probation, child psychiatry, marital counselling and gerontology. He has international consultative and teaching experience and has published books on groups and groupwork in most European languages. Currently, Ken Heap leads the Further Training Department of the Diakonhjemmet School of Social Work in Oslo, Norway.

Harold Marchant practised as a groupworker with adolescents, and for 15 years tutored on the Community and Youth Work Course at Goldsmith's College, University of London. He is now an independent trainer and consultant in London.

Nano McCaughan is Principal Officer Group Work for Croydon Social Services Department. She has long experience of groupwork practice and of teaching theories of group behaviour and social groupwork practice on basic social work courses and at the National Institute for Social Work.

Ros Muston teaches on a CSS course at Havering Technical College. She is a Senior Lecturer in Social Work specialising in groupwork. Previously she was Senior Lecturer on the Liverpool Polytechnic CQSW courses involved primarily in child care law. Her previous work experience, over many years, was in fieldwork settings. Her interests are in child care, adoption and fostering, and mental health.

Lynda Randall is a social worker in the Psychiatric Unit at Leicester General Hospital, employed mainly as a groupworker.

Clare Rhule has been in youth and community work, both part and full time for several years. For the past four years she has been employed by the South London Family Service Unit to work with women with children under five on the Myatts Field Estate, North Brixton.

Lawrence Shulman MSW, EdD is Professor of Social Work at Boston University. He is a groupwork teacher, practitioner and author. His many publications include *Skills of Helping Individuals and Groups* and *Skills of Supervision and Staff Management.*

Wendy Walker is an occupational therapist at Leicester General Hospital, working mainly with groups. She is particularly interested in the use of cognitive and behavioural techniques in group settings.

Jeremy Weinstein teaches on a CQSW course at South Bank Polytechnic. He is a Senior Lecturer in Social Work and teaches, amongst other subjects, groupwork. He was previously a specialist groupworker for the London Borough of Wandsworth.

EDITORS

Allan Brown is a Senior Lecturer in Social Work, University of Bristol. He is an established writer, teacher and consultant in social groupwork and has established links in Britain and the United States. His main experience and interests lie in groupwork with adults and offenders.

Andrew Kerslake is a Lecturer in Social Work, University of Bath. He has several publications in this field to his credit and has particular expertise in work with adolescent groups and in intermediate treatment and has produced a comprehensive computer consultancy package on working with adolescent groups.

NOTES FOR CONTRIBUTORS

Potential contributors

Articles are welcome from all who have an interest in work with groups (whether as practitioner, trainer, researcher, user or consultant) and who wish to contribute to the development of groupwork theory and practice.

Types of articles

The journal will publish two main types of articles:

i. practice-based papers
ii. theory-building papers

Although these two types of article will differ in emphasis and perspective, both are seen as equally important. The intention is that the practice papers will draw out general principles and the theoretical papers will indicate their relevance to practice.

i. PRACTICE-BASED PAPERS

These articles will be based directly on groupwork practice experience, but written in a way which is evaluative as well as descriptive. The material will make a direct contribution to practice theory in a way which will enable groupworkers to learn from it, and to develop their practice competence. The journal would like to receive articles from groupworkers from a wide range of settings working in different ways with people having different needs and circumstances. This range includes statutory and voluntary agencies, fieldwork, residential, daycare and hospital settings; members of diverse age, race and gender; and methods varying between discussion, structured activity, therapy and action. We recognise that many practitioners may not be familiar with writing for journals, and we wish to suggest the following guidelines to assist in this process:

(a) A brief summary of the contents of the article (100-150 words), drawing attention to any particular theme or emphasis.

(b) Background to the group, the context, e.g. agency setting, type of group, workers and members; group aims and objectives; and the theoretical/philosophical perspectives i.e. any particular principles or values central to the approach taken.

(c) A brief review of the group, content, methods and process.

(d) Outcome and analysis, specific topics of interest relevant to the focus of the article, e.g. key issues arising from this piece of practice; and evaluation of the group drawing out learning points for other practitioners.

ii. THEORY-BUILDING PAPERS

Each issue will carry several theoretical papers ranging over groupwork concepts, theory, research, issues and values. These papers will have no set format, but contributors are asked to begin with a brief summary of the contents of the article (100-150 words) and to include a section at the end which indicates the specific implications of the theoretical material for groupwork practice. Papers on the following topics would be especially welcomed:

(a) The current 'state of the art' of groupwork.

(b) Papers analysing the significance for the groupwork process of race, gender, class, culture and other social factors.

(c) Papers analysing key group concepts and issues.

(d) Papers from different countries, sharing current developments and theoretical concerns and preoccupations likely to be significant for groupwork practice in Britain and elsewhere.

(e) New sources of research evidence.

(f) Groupwork training and skill development, consultation/supervision.

We recognise that some contributors may wish to write papers which do not fall neatly into one or other of these categories, e.g. papers drawing out general principles from groupwork practice programmes. Such papers will, of course, be just as welcome in the journal.

Length of papers
The normal range will be 2,500-4,000 words, with practice accounts not longer than 3,000 words. Exceptionally, longer articles will be accepted and there will be a place for briefer contributions on new developments, responses to previous articles and other material of special interest.

Form of submission
Articles should be submitted in one of two ways:

i. typed on A4 paper, 3 copies, double-spaced with wide margins

ii. on computer disc. Materials submitted in this way should be for use on either IBM-PCs and compatibles (e.g. Amstrad 1512, Apricot PCs, or Amstrad PCW 8256), and should use either Wordcraft, Wordstar or Smart word-processing packages. Those intending to submit material in other formats should first contact the editors.

References
These should be quoted in the text by giving in brackets the author's name and year of publication. They should then be listed in alphabetical order at the end of the article as follows.

Books – author's surname, initials, date, title of book, place of publication, publisher's name, page if relevant.

Articles – author's surname, initials, date, title of article, title of journal, volume and number. Only those references which occur in the text should be listed. Where appropriate, additional resources may be listed separately as further reading.

N.B. It is important that punctuation and the use of capital letters should accord with the style used in GROUPWORK.

Assessment for publication
Articles submitted will normally be passed to members of the journal's panel of assessors, and decisions as to publication made by the editors in the light of the assessors' comments.

Publication
The journal will be published three times a year, in February, June and October.

Abstracts and information section
Any information for inclusion in this section, e.g. notification of conferences, network meetings, recent groupwork publications of particular interest, should reach the editors not later than two months prior to the publication month of the relevant issue.

Authors
Authors should include brief information – two or three sentences – about themselves and their background.

Enquiries
Any potential authors who would like to discuss their ideas prior to writing or submitting an article are welcome to contact either of the co-editors...

Allan Brown, Dept of Social Work, University of Bristol, 40 Berkeley Square, Bristol BS8 1HY
Tel: 0272-303030, ext. M208

Andrew Kerslake, School of Humanities, University of Bath, Claverton Down, Bath BA2 7AY
Tel: 0225-826826, ext. 5815.

ALL TYPED ARTICLES AND INFORMATION FOR THE ABSTRACTS SHOULD BE SENT TO ALLAN BROWN.

ALL ARTICLES ON COMPUTER DISC AND MATERIAL FOR REVIEW SHOULD BE SENT TO ANDREW KERSLAKE.

GCT

**GROUPWORK CONSULTATION & TRAINING
OFFER THE FOLLOWING TRAINING COURSES FOR 1988**

BASIC GROUPWORK WORKSHOP
17-18-19th February
20-21-22nd April
22-23-24th June
21-22-23rd September
14-15-16th December

MODELS OF GROUPWORK WORKSHOP
T. A. PSYCHODRAMA – GESTALT
13-14-15th April
7-8-9th September

GROUP WORKSHOP
INTRODUCTION TO T. A. (101)
26-27th May
6-7th October

GROUPWORK WITH SEXUAL ABUSE VICTIMS***
3-4th May – Women
26-27th October – Women Survivors
5-6th May – Children
24-25th October – Children

WOMEN AS RAPE SURVIVORS
A GROUPWORK APPROACH***
3-10th May
1-2nd November

GROUPWORK SUPERVISION/ ASSESSMENT
19-20th May
13-14th October

PREPARING THE CLIENT FOR GROUPWORK
18-19th April
14-15th November

CO-LEADERSHIP IN GROUPS
26-27th May
12-13th September

GROUP PROCESS OF CASE CONFERENCES
16-17th June
3-4th November

CONFLICT RESOLUTION IN MULTI-RACIAL GROUPS
25-26-27th April
28-29-30th September

GROUPWORK WITH YOUTH
1-2-3rd June
3-4-5th October

GROUPWORK WITH TRUANTS
23-24th May
26-27th September

MEN IN THE WORKPLACE – GROUP WORKSHOP†††
8-9-10th June
7-8-9th September

***Women Only Course ††† Men Only Course

COST: 2 day £60 3 day £90

ALL ENQUIRIES TO: GCT Greenwich College, Meridian House, Royal Hill Greenwich SE10. TEL.: 01-858-6627.

GROUPWORK

Volume 1 Number 2 1988

Editors: Allan Brown and Andrew Kerslake

CONTENTS

EDITORS:
Allan Brown, Andrew Kerslake

EDITORIAL BOARD
Jo Campling, Editorial Adviser.
Ken Heap, (International Editorial Advisor), Director, School for Advanced Training, Norwegian Lutheran School of Social Work, Oslo.
Nano McCaughan, Principal Groupworker, Croydon Social Services.
Rick Morgan-Jones, Consultant and Lecturer in Groupwork, National Institute for Social Work.
David Ward, Lecturer in Social Work, University of Nottingham.

ASSESSORS AND ADVISERS, Lucy Ball, Margot Breton, John Burton, Brian Caddick, Derek Carter, Tom Douglas, Sheila Ernst, Eric Ferron, Charles Garvin, George Getzel, John Harper, Peter Hawkins, John Hodge, John Hughes, Norma Lang, Jenny Lumley, Oded Manor, Harold Marchant, Catherine Papell, Michael Preston-Shoot, Sandra Regan, Kenneth Reid, Dudley Roach, Beulah Rothman, Paul Senior, Lawrence Shulman, Peter Smith, Theo Sowa, Christine Stones, Ann Walford, Dorothy Whitaker.

SUBSCRIPTION, ADVERTISING AND OTHER BUSINESS ENQUIRIES
should be addressed to the publishers, Whiting & Birch Ltd, 90 Dartmouth Road, Forest Hill, London SE23 3HZ. Telephone 01-699-0914 (Int'l +441 699-0914). Telex 8950511 ONEONE G. Quote Mailbox 39000001.

SUBSCRIPTION RATES
British Isles £27.50 Elsewhere US$60
Special reduced rates apply as follows:
Individuals to private address: £15 British Isles $30 Elsewhere
Groupwork is published three times per year.
Two and three year, and multiple copy rates on application to the publishers.

PAYMENT
Should accompany order. Cheque or banker's draft (made payable to Whiting & Birch Ltd) may be in any convertible currency to the relevant amount. Direct transfer can be made to either our Girobank account (no. 5440564), or bank account (Midland Bank, 20 Wimbledon Hill Road, London SW19 7BX, sort code 40-07-30, account number 91109693 78). The following credit cards are also accepted: Access/ Mastercard, Visa, Diners Club, American Express. Quote card number, expiry date and give cardholder's name and address if different from delivery address.

REPRODUCTION OF ARTICLES
© Whiting & Birch Ltd. All copyright reserved by Whiting & Birch Ltd. Enquiries regarding rights of reproduction should be addressed to the Publishers in the first instance.

PUBLISHED BY WHITING & BIRCH LTD, LONDON **ISSN 0951-824X**
Printed by Antony Rowe Ltd, Chippenham.

EDITORIAL

It is a familiar story in social groupwork experience that numerous projected groups either never materialise, or if they do get started, they fail to develop the climate and productivity anticipated by the workers. We can safely say that among the many different explanations of this phenomenon, will be the inadequate attention given to the fundamental, yet often neglected, practice-theory issues which are addressed by contributors to this issue.

Oded Manor's article on the *preliminary interview*, between groupworker and potential group member, illuminates the full significance of this initial encounter. Even at this early stage it is the worker's sensitivity and skill which may be crucial in enabling an uncertain individual to visualise how they may benefit from meeting with others in a group. Ken Reid's piece on *leadership* makes it clear that ambivalence about groups is not the sole prerogative of the potential member. His insights into the worker's ambivalence and skills are primarily for the 'neophyte' groupworker, but there is much there for all of us to ponder. The use of *programme* tends to be accorded low status as a practice skill, yet, as Sue Ross and Andy Thorpe demonstrate in their outline of a structured approach to programming, there are specific and important skills to be learned. In the fourth article on 'fundamentals', Michael Preston-Shoot tackles *evaluation*, demonstrating with helpful examples how it can and should be built into every piece of practice.

We are particularly pleased to publish articles addressing another basic and mostly neglected groupwork topic: *open groups*. Michael Henry reminds us that open groups are widely used, and are found in many different guises from 'drop-in' to quasi-closed. He opens up many of the theoretical and practice issues, which we hope will stimulate other contributions to our understanding of how to make the best possible use of this practice mode.

The two *practice based* articles are about meeting the needs of very different user groups, black children in transracial foster homes (Audrey Mullender) and older people in residential and day care (John Burton and colleagues). What emerges as common ground, however, is not only the opportunity that a group provides for sharing, support and creativity, but also the centrality of the institutional context in both creating the 'problem' and influencing the longer-term outcome.

We would like to thank all of you (British *and* overseas readers) who have welcomed the first issue of the journal as a promising foundation on which to build. Equally, we encourage readers to write to us with your suggestions for improvement and development in the future. And lastly, to those of you busy with your practice and wondering whether to write it up for GROUPWORK, please do!

Allan Brown and Andrew Kerslake

GROUPWORK (1988) 2, 100–114

PREPARING THE CLIENT FOR SOCIAL GROUPWORK: AN ILLUSTRATED FRAMEWORK

ODED MANOR

Many more social workers set up groups nowadays, but they still face a low turn-up to them. One of the reasons for this may be inadequate preparation prior to the first group session. A framework that may help prepare the client for social groupwork was suggested in a previous publication. The framework involved a spiral process of four 'rungs', and the skills associated with each. That framework is slightly modified in the present paper, but the main purpose is to demonstrate the spiral process through a transcript of a roleplay episode. It is hoped that the two papers together may help social workers to prepare clients more adequately and thereby encourage them to express their reservations early or turn up to the group more comfortably.

Low turn-up of clients to groups has turned many social workers away from groupwork. Many of us have been through it: all dressed up, ready for the first session, with nowhere to go. In spite of clients' promises they are not there, and the workers' skilful hiding of their own hurts does not convince the few who have turned up to 'try again next week'.

Some of the blocks which clients experience before they join a group may be better understood and differently handled so that such disappointments are prevented. For this to happen, more attention will have to be paid to the client's experience when she meets the worker on her own for the first time during the pre-group interview. The peculiar dynamics of this meeting and the skills needed to handle it were explored in a previous publication (Manor 1986). The purpose of this paper is to clarify the framework further and to demonstrate the spiral process involved in it.

Since the publication of the framework it has continued to be tested with many social workers in various workshops. The responses indicate that the idea has been found useful, and have also led to some modifications. This elaboration will be offered here first. It has also become clear that workers value seeing the spiral process for themselves. While a demonstration videotape does accompany the workshops on this topic now, it seems that writing it up, in a form of condensed script, might help those who have no access to the film itself. Therefore, the second part of this paper will offer a shortened version of the demonstration tape with comments explaining the spiral process step-by-step.

Four rungs for the interview

The preliminary interview in social groupwork may heighten the ambivalence between the wish to belong and the need for autonomy. These wishes parallel the 'social' and the 'personal' needs we all have. The ambivalence between social and personal needs is intensified during the preliminary interview for structural reasons that were discussed elsewhere (Manor, 1986, pp. 24-27). Briefly restated, pursuing the *goal* of joining a group is accompanied by the *anxieties* and concerns associated with the processing of new information about entering an unknown system (the group). The systems perspective (Balgopal and Vassil, 1983; Durkin, 1981) would suggest that two sub-systems, the worker and the prospective member, are meeting here for the first time to see whether they might join with others to form a 'meta system'.

The group as a meta system of workers and members incorporates the *personal* wishes of those involved and the *social* phenomena that evolve while those wishes are pursued. So, while the group is defined by its parts (members and workers) it is also a whole that is different from them. This delicate complexity has to emerge gradually. Very rarely will the process resemble a straight line beginning with 'selling' and ending with 'buying' a group. Rather, a relationship needs to develop between the worker and each prospective member whereby 'personal' needs are elevated to 'social' goals through trust and explicit communication. The transformation of such a relationship from an individual to a group oriented one is a subtle human endeavour that cannot be fully described in words. However, there seem to be some indications that may serve as the markers of this process. Such indicators for effective preparatory work seem to add up to a spiral process. It is convenient to talk about the process in terms of a spiral ladder of four rungs. These four 'rungs' are shorthand expressions that summarise the roles the worker assumes at different phases of the interview as she handles certain *goals* and *anxieties* related to *personal* and *social* issues. The interview will usually begin with a combination of personal issues and associated anxieties. The worker and the prospective member are both there as two people anxious to be accepted as such first: to be liked, trusted and respected. Therefore, the first step, or 'rung', is concerned with *engagement* between the two. Once engagement has begun to take place the interview may move to the next stage. 'Problems' may then be connected to 'tasks' which may alleviate them, and individualised aspirations may be extended into group oriented goals. The worker will then focus on *linking* by reformulating anxieties into tasks and individualised goals into those which may be achieved in group situations. If these connections begin to make sense to the prospective member the worker may move to combine goals with social issues more directly. She will enter an *induction* role describing concretely how the identified goals may be achieved in the proposed group. The exploration of social goals may well raise social anxiety in the prospective member. Groups can disable people and none of us is short of past experiences to confirm this. Faced with social anxieties the worker needs to accept them as part and parcel of the process of joining a new group. Rather than bypassing anxiety or supplying a blanket assurance of the 'this will be good for you' type, the worker would better enter the *mediation* role. This role may be assumed by inviting the prospective member to explore the fears fully. A new understanding may then arise between worker and client which will allow disabling behaviours to be handled differently. Figure 1 summarises the combinations of anxieties and goals in relation to personal and social issues as they call for different worker's roles during the phases of the preliminary interview.

Figure 1. The four rungs of the preliminary interview

	Personal issues	**Social issues**
Anxieties	i. engagement	iv. mediation
Goals	ii. linking	iii. induction

The spiral process

The preliminary interview may evoke intense ambivalence in the prospective member and call for a transformation of fears, expectations and goals from the personal to the social level. The systems approach alerts us to the difference between *convincing* people and enabling them to *transform* information (Wilden, 1972, pp. 125-201). Logical processes may convince people when the issue at hand involves adding or correcting information. Rational thinking of this kind can be described as a straight line from problem to resolution. However, when it comes to making different connections among different experiences the process does not seem to resemble a straight line, but rather that of a spiral (see for example, Juch, 1983, pp. 24-26). The spiral process often has identifiable 'rungs'. However, these rungs have to be climbed, so to speak, a number of times. Each time we climb the rungs the cycle is lifted to a different level of increased complexity of differentiation and integration between the parts and the whole.

Convincing a person of the general benefits of groupwork is a logical process that may resemble a straight line. Of course it should be part of the preliminary interview, but in itself it is not enough. Some transformational changes need to take place if the prospective member is to consider *this particular group for herself.* It is such a transition from understanding the possible benefits of the group to feeling that 'this specific group may be for me' which may lead to the act of turning up to the first meeting. Such transformation can emerge only during an interview that grows in cycles. However, speaking of cycles and spirals does not necessarily lead directly to mysticism. It is quite possible to describe a specific order in which spirals of relationships build up. Four 'rungs' through which these may emerge have been suggested in Figure 1. *Engagement* seems to be followed by *linking*, leading to *induction*, before *mediation* may bring about the need for more *engagement*, and so on. It seems possible also to describe skills that may help the worker at each of these four points. Again, these skills build up during the interview, layer upon layer, in aid of the transformational process. The skills were described in some detail in the previous publication (Manor 1986, pp. 29-37) and will not be discussed here.

An illustration of one spiral

The example used to describe the spiral process is artificial. It is a transcript of a roleplay episode conducted on a social work course. Three students agreed to act as a mother and her two children, with the author acting as the groupworker inviting them to join a group. This roleplay episode of 22 minutes is unrealistically short and far simpler than a real interview. However, perhaps because of that, it quickly shows a pattern that contains a number of the cycles described previously. For training purposes the illustrative nature was considered more important than full realism.

The full transcript of the roleplay was still too long to be contained in one paper. Therefore, some moments were summarised and others slightly shortened while the process as a whole was left unchanged.

In order to indicate the pace of this episode the timing of critical interactions was marked on the left side of the transcript, starting from the 14th second (i.e. 00.14). These time markers will also be used as reference points for understanding Figure 2. It may be helpful to examine Figure 2 before reading further, so that the 'map' (the overall process) is at hand while the 'territory' (the details of interaction) is explored. On the right are comments about the worker's interventions at each point.

Presenting situation: Ms Jones visited the social services office a few days earlier. She told the duty social worker that she was at the end of her tether and was afraid of hitting her children: Ruth aged four years and Danny aged two years. The duty social worker first assessed the risk involved and was satisfied that, given a concrete suggestion of help, Ms Jones was not likely to harm the children within the few days needed to organise a response. Since a single mothers' group was being set up in the high rise building where Ms Jones lived, the duty social worker decided it was the offer of choice. She then asked the groupworker to visit Ms Jones. The groupworker wrote to Ms Jones offering her a home visit first, and this is a transcript of that visit.

The groupworker had three aims for this preliminary interview:

i. to assess Ms Jones' parenting and the children's behaviour including the degree of risk to any of them now;
ii. to explore with Ms Jones whether the proposed group might help her;
iii. to find out if Ms Jones would want to join the proposed group.

The transcript begins a few seconds after the groupworker (W) knocked on Ms Jones' (J) door.

Time	Verbatim	Comments
00.14 W:	Hello, I'm Mr Manor from the social services. Did you get my letter?	
00.20 J:	Hum, I think so, yes. You can see the mess. Would you like to sit down?	
00.30 W:	Oh, that's alright. (to children) Hello. You are . . . ?	Introductions
Ruth:	Ruth	
W:	Hello Ruth, I'm Oded, and is that . . . ?	
J:	That's Daniel. He's only two, so he is a bit quiet.	
W:	Ah, hello Daniel	
01.10 J:	He's a bit shy.	
W:	That's alright. It takes time to get used to each other.	Assumes that Ms J refers also to herself; indicates a slow pace.
01.17 *W:*	(to J) I hope you remember that in my letter I said that following your visit to the office I thought we might have a chat about your situation. How is it now?	Clarifies purpose of visit. Offers a neutral starting point.
01.31 J:	It's the same. It's just the same. I've got many problems. I got the kids on my own. I don't go out, I don't talk to anyone, the lifts always break down. If I go out I can't always come back. so I'm frightened of going out. The kids drive me mad inside and . . .	
02.11 W:	They do	Stresses to allow focus.

02.12 J:	They don't mean it, but I do lose my temper, it's just that there is no other way round. People down there – they don't talk to you. Chains on the doors, you know?	
02.25 W:	It's like the whole world is chaining you...	Communicates empathy to enable elaboration.
02.28 J:	Coming in on me, there's no one to talk to. I'm sitting here smoking, watching TV, the kids are driving me mad...	
02.40 W:	Hum, what is it that they do when they drive you mad?	Draws conversation to more specific issues.
02.44 J:	Ah, they fight and argue, and .... They do play sometimes, but ... kids shouldn't be in a situation like this. I've written off to the Council, I phoned – they don't take any notice.	
02.59 W:	Hum. Let's take one thing at a time. Last time they drove you mad like that, what happened?	Orders issues. Draws out specifics.
03.07 J:	When they're arguing?	
03.09 W:	Hum, how does it happen?	
03.17 J:	Well, I've just given them dinner . . . (sighs) then she chucks something on the floor, blamed him. I smacked him and they both started...	
Ruth:	Mum, can I have a drink?	
J: (to Ruth)	In a minute! Wait. In a minute.	
03.40 W:	(to Ruth) Ruth, in a minute. We won't chat for very long, but I need to hear from your Mum how things are for you. I enjoy your play. Seems to go nicely.	Tests child's response to boundaries by reinforcing Mum and then reinforcing child.
03.50 J:	They're good kids really	
03.51 W:	Yes	
03.52 J:	But they do argue a lot and they drive me mad and I ... (sigh) I'm just frightened I'd do something to them...	

As can be seen, the interview up to now has been focused on *engagement* between the worker and the rest of the family. While using core skills for *engagement* the Worker also orders the issues (*02.59: 'let's take one thing at a time'*), begins to assess parent-child interactions (*03.17–03.52*) and hears enough 'group oriented' messages, that is issues that can be helped through groupwork, to encourage him to suggest the group. He will therefore *link* Ms J's situation to those of others on the estate and raise the idea of a group, thereby moving the interview into the *linking* 'rung' for about half a minute.

04.00 W:	Yes, you see, I'm visiting a number of women in your situation and they all describe the same things: being stuck in a very small flat, nobody talking, the lifts breaking down . . . and I thought that one possibility was for us to meet together, have a chat, see how to . . . make the most of it.	Links Ms J's situation to others' on the estate. Tentatively suggests a group.
04.30 J:	You mean, like meet the other women?	
04.31 W:	hum (pause)	

The worker's pause at this point is his response to the non-verbal cues from Ms J that she is worried. Even this brief mentioning of the group as a form of *linking* combined with some *induction* seems to raise social anxiety and the worker will now have to deal with that.

04.35 J:	Sounds a good idea, but I won't know anyone, will I (draws back)?	
04.40 W:	No, not yet. Although you'll all be living locally – people don't know each other here. That's quite amazing.	Confirms the validity of Ms J's fear.

The worker has begun the *mediation* between Ms J and the prospective members (*04.40: people don't know each other here'*), but has not involved the children sufficiently yet. Children always help the process when they stop it. They signal something about the process that most adults are slow to express. Often they sense that the adults are distressed and divert attention to themselves in order to ease the pressure. Such 'disruption' erupts now exactly 17 seconds after Ms J conveyed anxiety. Therefore, it is better to respond to the children in their own right (as in need of more contact with the worker) and as speaking for their mother at the same time. In such a situation the interview has to move back to *engagement*.

04.52 Ruth:	Mum! He's throwing things.	
05.00 J:	(to children) stop this arguing! (to W) See, they're at it now.	
05.07 W:	Danny, come and show me the one you like best. I'd like to know. (boy comes near with a toy). Ah, it says D, like Danny, isn't it?	Accepts child's behaviour as indication that the conversation is too uncomfortable. Slows pace down through play.
Danny:	Dee, Dee	
Ruth:	That's me	
W:	Oh yes, that's a bit like Ruth (continues play with children)	

After almost two minutes of play with the worker the children calm down. The worker sees this as an indication that the whole system of mother AND children are more at ease, so he can go back to *mediation*.

06.49. W:	(to J), Yea, you seem to be a bit worried about meeting all those women you don't know.	Reflects back to retrieve focus.
06.59 J:	Ah, yea – I do feel a bit frightened about it.	
07.02 W:	Hum, let's see, what's the worst that may happen?	Polarises, stressing the negative side.
0.710 J:	That I might not fit in, I think.	
07.14 W:	You'll be the odd one out.	Uses empathy to invite elaboration.
07.16 J:	I could be, and I wouldn't like that.	
07.20 W:	Yea, I wouldn't like to be the odd one out.	Offers support.
07.28 J:	No. Well, I may not find anything in common with the others.	
07.35 W:	I see, is it likely to happen? What would you enjoy doing, if you had the time that is.	Invites testing the reality of the group.
07.47 J:	Well, like going for a walk, reading books, but I don't get the time, or like having a chat, but I don't really meet anyone.	

Here, rather than deepening the relationship around more difficulties, the worker resorts to more *linking*, but this time drawing out strengths. This prevents the relationship from becoming too personalised and helps the orientation towards the future group.

08.03 W:	Aha, what books do you read?	Draws out strengths.
08.06 J:	Oh just novels, books I've seen as films.	

Again, rather than personalising prematurely, the worker now enters *induction* with more detail.

08.21 W:	Yes, one of the things I'll be trying to do is help the whole group with this. Each of us will have slightly different interests and we can learn to enjoy this. Like: 'that's a new hobby I can have' instead of pushing people out because they differ. There may be other interests you don't have. Myself and the lady working with me...	Describes own role in detail.
08.57 J:	Is there someone else?	
08.58 W:	Yes. Helen is going to work with me. We'll also have a crèche for the kids. We'll meet down in the Community Centre.	Introduces co-worker in relation to role. Introduces the rest of the system.

As *induction* becomes more specific it raises further anxiety. The children react again to slow down the process. The worker picks up the cue and *engages* them again through more play.

09.10 Danny:	(to W) Ruth? Ruth?	Engagement through play.
09.11 W:	Yes, that's almost Ruth. I think that's close.	
09.22 Danny:	(to J) Ruth! Ruth!	
09.23 J:	That's right. That's right.	
09.24 W:	We're getting there.	Alludes to group.
09.29 J:	Well, I'm interested (joint play continues)	
09. 44	They're both bright but I think they just don't have enough kids around.	

The worker sees this as Ms J's own *linking* and feels free to continue with more *induction* now.

09.50 W:	Yes. That'll be another thing. They'll play for some 90 minutes with other children of their own age.	Continues induction by describing the crèche.
09.55 J:	Oh, they'd love that!	

The non-verbal expression of Ms J at that point is assured and relaxed and the children continue to play happily. The worker reads the message as an invitation to go ahead and enter *mediation* fully, so he is turning to necessary practical arrangements. The proposed time and day are concretely agreed until entry 10.41 when social anxieties arise again.

10.45 J:	Hum, how many women would it be?	
10.47 W:	Around eight.	Responds to social anxiety with a concrete answer.
10.51 J:	Hum, that's not too big, is it? I'd be a bit worried if it was big.	
10.55 W:	Yes, many say it's better to keep it to a comfortable eight.	Validates social anxiety.
11.04 J:	Yes, 'cos you can get to know eight.	

Ms J is already doing some *mediation* work herself (*11.04: 'you can get to know eight'*) so the worker feels he can do more *linking* now.

11.12 W:	Yes, what . . . what do you think you may get out of it for yourself? I think if you knew why you were going there . . .	Goes back to *linking* Ms J with the group more concretely.
11.23 J:	I think . . . I didn't have any idea. From what you say . . . I may just feel less lonely, and . . .	

This hesitant response suggests to the worker that Ms J still does not have a full picture of what the group is for. He offers confirmation of what may happen resorting to *induction* that will have to continue later.

11.34 W:	Yes, that's very possible. It happens in groups. Just having somebody to have a chat with makes people feel . . .	Confirms realistic expectations from group.
11.40 J:	Yes, yes I'm sure I'll enjoy that, but . . . ah, if I don't fit in I needn't come again, need I?	

It can be seen that *induction* is still held back by social anxiety about 'fitting in'. The worker gives more attention to this anxiety first.

11.50 W:	You don't have to, but I'd like you to give it a go for some four times. Everybody will feel they are not fitting in at first. We'll all need time to find out.	Begins to offer a contract for dealing with the anxiety.
12.00 J:	Others too?	
12.01 W:	Oh, yes.	Stresses issue as a task for the whole group.
12.02 J:	Is this usual? I'm not odd?	
12.04 W:	No, not at all.	

The conversation is becoming quite personal now and, as before, the children intervene. The worker is not worried, but rather *engages* them yet again in play and conversation. When it is over he fills the gaps of *induction* with concrete tasks that may be pursued in the group.

12.48 W:	We have a number of ideas we could try together. Some things cannot be solved, but others . . . eventually, people may start helping each other, with shopping perhaps . . .	Offers *induction* in describing concrete tasks that may be pursued by the whole group.
13.07 J:	That'll be useful	
13.10 W:	Maybe together you could do something about the lifts, coping with DHSS, visits to clinics. Do you take them to the health centre?	Reformulates problem as social instead of individual.

The worker makes a detour into health just to be sure there are no pressing problems there, and continues with *induction* talking about finding more ways of coping with two young children alone and adding more games that can be played with them. As he describes his hopes that the group will learn to work together Ms J adopts a withdrawal position holding her head in her hands while she says: *'Well, I do feel interested anyway'* (14.32). It sounds as if not all is well yet.

14.36 W:	Aha	A neutral response to enable elaboration.
14.40 J:	As I said, I feel a bit frightened.	
14.44 W:	Yes, in case you don't fit in. One of the things Helen and I will do in the first meeting is to help everybody with this.	Empathy followed up with description of workers' responses to the anxiety as a group issue.
15.17 J:	You'll talk about it, will you?	
15.19 W:	Hum, maybe we'll also see a film, perhaps about playing with children, and then talk about that.	More detail about workers activities and group participation.
15.35 J:	That'll be interesting.	

The worker has sensed that Ms J's social anxiety has not been allayed and offers more details about help with it. He then stays with *mediation* for the rest of the interview. Step-by-step he then covers other anxieties, particularly about leaving the children alone in the play room. Not only does he explain to Ms J that the children will be introduced to the experience gradually, each time spending more of the session on their own. He also describes the play room and talks about the play leader to the children themselves. The worker assumes his position to be at the interface between the sub-system he is meeting and at least another three. The other sub-systems are: his co-worker, the other group members and the play leader. He does his best to show he listens to the Jones' feelings. He then represents the missing sub-systems by describing in concrete terms what each may be expected to do. Since Ms J and the children convey relaxed interest, the worker moves on to clarify practical arrangements for getting to the group:

19.55 W:	Actually, do you need any help getting there?	Specific contracting about turning up.
20.00 J:	No, I know where it is. That'll be alright so long as the lifts don't break down.	

20.07 W:	Right. So, I expect you one o'clock. Is that right?	Contracts a specific starting time.
20.12 J:	One o'clock. Till what time?	Contracts time limits.
20. 14 W:	Two thirty. I think we need an hour and a half by the time they settle down and we have a chat. Oh yes, if there is any problem, can you give me a buzz at the office? Otherwise I'd be worried about the three of you.	Contracts how to communicate about difficulties.
20.32 J:	Yea, is that the number I've got?	
20.32 W:	Yes, at the top of the letter I sent you.	

At this point the interview has clearly moved to the end of *mediation* when some form of contracting is taking place between the worker and the Joneses. The worker goes over the major purposes of joining the group, finalises arrangements for getting there and says goodbye to each member of the family 'till Thursday'.

Figure 2. The spiral of interactions during the interview

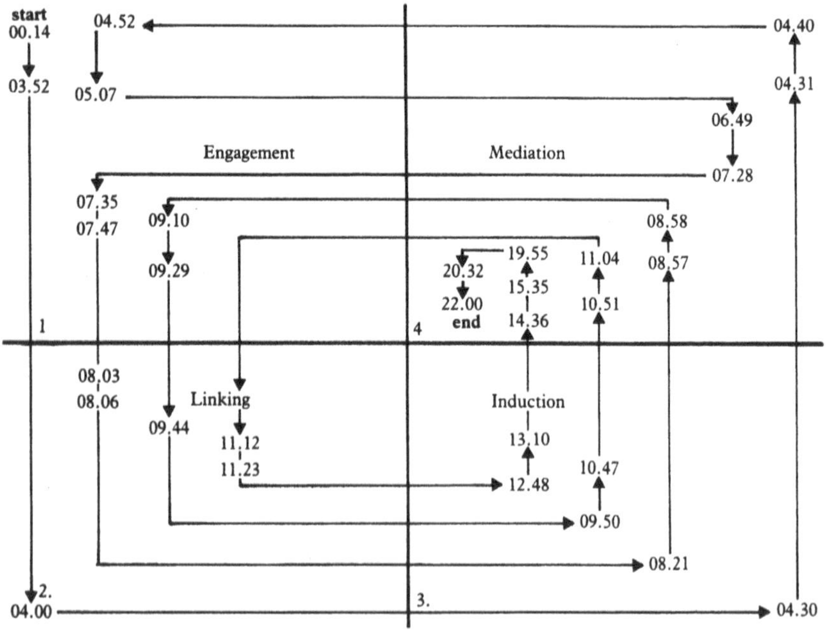

Discussion

It is easy to see that the spiral is not perfect. It goes into a 'loop' between 05.07 and 07.35. This loop is likely to emerge when the worker engages two sub-systems, such as a parent and the children. The children needed attention at a different level from the adult, thus shifting the interview into *engagement* between 04.52 and 05.07. Some tend to ask children to play in another room while they talk to the adults, and this would have probably produced a smoother spiral. However, in groupwork it is better to work with the system as a whole right from the start. In fact, children always help in this. Due to their sensitivity to non-verbal behaviour they always react to the dynamics in the room and show, by their behaviour, some needs that adults are slow or unwilling to express. A child playing more vigorously or coming with a request is not 'disruptive', but rather helpful. The child is signalling to the worker that the conversation is becoming too intense for comfort and that the pace should be slowed down to allow better engagement. In addition, many parents are anxious, as Ms Jones was, about leaving their children to join other adults, and many children are not used to playing in a crèche without their parents. Including such anxieties in the preliminary interview prevents them from surfacing later and cancelling attendance in the group. Of course, working with such two sub-systems during the same interview will create 'loops' in the spiral, but as long as the worker has a clear sense of the meaning of such detours the whole process is not lost. On the contrary, firmer and fuller engagement may evolve.

It is also noticeable that the spiral skipped the phase of *engagement* between 11.04 and 11.12. This often happens later in the interview when the relationship has been, so to speak, elevated from the individualised to the social level, that is to the proposed group. The worker can then see the prospective member communicating about the proposed group 'congruently': the words matching well the non-verbal expressions. When this happens, there is, of course, no need to deepen *engagement* further. Indeed, added depth may make it difficult for the member to share the relationship with the worker in the group session. Therefore, at the later stages of the preliminary interview there will be leaps in the spiral to allow focusing on the future group more than the present relationship between the worker and the prospective member.

Finally, it should be stressed that the spiral takes longer in real interviews. In fact, it may have to be carried over two or sometimes even three interviews before meaningful contracting is possible. Prospective members often do not know enough about groupwork and need far more time for *induction*. They also have legitimate fears of social workers, particularly of those working in statutory settings. The latter would better respond to adults' fears of their powers to remove a child from home or to effect compulsory admissions. It seems better to acknowledge such fears as valid social anxieties and to allow time for concrete exploration of their implications during the preliminary interview.

Of course, the present scheme is only a very general one. Experience and training are needed to apply it to various situations. The first paper (Manor, 1986) provided concepts and the present one demonstrated the process involved. It is hoped that the two papers together may encourage social workers to pay the preliminary interview the attention it needs so that more clients turn up to their groups. It would be most encouraging to see the framework tested with different clients presenting various needs. Inevitably revisions, modifications and substitutions will be suggested that could only improve our work with groups.

Acknowledgements

Thanks are due to Karen Cooper, Keith Benniston and Rachel Richards for acting the Jones family, and to Vic Croucher, Middlesex Polytechnic Media Service for producing the film.

References

Balgopal, P.R. and Vassil, T.V. (1983) *Groups in Social Work: An Ecological Perspective*. London: Collier MacMillan.

Durkin, J.E. (ed.) (1981) *Living Groups: Group Psychotherapy and General Systems Theory*. New York: Brunner/Mazel.

Juch, B. (1983) *Personal Development: Theory and Practice in Management Training*. New York: John Wiley & Sons.

Manor, O. (1986) 'The preliminary interview in social groupwork: finding the spiral steps', *Social Work with Groups*, 9(2), pp. 21-39.

Wilden, A. (1972) *System and Structure: Essays in Communication and Exchange*. London: Tavistock. Second edition.

GROUPWORK (1988) 2, 115–123

GROUPS FOR OLDER PEOPLE IN RESIDENTIAL AND DAY-CARE: THE OTHER GROUPWORKERS

LORRAINE BERNARD, JOHN BURTON, PHYLLIS KYNE and JUNE SIMON

The following article recounts the progress of four groups: a core group of workers on an in-service study course and three projects undertaken by course members in their work places with various groups of older people.

We demonstrate the viability of groupwork by skilled, but not formally trained, basic grade staff: the uses of groups in a variety of residential and day care settings; the therapeutic use of groups in work with older people; the importance of support groups for groupworkers; the feasibility of groupwork even in social services settings which are badly understaffed and have an undeservedly low status; and the place of groupwork practice in social care teaching and training.

The core group is part of the In-Service Course in Social Care at Southwark College and the groupwork projects were undertaken in a South London Borough.

A learning and support group

On Friday afternoons we meet for nearly two hours. We are a group of ten workers whose common concern is social services for older people. Each week we have a theme for the session, but we spend the first half of our time picking up and discussing issues which have arisen at work in the intervening week or during the morning's course teaching.

The purpose of the group is to learn about and work on major issues in social care for older people. Conventional teaching and lecturing in such a group would be counterproductive. All members are working in highly charged and very difficult environments. Some have been moved around from job to job; some of their homes have been closed, are under threat of closure, or are undergoing some sort of inquiry or investigation. For most there is precious little management guidance, support or encouragement. They come to the course with desperate immediate needs and concerns, and nearly always with experiences during the previous week which need talking about.

They also bring with them a lot of good experience, knowledge of the work, commitment to good practice and skills in helping and communicating both individually and in groups. The tutor's (or group facilitator's) job in these circumstances is to create a context in which learning and development can happen, and in which the angry, but creative and supportive, energy of the group can be productively released and used for the benefit of the members and their work, not simply dispersed.

There is another aspect to the circumstances of the group which is very important to its operation. This group is broadly representative of the workforce from which it is made up. All members are women; many are black; many are in their middle or later working lives; many have their own dependants to care for. They are in low status, low paid jobs, and all of them work with older people (mostly women and many disabled). Their conditions of work, the jobs they are expected to do, their lack of support and resources are inextricably bound up with who they are.

We use all of this. There is never a session when the impact of trying to do this work in an ageist, racist and sexist society is not only referred to but is embedded in our discussion. And in this area, as in several others, the tutor, a white man, is far from being the group's expert.

So just how do we use this wealth of skill, experience, knowledge and feeling to achieve the learning objectives of the course and to initiate and support the group projects recounted below?

Setting the tone, opening areas of discussion and leaving them open, encouraging trust, confidentiality and disclosure are essential. The material is abundant. So statements about age, race, and gender, disclosure from the facilitator about his own experience and practice – good and bad, acknowledgement of discrimination and working conditions, careful listening to and taking mental note of people who offer their own experience early on, an open respect for, care for and interest in each individual in the group, all set the ball rolling. In addition, such mundane but important details as arranging seating, keeping an eye on the time, and then commenting on and discussing these arrangements very quickly start the group adding to their already extensive, but often 'unthought out' knowledge of group processes and practicalities.

There should be nothing mystical or hidden about groupwork practice. The growth of a discipline, theory and special language, while in some ways helping the 'thinking out' process with which our group is involved, has also done much to increase distance and confuse people.

In the introductory, initial meetings, we concentrated on working together in a democratic and self managing way. This practice was led by the tutor who took every opportunity to comment on process but also encouraged such observations and reflections from other members. There grew a common awareness of, and conscious attention to, non-verbal and verbal actions and expression of attitudes.

The training for groupwork practice was going on as we proceeded with the other business of our course. Early in the year we constructed an agenda: a large sheet of paper on which we noted topics for further discussion as they arose. We took care to spend time planning our sessions so that some of those issues did not get lost and to prevent our getting stuck in a depressed and angry state which, if accepted long term by a group, leaves nowhere to go, and becomes mutually destructive and very boring.

We have covered a lot of ground in our presentations and discussions. We have ranged over the issues of black elders – their use of and exclusion from services, risk, motivation, incontinence, confusion, quality of staff, sexuality and age, violence and physical abuse and many others. A guest speaker was invited – the head of a residential home, who told us about his struggles to change practice. A visit was made to a home which is pioneering new work, particularly around staff and user groups.

The group was considerably threatened by the prospect of being joined by a new member who was initially viewed as too powerful and in danger of disturbing the trust and cohesiveness which had been established. However by talking about and working on their own attitudes, the members both adjusted and planned their responses so that, far from being a destructive influence, the newcomer was welcomed and allowed to make the creative contribution she was capable of, and this has added considerably to the group's resources.

Groupwork practice and training, without ever being on our agenda, was the source of the strong current which bore the rest of the course along, and helped to launch and support the project work which members undertook in their own workplaces.

As the year has progressed members have become increasingly involved in and responsible for leading discussions, chairing sessions, bringing information, and planning our programme. Experience, knowledge, group skills and the confidence to take the lead have grown even when the workplace has been barren and dispiriting. People have had the belief and courage to discover small areas of fertile ground in the midst of wasteland, and to set out and cultivate their fragile plants.

JB

THREE GROUPS FOR OLDER PEOPLE

A group for independence

I decided to set up a small group to aim for the regaining of some independence by residents of a large residential home through preparing and eating their own meals. I had to make quite complicated arrangements and to negotiate rooms, times and resources with management and colleagues. This is an account of our first two meetings – shopping, cooking and eating.

I asked four residents if they would like to take part and explained to them that I would assist them as best I could. There were conflicting reactions: two ladies were extremely eager to proceed with the project, whereas the other two were very apprehensive. One had not been to the supermarket for 14 years and one said she couldn't manage to walk around the shops. I felt these anxieties, although very real, were more in the mind than in the body. After a lot more discussion, they agreed to meet at ten o'clock one morning for our shopping expedition.

I am a night care assistant so I was off duty when I arrived to collect the group. Mrs M was adamant that she wouldn't go. She stated that someone had stolen her glasses and all her money. She couldn't see because of dizziness, had a bad chest and was waiting to see the doctor. Mrs C was also reluctant to go, saying she had bad arthritis and it would be absurd to involve her in the project. I collected the other two ladies and brought them down to where Mrs M was. On seeing them she immediately rose to the occasion, put on her coat and we were on our way.

After an eventful and talkative car journey, we arrived at the supermarket and found a trolley. Mrs T said that her feet were giving her trouble, whereupon Mrs M suggested that we push Mrs T around in the trolley. All three ladies burst into laughter.

Our first purchase was a bottle of wine. We then went to the meat counter to choose a joint. The ladies practically tore the display counter apart. I got involved when I saw the angry glare of the shop assistant, only to find that they were looking for a joint for two pounds or under in price. I explained to them the current price of meat; they agreed on a joint costing five pounds and went on to do the rest of the shopping.

We returned to the home in time for lunch. Mrs C was waiting for us and asked if she could help with the meal. It was very pleasing to see her renewed interest, and I welcomed her offer. The ladies were very tired and we agreed to start preparing the meal the following morning in the staff flat. At 11 am the next day, Mrs C was seasoning the meat and putting it in the oven and the rest of the group were peeling the potatoes and preparing the other vegetables. They were eager to sample the cabbage for they said when it was cooked at the home it was overdone and quite tasteless. Mrs C asked for flour and eggs for the Yorkshire pudding and to watch her make it you would have thought she did it every day. Mrs H asked for bicarbonate of soda saying she always used it so that cabbage would keep its colour. Mrs F prepared the prawn cocktail starter. This was something of a special occasion so we set a restaurant style table with wine glasses, serviettes, a new table cloth and best china.

The ladies kept popping into the kitchen checking the food. Mrs C had now assumed a management role, taking the lead in the cooking and she knew exactly when everything was ready. We dished out the meal: prawn cocktail followed by roast beef and Yorkshire pudding, roast potatoes and a choice of vegetables, and finally strawberry flan and fresh cream.

The meal was first class and a credit to the cooks. As we sipped our wine afterwards, the ladies talked about the days when they cooked for their families. They said they would like to do their own cooking occasionally. They felt that food was wasted, mainly due to the way it was presented with plates overflowing with overcooked food. They thought a self service arrangement would be better as they could take what they wanted.

During the five hours we were together that day all the ailments previously mentioned seemed to disappear or were forgotten. It made me realise that, although the provision of care is necessary, these residents were very capable in many ways of managing themselves; and I noticed the satisfaction, pleasure and purpose it gave them to do so. We are now discussing the possibility of further meetings on a weekly basis.

PK

A 'memory diary' group

My group was of four clients in a special day centre for elderly mentally infirm people. The 'memory diary' is the combination of scrapbook and diary. It is a very personal and individual way of talking about, writing and recording life events, past and present. It works with each client's memory of childhood, family, occupation etc. and the details are written in the diary along with photographs, if available. The ideas and memories for each diary can provide stimulation for wider use in the rest of the day centre.

Before beginning the diaries with my four clients, I took care to explain and show them an example of a diary, to make clear that each would have her own diary to keep, and to give them some idea of what we were going to be doing twice a week for the next few weeks. Each session was planned to last about an hour and a half. All four clients seemed interested and happy to take part.

We started with the personal details, the first page of the diaries being headed 'The beginning of my life'. Three out of the four had immediate difficulties. They could not remember their surnames when they were children; some said their married names. But when I asked them what their mum's and dad's married names were the memory came flooding back, and brothers' and sisters' names and schools followed quite easily. Mrs H's memory was very clear; she didn't seem to have any problems, and she was a great help to me with the other group members. This lady is 69 and suffers from diabetes; she is often very confused about time and place, lacks concentration, and is said to have severe short term memory loss. However in our group none of these things seemed to hinder her. She just went right ahead and, after discussing each topic, she wrote it all in her diary. She brought in photographs and her baptism certificate and stuck them in the book.

Some of her memories were clearly painful but at the same time she was proud to remember. She felt the loss of memory very keenly and did not like to be told she was 'confused'. She took her diary home to show her family and friends. Her son-in-law was very surprised at what she remembered – in the past and the present, family history, achievements, and details that only she knew. Mrs H took much pride and pleasure in the diary; it helped to stimulate and encourage her in many ways, and gave her a sense of purpose.

Mrs S aged 81, has a short term memory loss and is very hard of hearing but will not wear a hearing aid. It is difficult to communicate with Mrs S but her long term memory is vivid: her childhood, having her own children, her father, where they lived, schools. Some of the unpleasant memories she blocked out. She talked most interestingly but when it came to writing it all down she had forgotten, so I took notes and then after the session I spent time with her individually and we went over it all bit by bit, and then I helped her to write it. She enjoyed the sessions because she loved talking, and I thought that it might be better to use a tape recorder in a one to one situation with her. When the other group members were talking, I had to sit near her and repeat everything that was said close to her ear to keep her involved and part of the group.

Mrs F aged 79, is very lonely and disorientated, and has a poor short term memory. She was very apprehensive to begin with and started by saying she could remember nothing of the past, but once the others got going she too began to remember; she even recalled her first date up on Blackheath Common. This lady has a great sense of humour and was a valued member of the group, often helping to jog others' memories by what she said.

Mrs E, who is 82, suffers from depression, has a very poor memory and often seems very confused. She was quite willing to join the group when asked, and seemed happy during the first two sessions. She joined in, remembering her school days in Wales and working in a tin can factory. She explained how she had to wear rags on her hands to prevent them getting cut by the tins. She couldn't write in her diary so I wrote for her.

To my surprise Mrs E's daughter rang to say her mother didn't want to come to the centre any more because she couldn't sit next to her friend in the coach in the mornings, and also she didn't like the memory diary group because she couldn't remember anything about her life and didn't like the writing.

Our deputy manager persuaded her daughter to try to get Mrs E to come back. She did and I asked her if she wanted to rejoin the group; she was keen to.

In the next session I tried to reassure her that her contribution was very interesting and stimulating, and that we valued her taking part. I asked if she would like me to read back what she had told us. She agreed and when I had done so, she said she couldn't remember telling us all that but said she must have done because it was all true. She told us that while she was in bed, the night of the second session, a lot of the past came back, but by the morning she couldn't remember anything. She is deeply upset by her memory loss and can't understand why it is happening.

I enjoyed running the group and although it was not apparently a great success with all the members, I feel everyone benefited to some extent. This experience has convinced me that this method of work has a lot to offer older people who through their mental frailty and forgetfulness tend to be written off as just 'confused' and have their lives and history, and therefore who they really are, ignored.

LB

A social group in a residential home

I made careful preparations before starting the group. On the advice of my study supervisor, I contacted a specialist groupworker in the borough and was able to discuss with him such questions as suitable numbers for membership, leadership, aims and objectives, and whether to record or not and how. I visited the Age Exchange reminiscence centre in Blackheath which stimulated my own thoughts about the potential areas for discussions and activity.

At this stage I was 'acting up' as a temporary assistant officer in charge in a large home. I had discussed the group with staff and residents, and was about to start when I was suddenly asked to move to another home. I immediately contacted the officer in charge there to explain my predicament. She welcomed the idea but said that another member of staff was also thinking along the same lines. I consulted the person in question and we decided to work jointly.

We selected our six residents and three care staff; all were eager to join in, and we found a small, intimate room for our meetings.

After much discussion we decided on a date to begin. Although it was 'pay day' when everyone gets their pensions, and the day when the shop trolley goes round – the only chance many residents get to buy such things as sweets, cigarettes, and toiletries – it was still the most suitable day we could find.

My colleague who was doing the 'sleeping in' duty that day had to come in an hour early and I had to stay on an hour later in order to fit in the hand-over. As the time drew near I got very anxious. Will I have enough ideas to put forward? Will everyone look to me for total leadership and control? Will we be able to hold their attention and make conversation lively and interesting? Will our inexperience be noticeable?

I was the last to enter the room; everyone was waiting quietly and expectantly. I broke the ice by clasping my hands together and, in the tone of a clergyman, I said *'Dearly beloved, we are gathered here today...'* There was laughter; the atmosphere relaxed and our meeting began.

We started by explaining what our intentions were but also that this was their group and that we would welcome any ideas for future meetings. We also let it be known that this was for a trial period of six weeks but we could extend the time if required. A lot of ideas were put forward: outings, picnics, card playing, music, dominoes, fashion – now and then. Everyone had an idea or comment to offer. We had tea and biscuits, but I kept an eye on the time, and we spent the last 15 minutes discussing our proposed visit to Age Exchange.

All but one member were keen to go. Later my colleague discovered that she was anxious about her incontinence, and for that reason she had never been out of the home since she had arrived there to live.

The next week as we were about to leave for our visit, one of the residents came up to me and asked: *'Does one have to belong to some special club to get asked out? I never get asked to go anywhere.'* My heart sank, wishing there was something I could do but it was too late. As we arrived at Age Exchange the live music performance we were trying to catch had just finished. The residents were so pleased to be out and doing something that they didn't mind. Two of the staff at the centre made us very welcome and took us round. Old, but everyday, objects were delightedly recognised and discussed – sock darners, butter pats, potato and vegetable mashers, ration books – and then the group was asked to identify smells. More memories came flooding back – like oil of cloves for toothache and snowfire for chilblains! We had tea and coffee but our time slipped by and before we knew it, it was time to go.

Our third group had to be cut short because two of us were summoned to a meeting about our previous place of work. However we managed to talk about our trip; the residents were full of it and were keen to plan the next session which was to be a visit to the theatre.

I was off duty so I had arranged to meet the group at the theatre but spent a very anxious half hour waiting for them. They had been caught up in traffic and we were just moving into our seats in the front row as the curtain went up. The show, 'Bugsy Malone', was a terrific success with the group not least because it was set in the Thirties and the accuracy of the costumes was of particular interest and was the starting point for discussion in our next meeting.

We have only just begun, but at this stage I have some thoughts about starting such a group. It is important to keep the group quite small because it may well be that some of the members are speaking to each other for the first time. It helps to make the purpose of the meetings clear from the start and to invite and encourage participation in all aspects of the group's activities. Be prepared with various ways of breaking the ice in the early sessions. The group leader's role is crucial in the above but also she needs to nurse the group's existence to begin with, to be very attentive to individuals and to help every member to feel that she or he is as important as the next person. The next time, I would like to have more time to plan, prepare and to get to know group members better before starting.

JS

GROUPWORK (1988) 2, 124–134

'BUT I DON'T WANT TO LEAD A GROUP!'
Some Common Problems of Social Workers Leading Groups

KEN REID

There is a general fear by both social work students and practitioners of leading groups. One result is that a majority of social workers do dyadic or family counselling and avoid groupwork in their practice. The article deals with fears and fantasies, linked to a perceived loss of power and control, experienced by the social worker leading groups. It also addresses some of the common problems workers face in creating and maintaining groups, including lack of authenticity, misuse of techniques, ignoring process and reluctance to confront, and suggests practical ways the problems can be addressed.

The use of groups as a means of helping has been part of social work methodology for four decades. Along with individual and family therapy, groups have demonstrated their usefulness as an effective vehicle for prevention, rehabilitation, education, social change, and treatment. All schools of social work in the USA require students to have basic knowledge and skill in leading groups and generally require that first and/or second year graduate students lead groups as part of their field work training.

In spite of this acceptance of groupwork within the profession of social work, practitioners are reluctant to work with groups, preferring instead dyadic or family treatment. While the reasons for this reluctance are many and include lack of agency support and limited academic preparation, there are basic fears and apprehensions associated with a loss of control and decrease in power as perceived by the worker when they venture into groupwork. The anxiety linked to these fears and fantasies leads to defensive manoeuvres and security operations by the worker as a means of maintaining control (Barr *et al.*,1981). While a modicum of anxiety in leading a group has value, severe anxiety impedes the worker's effectiveness, and negatively influences the group's development.

This paper examines worker fears, apprehensions and fantasies, and explores problems frequently experienced by neophyte groupworkers. The observations upon which this paper is based are derived from the author's experience (in the USA and England) as a teacher of groupwork within a school of social work and as a consultant to professionals leading groups. It is also based on the author's intimate (and sometimes painful) personal experiences as a practitioner working with groups in both institutional and outpatient settings.

Fears and apprehensions

The beginning worker usually has had experience working with clients on an individual basis. As they begin to work with groups, he or she gives up the relatively secure one-to-one or one-to-two worker-client ratio for the less secure ratio of one-to-eight or one-to-ten commonly found in groups. With the increase of each additional member, the number of interactions the worker is required to keep track of expands rapidly.

Those working with groups, whether beginners or seasoned practitioners, must cope with the problems that are a part of all social work and also with the problems that are unique to this aggregate of people who have come together to meet their personal needs and accomplish the group's goals. The worker must also deal with the dynamics of the group and the multiple relationships between worker and members, and among members.

Whereas in the more traditional practice of casework the practitioner can close his or her office door and be on one's own 'turf,' in groupwork this touchstone is usually absent. Seldom are group sessions held in the worker's office but are more likely to be held in some other room within the agency or another location in the community. Familiar artifacts such as books, diplomas, and family pictures are absent and the worker is forced to find silent security in a pad of paper, a styrofoam coffee cup, or whatever happens to be close at hand.

The worker also gives up power and control that is very much a part of dyadic counselling. Rather than the practitioner being *the* helper, other individuals share in the therapeutic endeavour. The worker, while still in a position of prominence, is but one part of the treatment process. If the worker's ego is fragile, the worker desires excessive recognition, or the worker needs to be the star, he or she will experience frustration as suggested in the following observation by a newly graduated social worker.

> Whenever Flora speaks, the other members pay attention to her and take serious what she says. If I were to say the same thing, they wouldn't consider it as valuable. What really bothers me is that Flora only has a tenth grade education and has held only menial jobs. Even though I'm the leader and have gone to graduate school, I'm embarrassed to say that her advice and interpretations are sometimes more on target than mine.

In this example, the novice worker was threatened by the member. She wanted very much to be accepted by the group and to be thought of as adequate. In such a situation, it is not unusual for the practitioner to find him/herself in a competitive struggle with the member which becomes non-therapeutic and destructive.

Beginning workers frequently become emotionally unhelmed by the fear that they will be made to look bad or lose face in the group. It is as if they are under constant scrutiny and need to do the correct thing at all times. When there is premature attrition, for example, the worker becomes fearful that this will be a reflection on his or her leadership, and the members' confidence will diminish. When there is silence in the group, the worker feels compelled to change the subject or fill the void so as not to give the impression of wasting time, or appearing incompetent.

When members express honest opinions and share painful feelings there is fear on the worker's part that the group is getting out of control and the result will be chaos. Aware of the powerful nature of the group effect, the worker anticipates unbridled conflict that he or she will not be able to manage. There is also fear that because of the group's capacity to collaborate and to establish shared defences, aggression will be directed at him or her in the role of worker. As a means of countering this threat, the beginning worker may display his or her superiority using technical language and interpretations, or becoming quasi-profound and intellectually enigmatic.

Nearly every beginning worker harbours the fantasy of having to deal with uncontrollable resistance during group sessions. In supervision these fantasies are prefaced by 'what if' followed by some potential action of a member or a group, that results in the worker feeling helpless. For example, 'What if no one shows up?' or 'What if they don't talk and just sit there and stare at me?' or 'What if they don't listen to me but take the bad advice of a more disturbed member?'

Williams (1966) has observed that fears, particularly those of beginning group therapists, are often tied to the individual feeling socially impotent, and also being doubtful regarding the value of the group approach. The professional is so impressed by and anxious over the massed psychopathology that he/she loses sight of the underlying community of human feeling and thought processes. '*It becomes apparent that the therapist is resistant to the notion of being treated in a group and projects this resistance upon the patients.*' Thus while giving lip service to the principles and rationale of group treatment, the individual finds him/herself trying to carry out a procedure which is ego threatening, and of which he or she has no faith.

Helping professionals, raised in a family situation where there is an emphasis on rationality, moderation of feelings, and the suppression of hostile communications, are frequently preoccupied with the fantasy of excessive hostility breaking out in the group. This is evident in such questions as: 'What do I do if they begin to yell at me?' or 'What do I do if they start fighting?'

Conflict is not perceived as something that is a natural and normal part of the group process, but rather something akin to violence that is to be avoided and extinguished when it arises.

Lacking authenticity

For a member to derive maximum benefit from group treatment, he or she needs to present thoughts and feelings in an open, honest, and non-defensive manner. The degree of openness and candour will be facilitated or perhaps extinguished by the actions of the worker. If the worker is open, genuine and honest, the participants will be more willing to take risks in expressing feelings and concerns. If the worker is defensive, artificial and judgemental, the members will hold back and resist meaningful participation.

The worker, ideally, brings to the group as much of his or her own self as he or she possibly can, stopping at the point at which this hinders the individual member or the group as a whole. They are not afraid of revealing their imperfections and humanness and invite the clients to do likewise. They have a 'stance' and are clear as to who and what they are as helping professionals. Ideally, they know their function and the goals in which they believe. They are aware of their own pre-dispositions, modes of adaptations, and demonstrate congruence between what they say and what they do (Reid, 1977).

These ideal traits, unfortunately, are not something that one is born with, and while approximated, in reality are seldom totally achieved. Through the process of trial and error, false starts, awareness, discomfort, positive and negative reinforcers and feedback, the worker increasingly expands his or her repertoire of skills, techniques, and methodology. As with most forms of social work, however, there are no formulas the worker can fall back on, and something that is appropriate in one situation may be inappropriate in another.

As a means of dealing with the anxiety common to a beginning worker, he or she may present a facade or front rather than being him/herself. Rather than trusting their natural curiosity, spontaneity, warmth and the ability to listen, they take refuge in the role of therapist, accentuating differences rather than similarities. By playing a role, clients are kept at a safe distance with psychological intimacy avoided.

Some novice workers report that they feel like an imposter in the group and are concerned that the members will soon discover their inadequacy and inability to lead. As a means of protecting themselves, they go to the other extreme appearing as all-wise, all-knowing, and healthier than healthy. During group sessions they become so concerned with what they will say next that it becomes difficult to listen and absorb what is going on.

Others keep rigid control of the group and are quick to fall back on textbook knowledge or their position of credentialled worker when questioned. If members disagree or challenge their authority, it is interpreted as defensiveness or resistance. Or, the beginning worker may remain unexposed saying very little in the group, so fearful they will be viewed as being limited as a professional that they engage in psychological withdrawal within the group. Verbal contributions become that of agreeing with what the more accepted members have said and 'piggybacking' on comments or observations that are safe and unprovocative.

Misuse of techniques and gimmicks

The seeming lack of structure and ambiguity of group treatment can be as uncomfortable for the beginning worker in a group as it is for the participants. Periods of conflict which seem interminable and moments of resistance when the group appears likely to collapse generate a sense of urgency. It is during these times the worker longs for the security of individual sessions and the comfort of his or her office – with the door closed.

It is also during these times that those leading groups crave some form of technique or gimmick that will resolve the particular isssue. They may rush to the library for a 'cookbook' on group activities, seek consultation from someone more experienced, or enroll in a workshop on group leadership. Silently they rue the day they ever decided to lead a group.

Once they have obtained their new found knowledge, they return to the group with 'recipes' appropriate for all occasions. With a flick of the wrist they can lead a 'trust walk,' have members fall backward and caught by the group, and do sentence completions like a pro. After the first technique has been accomplished, they quickly move on to another technique without batting an eye. The worker eventually runs out of techniques but now has become a 'technique junkie.' Rather than serving as a means to an end, techniques have become the end.

While techniques are not bad in themselves, they may mask a situation and hinder the group's development. This is illustrated in the following situation in which a young worker was concerned with silences which she described as going on for three or four minutes at a time. It was her assessment that the silences were due to resistance on the part of the members toward her and an expression of their hostility. In hopes of increasing trust, the worker was planning on having the members lie on the floor, each with their head on someone else's abdomen. Then, the worker, would have them close their eyes and share fantasies about the group.

After some consideration, the worker, at the suggestion of her supervisor, decided to examine the silence both as to its quantity and quality. Upon monitoring several sessions of the group, it was discovered that the silences were no longer than 90 seconds in duration and occurred less frequently than the worker estimated. When members were subsequently asked to share their feelings about the silences and the thoughts they were having, the general response was that they were feeling comfortable and had been thinking about what had just been said.

The activity that the worker had planned probably would not have done any damage *per se* but could easily have distracted from the flow of the group rather than enhancing the flow. Techniques can be powerful sources for emotional release and generate tremendous energy in the therapeutic group. They also have the potential of masking the relationship between the leader and the members. When the storm has subsided, any insights gained can easily be dismissed by the client as having been brought about by something foreign to the client's own resources: the power of a special environment or the magic of the leader's technical skills (Corey *et al.*, 1982).

Accentuating of content and ignoring process

Beginning workers often have difficulty in understanding the concept of using the group method in doing group treatment. Rather, they do individual therapy within the group with the other members serving as observers. Closely resembling more classic psychotherapy, emphasis becomes that of catharsis with the person gaining knowledge of self, i.e., understanding unconscious motivation, eliminating personal barriers with family members, etc. Taken to an extreme, the worker misses the relationships that go on between members and does not address the barriers which prevent honest, open and genuine communication.

Inextricably connected is a 'there and then' or historical focus rather than a 'here and now' or immediate focus. An outcome is digression into storytelling and personal histories having to do with people and situations unfamiliar to most members of the group. The beginning worker, assuming this is helpful, encourages the client to tell his/her story, and the client willingly obliges. The other members, not wanting to be rude or 'bad' members, obediently listen, anticipating the moment when they too will be expected to share their past. It does not take long before members, as well as the worker, are bored. But by now, the group is into a pattern which everyone assumes to be helpful but silently recognises as having little or no real value.

One of the most meaningful contributions the worker can make is that of being open and honest, and sharing genuine feelings in a 'here and now' manner. This, of course, means that the practitioner is in touch with his or her feelings and willing to take the risk of self-disclosing them to the group. So often, beginning workers have some insight into what is happening in the group but are unwilling to act on their observations. In reflecting on this reluctance, Jourard (1971) has observed:

> Resistance to being, to being oneself with the patient, seems to be quite as characteristic of beginning therapists and of experienced 'technicians' of

> therapy as it is of patients and often for similar reasons, i.e., latent fears of how one will seem to the other as well as how one will seem to one-self, or dread of what will happen if one 'let's go' of one's tight self-control.

By self-disclosing thoughts and feelings, the worker puts him/herself on the line and conveys the message. 'I want to be open and honest in my relationship with you and am willing to share what I think and what I feel even though you may not want to hear it.'

Clearly one of the advantages of group treatment is that a vast array of problems clients have in their day-to-day relationships are replicated in the group. If the person has difficulty with authority figures outside the group, they will generally have problems with the worker. If they tend to be scapegoated by their peers, there is a good chance they will be scapegoated by the other members. If they are excessively compliant in their job, they will be excessively compliant in the group. The group, therefore, has the potential of serving as a laboratory where the member's interpersonal style can be examined and positively influenced so as to enhance his or her life outside the group.

Misreading structural realities

Structural properties such as room size, format of the group, and composition can facilitate or inhibit the group's development and the accomplishment of its purpose. The beginning worker who is unaware of the impact of these structural properties may erect situations which will be self-defeating and come back to haunt him/her throughout the life of the group. While many of the structural properties can be determined and modified before the first group session, the beginning worker often comes to appreciate their impact *ipso facto*.

One example of this is the size and make-up of the room where the group will be meeting. Too large a room can distract from the feeling of intimacy while too small a room may, for some members, generate a sense of violation of their personal space. A table may provide a place to put one's coffee cup but also serves as a barrier for participants symbolically to hide behind. Under certain circumstances, the worker may feel that having a place to hide is appropriate while at other times it may be less desirable. Soft over stuffed chairs and couches, while comfortable, may be perceived by young children as a trampoline to be jumped upon, with the worker having to spend an inordinate amount of energy trying to convince them to stay seated.

Whether the group is open or closed ended will also have impact on the group's development. Closed ended groups, in which everyone begins and ends at the same time, provide greater opportunities for group cohesion and member intimacy. But not everyone in the group can accomplish their purpose and goals in the same or a similar period of time. Open ended groups, generally have the potential of serving more clients but seldom reach a point where there is real cohesion. Groups that are open ended can also be frustrating for people who have been in the group for some time. As new members join, the 'old timers' have to repeat over again material they have already shared and what no longer seems relevant to them.

Selection of members and composition of the group can also be a factor in the group's success or failure. Often beginning workers, in an attempt to find a common denominator for the group, bring together individuals that have behaviours or symptoms that are too similar or too different. For example, a group of hyperactive eight-year-olds who cannot sit still, can leave the worker physically exhausted in trying to organize meaningful and enjoyable activities. A group of withdrawn, passive, non-spontaneous adults may leave the worker emotionally exhausted merely out of an effort to get something going in the group. On the other hand, if there are too many differences, the members will feel estranged from each other and find ample excuse not to participate.

In planning activities, the worker needs to take into consideration the social-emotional capacity of the clients in the group juxtaposed against the particular activity and its inherent dimensions such as rewards for participation, competency required, and degree of interactiveness. In short, some activities, by their very nature, are more frustrating than others and require greater ego strength and skill for participant success. Lack of attention to the social-emotional capacity of the clients will lead to frustration for the worker and the group.

Size of the group will affect the members' interaction and the quality of their participation. In small groups, less than ten, there is greater individual involvement, with face-to-face communication more intensive. There are less chances of harmful subgroups forming and more pressure to attend the group. At the same time, the intimacy that occurs in small groups can also be threatening to certain members and result in premature termination. When one or more members are absent, there is the very real risk that the group will fall below the point needed for meaningful interaction.

Large groups on the other hand provide a treatment resource for a larger number of people. There are more individuals involved which offer the possibility for support, feedback and friendship. Participants can occasionally withdraw to reflect, and experience less pressure to speak or perform. But, large groups have the disadvantage of having a lower rate of involvement by members, and require higher demands on the workers. There is less flexibilty in modifying goals to meet changing needs of members and it is more difficult for the worker to manage acting out behaviour.

Reluctance to confront

In observing beginning workers in action, helping skills such as empathy, concreteness, respect, and warmth are generally visible and performed in a manner that has positive meaning for both members and the group. On the other hand, there appears to be a reluctance on the part of many practitioners working with groups to challenge and confront behaviours that are thought of as either self-defeating or dysfunctional to the group's development. The reasons for this reluctance to confront are varied, and include the worker's discomfort with conflict, an overriding need to be liked, and the kind of person who is attracted to the helping professions. Another reason may be the worker's fear of verbal retaliation by the members if they are confronted.

Confrontation is a conscious act initiated by the worker to bring the client and the group as a whole into direct contact with strengths, weaknesses, blind spots, and resources. When done skilfully, it serves as a way for the individual members and the group as a whole to address inconsistencies, clarify perceptions, and to assume a proactive rather than a reactive posture. When done awkwardly, it leads to fear, anxiety, and heightened defensiveness on the part of the participants.

Challenges can be directed at the actions of the group, or one or more of the members. When directed at the group, the focus is generally on themes and processes, particularly communication patterns, roles, decision making, and resistance. The overall objective is to facilitate interaction so as to enhance effective communication between members and to meet the purposes of the group (Reid, 1986).

Challenges directed at the actions of an individual tend to be focused on discrepancies between what the person says and what they do; distortions of their view of themselves and the reality of their life; resistance to the treatment process; and games and smoke-screens used as a means to avoid intimacy.

As beginning workers gain confidence in their skills and abilities to work with groups, the question of whether or not to confront becomes reframed to 'how can I confront in a manner that is responsible, and does not result in the member erecting thicker barriers'.

Dependancy on talk therapy

To the general public and also to many inexperienced clinicians, group treatment consists of children or adults sitting in a circle, talking about life experiences, sharing feelings, and problem solving. The worker, perceived as a calm, benign, parent figure, guides and directs members through interpretations, the offering of insight and sage advice. While this pattern is not necessarily inaccurate, it is but one of many forms of group treatment available to the worker. This particular mode is most appropriate for clients who are able to articulate feelings, conceptualise ideas, and who have a fairly high frustration threshold.

Unfortunately, this template fits only a segment of the clients social workers deal with in their practice. It does not fit children with limited verbal development, and whose most significant life experiences, heretofore, have centred around play. It does not fit many of the aged who have difficulty communicating ideas, feelings, and experiences using words. It does not fit the aggressive, 'acting out' adolescent who chooses not to self disclose, and who is resistant to seeing a counsellor at a social agency. Nor does it fit the hyperactive child who cannot sit still for more than three or four minutes at a time, and who feels a compulsion to get up and run around the room.

The use of talk therapy for many individuals only increases their sense of frustration, isolation, and inadequacy. They would like to please the worker but are incapable of communicating feelings, ideas, and experiences on a verbal level. Similarly, the neophyte worker, wanting to do a good job and genuinely assist the members, increasingly comes to feel overwhelmed and convinced that groups are ineffective and a waste of the agency's time.

Activities should not be thought of as secondary to 'talk' therapy, but rather an essential and valuable vehicle to facilitate interaction, strengthen cohesion, reduce isolation, and provide opportunities for mutual aid. It can be used for assessment purposes and reveal different aspects of group members to themselves and to other members so that the material can be worked on in the group. Activities can also serve as a powerful attraction factor for individuals, particularly children and adolescents, who are reluctant to sit and talk about problems but are drawn to experiences that sound creative and fun.

Practical implications

In spite of fantasies to the contrary, no one is born with the natural ability to work effectively and successfully with groups. As in any meaningful therapeutic endeavor, to reach a level of proficiency requires time, patience and feedback. For many workers they have been pushed to start a group by an agency administrator before they are ready, and the experience has been disastrous. Or they have decided to lead a group because it's fashionable and found they were over their head in dynamics they could not comprehend or comfortably deal with.

Presuming the individual has had basic didactic instruction on group dynamics and the principles of groupwork, and examined the literature regarding the type of group they are considering, it is essential that they have ongoing supervision by someone who is more experienced in leading groups. This can be done on an individual basis or along with other workers who are also interested in deepening and broadening their experience with groups. The discussion may centre on verbal reports drawn from memory, or from a video or audio tape of the session, or the supervisor's observations from viewing the session from behind a one way window. It should be assumed that the learner has certain *lacunae* or maladaptive patterns which need to be modified or at least brought under control in order to become an effective groupworker.

It is also helpful for the individual to be in a group where they are a 'member' rather than the worker. In addition to assisting the person work out personal problems, in relation to peers and authority figures, it gives firsthand knowledge of group treatment from the inside rather than a position of control. The knowledge gained from being in the member role will be of real value as he or she begins to function as the worker with a group.

Co-leadership is another valuable way of learning about groups. This can be done with the individual's supervisor or with a colleague who has had more experience in leading groups. It is important that at the end of the meeting both sit down together and process the experience as to what occurred, patterns of interaction, contribution of the various members, and their own feelings and activity as workers. It is also helpful to sit down before a meeting and discuss ideas and expectations and any anticipated difficulties.

Finally, discussing the process of becoming a writer, Flannery O'Connor has observed, *'One thing that is always with the writer, no matter how long he has written or how good he is, is the continuous process of learning how to write.'* This axiom also holds true for someone becoming a groupworker. One thing that is always with the practitioner, no matter how long he or she has done groups or how good he or she is, is the continuous process of learning how to lead.

References

Barr, D., Greene, P., Kurtz, M., Olds, B., Rich, M., Teah, C., Ulrich, M., Van Slambrouck, C. and Reid, K. (1981). *An Investigation of Social Workers' Attitudes Toward Group Leadership.* Western Michigan University: School of Social Work.

Corey, G., Corey, M., Callahan, P. and Russell, J. (1982). *Group Techniques.* New York: Brooks/Cole.

Jourard, S. (1971). *The Transparent Self.* New York: Van Nostrand.

Reid, K. (1977). 'Worker authenticity in group work.' *Clinical Social Work Journal,* 5 (1), pp. 5–16.

Reid, K. (1986). 'The use of confrontation in group treatment: attack or challenge?' *Clinical Social Work Journal,* 14 (3), pp. 224–237.

GROUPWORK (1988) 2, 135–146

PROGRAMMING SKILLS IN SOCIAL GROUPWORK

SUE ROSS and ANDY THORPE

This article offers groupworkers a way of tackling the tasks of drawing up a programme of work in a group. It uses groupwork theories about group process and leadership to help the group leader think about how best to use the group sessions to bring about changes in the group members. The technique of linear programming, which it describes, gives a framework for thinking about, and working on and evaluating, the work of a group within individual sessions, over a whole group session and over a total programme of groupwork. It is based on practice – the authors' and other groupworkers' – who have used it and found it helpful in looking at the complex issues involved in working out group programmes. It is not offered as a prescriptive model in groupwork, but rather as a way of developing links between theory and method which should lead to better more effective groupwork.

Developing programmes for groupwork with social work clients is a part of social groupwork which takes time, effort and skill. There are a range of books about using techniques such as games, drama, role play, psychodrama, and discussion work in groups, but there is an absence of material on how to draw up programmes for groupwork sessions, and no theoretical frameworks which allow this complex procedure to be made easier. This article attempts to outline one way of working out a programme for a group. It synthesises many of the theories and practices of other writers and groupworkers in the field of social groupwork, particularly the work of Schutz (1961, 1973) and we acknowledge our indebtedness to their work here. It is applicable and has already been used in devising groupwork programmes in a wide range of social work settings, including work with people who are mentally handicapped, elderly, psychiatric patients and young offenders. It is intended to be a practical tool for use in social groupwork and it is hoped that in using it, groupworkers will find it sharpens their awareness and their skills in overall programme planning and evaluation. It is offered, not as a theoretical model, but as a practical aid to good social groupwork programming.

When programming for a group, the workers have to make a series of subtle and complex decisions. They attempt to do so by defining and thinking about the needs and aims of the group, the constraints – both positive and negative – which exist on the group, the objectives and value-base of their agency and the developmental stages of the group. The mixing of these four variables is the same, whether the programme is for the overall sequence of group sessions or for each individual session or for part of a session and, indeed, the groupworker's task is to plan both the overall outline, the individual sessions and the constituent parts of individual sessions (see Douglas, 1979).

Before the linear programming method is outlined, it is important to consider some of the issues introduced above – *aims, constraints, value-base and objectives of the agency, and group processes* – so that the implications of these vital issues for the programming task can be understood.

In considering *the aims* of the group, the groupworker is immediately beginning to define the parameters of the group activity. The aims that a group has, need to be clearly defined both at the outset of the group and throughout its life, so that the groupworkers and the group members are clear what can and cannot be achieved by the group. Tom Douglas talks of the problems caused when groups are made to fit certain aims rather than aims being designed which are truly those of the group. He expresses the hope that groupworkers '*can be encouraged to work with collections of people in fuller understanding of what such entities can achieve, and what they cannot*'. They can be freed from the necessity of using 'off the peg' group approaches designed by others with particular theoretical or methodological axes to grind. These 'off the peg' groups will have particular programmes, not because they meet the aims of the group and its members, but because they reflect some model of groupwork which has been designed to fit in with their theoretical model. This severely restricts the effectiveness of any social groupwork group.

What is achieved, and achievable in a group, should be realistically and specifically defined by the groupworkers. It should not be an abstract statement of aims such as 'the group will aim at raising the self-esteem of the group members', the logical extent of which could be that the programme might include anything from ice-skating and pool playing to psychodrama. Since such an aim is ill-defined, unable to be measured and highly subjective, the programme cannot be linked clearly and directly to the aim. A more appropriate definition of aims might be, for example, 'this group is aimed at helping its members to practice the skills involved in going out and meeting people'. The programme implications for such a group might be that the programme would consist of looking at skills and communication, followed by a series of role plays around various social situations, followed by some real life social situations with feedback and help from the group. This example shows a clear link between the stated aims and the designated programme, and this is the kind of link which is required in an effective social groupwork group. It ensures that the group will be relevant to the aims of its members and will be clear in what it is attempting to produce.

The linear programming mode for social groupwork being proposed here attempts to blend an understanding of these four difficult areas of groupwork judgements in a way which allows for a dynamic and flexible programme to be developed. It also has to take into account that any groupwork programme has to be flexible. All practitioners and their managers in social groupwork know that groups are dynamic and difficult to predict at any time. It is necessary to plan programmes for the group sessions because social groupwork is an active, inventive way of bringing about change rather than a reactive, reflective one. The workers need to know what they are doing and when. Programming is the major way to achieve this. Yet, at any point in the group, crucial decisions may be taken to divert from the planned programme to take up an issue raised by a group member, or to concentrate on an immediate concern. Then the importance of programming is to know what has been omitted, how it affects the total and what does it tell the groupworker about the work of the group up to that point. This demonstrates the value of linear programming as an evaluative tool. In some senses, it would be true to say that in social groupwork, the purpose of a good programme is to give the groupworker something from which they are able to divert. Such is the organic nature of groups that the leaders need to be clear about the direction of the work, or the ways they hope to bring about change.

Another purpose of the programme is to help the workers decide what tasks have to be performed before, after and during the groupwork session. Preparation for the session in a practical and emotional sense is extremely important for the groupwork, and this can only be achieved through good programme development. It is a universal experience for groupworkers to find themselves burdened with a faulty video machine, no materials for a particular game (blindfolds seem particularly elusive in our experience, and unless the weather is harsh when scarves are in evidence, substitutes are difficult) or inadequate materials for the session. Part of the function of programming is to define clearly and assign the tasks that will ensure materials are available and preparation takes place for each session. Likewise, preparing yourself psychologically for the issues that may arise in each session, particularly around ending groups, is supremely important.

A final function of good programming concerns the co-worker relationship in groupwork. Where the session is led by two or more groupworkers as is usually the case in the social groupwork group, it is important that they complement each other and do not 'trip over each other's feet'. The ideas of functional leadership are important here in that, according to this model, leadership is seen to be a set of functions which are performed throughout the group to a greater or lesser extent by the group leaders and the other members. These functions fall into two main categories: those which are about the tasks of the group (getting information, collecting opinions, summarising what has been achieved etc) and those which are about the maintenance (valuing peoples' contributions and feelings, helping resolve differences of opinion between members, harmonising in the group, lightening the atmosphere where appropriate etc). The leaders' tasks are to ensure that these functions are performed by them or by the other group members.

There is a need to programme what each group leader is doing, especially at the beginning of a co-worker relationship. Sometimes, rather more rarely than is generally assumed in social groupwork, co-workers develop an understanding between them of what to do when the other is leading the group. But when this *is* achieved, it is only by a great deal of effort in planning and in feedback, and it is rarely achieved by some form of 'social chemistry'. A good co-worker relationship looks effortless, but seldom is, and represents many hours of hard and demanding effort in programming discussion, feedback, evaluation and sharing of ideas. We have found it helpful to assign tasks and maintenance responsibility in our programming so that when one leader is leading a discussion, for example, the other is taking into account the maintenance functions needed in the group – checking to see if group members are understanding the material; watching the reactions of the group members; lightening the tone of the group where appropriate.

A helpful rule of thumb which can be adopted for co-work is that the maintenance needs of the group will always predominate over its task needs, and therefore the worker responsible for ensuring that the maintenance functions of the group are carried out, can take over from the task person when she feels it is appropriate to do so. For example, in a group where discussion is being led by one worker and the other co-worker notices that a group member is upset by a hurtful comment made in the group, then it is incumbent on the worker responsible for the maintenance functions to intervene as she sees fit. Should she decide to interrupt the group to discuss this issue, then that becomes the task and the other worker becomes responsible for group maintenance while that issue is being discussed and resolved. It is always hard to develop 'rules' in groupwork, but the development of a successful co-worker relationship requires a careful distribution of task and maintenance responsibilities between the workers.

The constraints exerted on a group in social groupwork are the factors which shape its nature and may have positive or negative characteristics, or both, depending on the aims of the group. The constraints most relevant to groupwork planning are the size of the group, the numbers of meetings planned, their length, the abilities and resources of the group members and leaders (intellectual, social, emotional and physical), the venue and environment for the group. It should also be remembered that the aims themselves are primary constraints for any group.

These are all critical factors in programming because, for example, it would be absurd to plan a very active session of group games which took up a large space if the room available was too small, and it would be pointless to plan a session using very difficult verbal techniques for a group of predominantly non-verbal clients or a session using psychodrama if none of the leaders were trained in its use. These seem rather simplistic examples, but they are familiar experiences in social groupwork and hindsight makes groupwork look more straightforward than indeed it is. For example, one of the authors was involved in a group consultation for some groupworkers working in a high security hospital for the criminally insane. The group members were involved in a programme of 'social skills training' which involved learning how to order meals from restaurants, whereas, in reality all of the patients in the group were serving life sentences and were unlikely to be released and would not be using restaurants. In such a situation, a groupwork programme could be much more relevantly constructed around ward régimes or social situations in a hospital such as telling a nurse that you do not wish to take a tranquiliser, or fending off another patient's sexual advances when they are unwanted. Common errors, particularly with relatively inexperienced groupworkers, are either very restricted programming because they overestimate the difficulties group members might have with particular material – for example it is not uncommon for inexperienced groupworkers to say things like 'elderly people never want to do any physical activities in a group' or 'adolescents will never use any written material' – or programming which tends to try to achieve more than is feasible in a restricted number of sessions, which is inevitably going to leave group members with a sense of disappointment and failure. Dealing with these kind of constraints is a crucial factor in social groupwork planning.

A responsive programme will evaluate the constraints in the group and will be a creative, imaginative and full response to those constraints. The formula can never be perfect, but the skill is in making successive approximations towards the optimum programme open to the group.

The value base and aims of the agency for which the groupworkers work, is also an important factor in programming issues. Sometimes, social groupworkers try to act as if they are not part of the agency for which they work, and such groups are doomed to failure. For example, prisoners groups or groups formed of young people on Supervision Orders with Intermediate Treatment requirements have a statutory existence, and the groupworkers, therefore, have some sanctions open to them if members do not co-operate within the group. Such groups have to explore, early on in the programme, issues of control, of coercion and of voluntarism; and any programme of groupwork which does not contain material which allows these issues to be explored is going to be unable to move through them.

Lastly, *the developmental stage of the group* is vital in programming, and again the skill of the social groupworker lies in being able to define what is possible at various stages of the group's life. The processes of group development are widely described in the groupwork literature, but we shall restate here Schutz's model (1961, 1973) which describes the process of the group as containing three elements, that of inclusion (I), control (C), and affection (A). The first issue that a group works on when it comes together is the inclusion elements of the group e.g. are we a group?; who is 'in' the group and who is 'out' the group; to what extent are people included or excluded in this group? The second issue, that of 'control' is then worked on. Who is most influential in the group and who least? Who is to be followed and who is to be led? Very often, this control phase will begin with a centring around the leader's power and authority with group members, testing out how far they can go in doing what the groupworker suggests. The third stage is 'affection' when the issues are about who is closest to who, and who is distant from whom? These affective bonds are powerful and 'real' at this stage of the group's life and can have very important influences on the behaviour of group members and groupworkers alike.

Schutz's model suggests that the group progresses in this manner through a primary resolution of inclusion, control and affection issues, in that order. Then it will work at the same three issues only in a deeper and more concentrated form. This process will continue until the phase of the group known as 'termination', when the formula will go into reverse. At that stage, the affection needs and issues will be taken outside the group, then the control and then the inclusion needs. The model is symbolised as I.C.A. . . . (I.C.A. . . . I.C.A.) . . . A.C.I. (For a fuller discussion of his model, see Schutz 1961, 1973).

If this mode of group process is considered, it has implications for programme planning. It would not be advisable, for example, to plan a programme in the primary inclusion stage which used high risk personally demanding structures like some of the 'hard encounter' games or structures which require members to act independently as a group, because the needs of the group members, at that time, are about working out whether they want to be 'in' or 'out' of the group. Members experience high degrees of personal security needs at this stage of the group and, if inappropriate pressure is applied, it is unlikely that members will actually agree to participate and may leave the group. Likewise, structures or events which pull the group members closer together are inappropriate during the A.C.I. or 'termination' phase. Very often, the insistence on a party at the end of a group can lead to this fundamental programming error, if it omits to take into account an appreciation that group members are trying to break affective bonds with the group and move out to other groups and to relationships outwith the group. (For a fuller discussion of how to link group programming with group process, see Ross and Bilson, 1980).

Linear programming is a way of linking all the aspects discussed above and trying to write down what should happen in an individual session in groupwork and in a whole series of groupwork sessions, or even a segment of a session. It is important in groupwork to see how each part contributes to a whole. It is very clear however, in reality, that groups do not fit into a linear pattern, but rather evolve in a kind of circular dynamic of interaction between the members. Linear programming is, therefore, a device to help planning to be undertaken rather than any attempt to represent 'real' social events in a group. The usual groupwork practice of writing a list of the programme for a session seems to make programming very difficult conceptually. The programming task starts with a definition or a re-statement of the aims of the group and defines the overall frame of activity for the piece of groupwork by a thorough consideration of the group's constraints. This starts by a horizontal line, as below, with the starting date and finishing date marked along the axis. Figure 1 demonstrates very simply how to do this. In this example, the group starts on 2 May and ends in July, and there are to be 12 sessions with the dates on them.

Figure 1

	2 May					Sessions						18 July
Sessions	1	2	3	4	5	6	7	8	9	10	11	12
	Beginning											End

Adding to this material, the groupworkers then write down the aims which are clearly stated above the line so that a clear relationship is drawn out between what the aims are for the group and the time scale for the group. Also added before the starting date, are any planning meetings, consultancy sessions, reviews, meetings with social workers etc, and at the end of the 12 sessions are marked any planned evaluation, consultancy, follow-up or supervision sessions. Figure 2 demonstrates a simple example of this type of planning:

Figure 2

Aims:

i) To help members develop their skills in making conversation, meeting people, listening and assertion.

ii) To provide an enjoyable group experience.

iii) To help members learn to relax in the company of others.

Planning Meetings		1	2	3	4	5	6	7	8	9	10	11	12	Evaluation	Follow-up
		2 May 1982											18 July 1982		
11 April 1982	18 April 1982													4 September 1982	July 1983

The aims may subsequently be modified and adapted, but the workers and group members have to know from the beginning of a group what the work is designed to achieve if social groupwork is to be effective in its planning and programming. Above the horizontal axis there also goes an assessment of the various developmental stages that the groupworker would expect the group to work through at various times. This is to link the programme with those developmental processes which are so important in groupwork phenomena. Figure 3 demonstrates the same group with Schutz's developmental stages marked into the programme. This gives the workers an opportunity to predict, albeit very speculatively, the developmental stages the group might be expected to go through at different times, and to plan their programme around those developmental stages. (For further examples of this type of programming, see Ross and Bilson, 1980).

Figure 3

Aims:

i) To help members develop their skills in making conversation, meeting people, listening and assertion.
ii) To provide members with an enjoyable group experience.
iii) To help members learn to relax in the company of others.

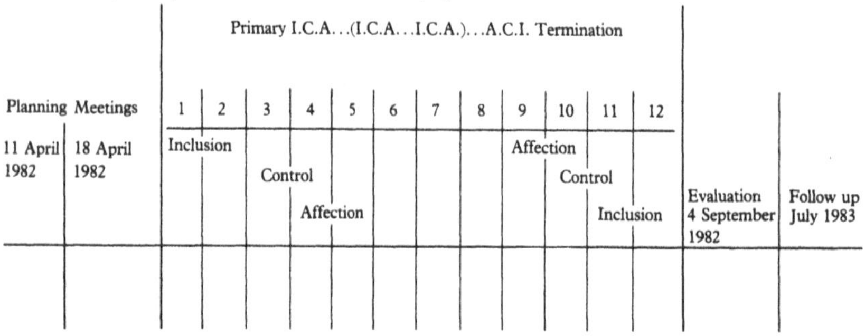

Below the horizontal axis goes all the specific material about who does what and the particular activities that go into each session. The total programme for the group, therefore, might look something like that which is illustrated in Figure 4.

The more ideas that can contribute to the major programme, the better the programme is likely to be, and then each session can be broken down more closely, and detailed more fully, before it occurs, using the same linear programming techniques. For example, Figure 5 illustrates a linear programme for session one of the group illustrated in Figure 4. Again, the aims are specified above the line, the developmental stages of introduction, communication and evaluation are set out, as are the time scales and the detailed planning of who does what.

Figure 4

Single parent's group

Aims:
To help group members develop their skills in making conversation, meeting people, listening and assertion.
To provide members with an enjoyable group experience.
To help group members learn to relax in the company of others.

Planning Meetings		2/5/82 I.C.A.				(I.C.A. . . . . I.C.A.)			
11 April 1982	18 April 1982	(1) Introductions Name games	(2) Input on Communications	(3) Trust work	(4) Contracts 'What I want to achieve between now and July'	(5) Input on Assertion	(6) Role plays	(7) Review of contracts	(8) Role plays
Video to be booked – Sue Room checked – Andy Stationery and materials ordered – Sue Group members interviewed – Andy		– Sue (task) – Andy (maintenance)	– Andy	– Andy	– Sue	– Sue	– Sue	– Sue	– Andy

A.C.I. 18/7/82					
(9) Begin ending work 'Where now?' 'What has been achieved?'	(10) Group feedback	(11) Games about saying goodbye	(12) 'Hot seat' about where people will be in: 1 Year, 5 Years, 10 Years	Evaluation 4 September 1982 Write-up to be completed	Follow-up July 1983 Meet with Supervisor/consultant for area review – Sue to book date
– Andy	– Andy	– Sue	– Sue		

Figure 5

Session 1

Aims:

i) To get members to learn and remember each others' names.
ii) To introduce the aims of the group.
iii) To get members relaxed in each others' company.
iv) To have fun but establish a pattern of work.

6.00	7.30	8.00 Introduction	8.15
Staff planning meeting	Coffee	Intros Game	Feed back
– Andy to collect video – check room – bring equipment	Sue to talk about the group – Andy to introduce name 'rounds'	'Why am I here?' game – Sue (task)	Andy

8.30 Communication	8.40	9.00	9.10	9.30 Evaluation
Input	Games about listening	Feedback on game	Feedback on session	Staff feedback
Listening skills – Andy	'Chinese whispers' – Sue (task) – Andy (maintenance)	Andy	'Resent' and 'Appreciation' rounds – Sue (task)	Fill in recording form

It can, therefore, be seen how this would fit into the complete plan and should interlock with all of the other sessions as outlined in the overall programming planning. If necessary, it is possible to break the programme into even smaller parts so that very detailed planning can be undertaken. Figure 6 attempts to show the last hour of the session described in Figure 5 to give an idea of how this detailed plan could be undertaken.

Figure 6

Aims:

i) To introduce the idea of 'listening' as a skill and practice it.
ii) To wind up and review the session.
iii) To get feedback on how it has gone.

8.30	8.40	9.00	9.10	9.30
Input	Structured experience	Feedback	Total feedback	
Explain listening skills – Andy (task) – Sue (maintenance)	'Chinese whispers' game – Sue (task) – Andy (maintenance)	'I noticed' ………………… round – Andy (task)	'Resent' and 'Appreciate' rounds – Sue (task)	

(*For a description of these games, see Brandes and Phillips, 1978)

When that small section of the programme is broken down, it may well be the case that the programme is far too full. For example, the feedback 'rounds' on a first session are very important in helping the group members to begin to develop ideas of how to give, and receive, feedback from other members of the group. Therefore the time allotted to them in the early stages of the group may, in our experience, need to be quite considerable and so ten minutes of feedback on a game may not be adequate, given the stage of the group. Where the groupworkers feel the need to programme very carefully – (particularly in the first sessions and the last few sessions of a closed group) – it is worth going into this kind of detail as problems of timing overcramped programmes or lack of structural variety can be thus avoided. Two episodes of 'feedback rounds' in that programme may be rather boring, and perhaps an alternative type of feedback structure like a 'continuum' would be much more effective (see Brandes and Phillips, 1978).

In conclusion, linear programming is an attempt to get groupworkers to focus on a wide range of variables that need to be talked about and discussed and examined when groupwork programmes are drawn up. There are a wide range of activities, structures and techniques that can be used in social groupwork, and the range of available material is vast. However, it is the problem of deciding on the applicability of this material that causes difficulties. Linking programme content to the developmental stage of the group is a fundamental groupwork skill. Linear programming helps workers to try to develop realistic aims, to examine the constraints on the group, and to take into account group processes, whilst drawing up a programme. In our experience, the drawing up of linear programmes focuses the groupworkers' minds on these issues in their planning, and gives the basis on which to develop feedback and recording after the group sessions, and it should help them make and form decisions about their options at each point in the group.

Programming skills in groups remain complex, but ought to become more accessible if methods such as the linear programming one described here, are adopted. This technique has been found helpful by many groupworkers who have trained with us, or been present in groups we have run. But it is not given as any kind of theoretical model upon which to construct a groupwork theory or methodology. It is offered here for practitioners to consider, practice, modify, and develop in their own work in groups with a range of social work clients, and it is our hope that it generates increased clarity in the area of planning in social groupwork.

References

Bertcher, H. and Maple, F. (1977) *Creating Groups.* London: Sage.

Brandes, D. and Phillips, H. (1978) *Gamesters' Handbook* London: Hutchinson Press.

Cohen, A. and Smith, D. (1970) *The Critical Incident in Growth Groups, and Theory and Techniques*. California: California University Associates.
Johnson, D. W. and Johnson F. P. (1975) *Joining Together: Group Theory and Group Skills*. Hemel Hempstead: Prentice-Hall.
Douglas, T. (1976) *Groupwork Practice*. London: Tavistock.
Douglas, T. (1979) *Group Processes in Social Work*. New York: Wiley.
Douglas, T. (1982) 'Made to measure', *Social Work Today*, 13 (36) pp. 7–9
Schutz, W. C. (1961) *Joy*. New York: Grove Press.
Schutz, W. C. (1973) *Elements of Encounter*. California: Joy Press.
Ross, S. and Bilson, A. (1980) 'Playing the game', *Community Care*, 31 July.

GROUPWORK (1988) 2, 147–157

A MODEL FOR EVALUATING GROUPWORK

MICHAEL PRESTON-SHOOT

For groupwork to secure a place among the methods used by social workers, evaluation must become an essential component of groupwork practice. Further, its findings must influence future planning and practice. This paper outlines the importance of adopting a consciously evaluative approach to groupwork practice. A model is then presented which, together with examples of this approach in practice, aims to convey a sense of the feasibility of evaluating the process and outcome of groupwork. User participation is regarded as central to the model.

The importance of evaluating groupwork practice, where to evaluate is to seek the value of practice, cannot be emphasised too strongly. There are several reasons for this. First, groupwork remains largely a fringe activity, dependent on individual initiatives and incorporated into overstretched workloads, rather than being one of a range of interventions available to and offered by practitioners (Preston-Shoot, 1987a). This position will alter only when practitioners can demonstrate the value, effectiveness and appropriateness of groupwork, its potential contribution. This requires that results are presented in an accurate and communicable form. It will be insufficient to rely solely on the banner headline that groupwork is a 'good thing.'

Secondly, there are many questions for social workers intending to use groupwork in their practice. For example, are there particular needs and problems for which short term groupwork is appropriate (Brown *et al.*, 1982)? Groupworkers often underestimate the time required either to achieve particular objectives or to consolidate progress. Adopting a consciously evaluative attitude to work, and being able to refer to practice which has been demonstrated to have been effective, will enable social workers to avoid having to reinvent the wheel with each groupwork experience. Put another way, evaluation will inform groupworkers about what approaches work and for whom, about who can be be helped and how (Preston-Shoot, 1987b).

Thirdly, evaluation can improve the quality of services. A clash in perspective (Mayer and Timms, 1970) is not uncommon between social workers and service users, either relating to possible targets of change and/or to how that change is to be accomplished. Evaluation provides a structure for ensuring that activities are directed towards purposeful, achievable outcomes and for negotiating the objectives of the work. In respect of process, Sainsbury (1986) has pointed to a tendency, over time, for social workers and users to lose sight of the clarity of purpose with which the work begins, to lose touch with each other's feelings about their relationship and to find increasing divergence in the reported utility of certain inputs of work. The effect of this can be both to demoralise and to restrict change. Evaluation may provide a welcome counter to these tendencies by reviewing movement towards or away from set objectives prior to any necessary redefinition of desired outcomes. Finally, when approaching termination, the information collected during the task will enable participants to recognise and measure the amount of movement and change. This will suggest areas where groupworkers may usefully focus, where groupwork is especially effective. It will add substance to anecdotal accounts and impressionistic assessments. It will provide grounds either for terminating a group positively or for identifying not only the extent to which objectives have been achieved and why but also the areas of work which remain and those changes to the set objectives which are required. However, little evaluation appears to be undertaken (Sheldon, 1982; Preston-Shoot, 1985) because social workers are unclear what methods to use and are unsettled by the complexity of the processes and problems to be addressed. Furthermore, Sheldon (1986) has suggested that social workers are unused to saying in advance what they want to achieve and what tests of comparative success or failure they would accept.

Initial guidelines

It is particularly useful to distinguish between aims, broad statements of purposes, and objectives, specific targets which together comprise the aim (Preston-Shoot and Williams, 1987). They are not interchangeable. Thus, it follows that broad aims, such as keeping a child out of care or enabling users to establish a self help forum, and vague concepts like self-esteem or support should be reframed into clearly articulated objectives and indicators of progress which lend themselves to specific meaning and measurement. It follows also that evaluation should be a continuing, integral activity within the task, and not something which follows the termination of the group. By that time, if groupworkers have not determined what information they require to evaluate their group, much potential material will have been lost.

The concepts of subjectivity and objectivity appear less helpful than a view of evaluation as a continuum. This runs from precise measurement to impressionistic assessment and description; from rating scales, questionnaires and controlled observation to professional judgement and opinion (Preston-Shoot, 1987b; Preston-Shoot and Williams, 1987). What practitioners use from this continuum will be influenced by what they want to know and what degree of rigour they want to enter into. A variety of approaches will produce a fuller picture.

Sainsbury (1986) has argued that social work is especially effective where targets of change are small and precise enough to be managed. This accords closely with Sheldon's view (1986) that effectiveness stems from 'problem cornering' where the work is focused and the problems well-defined and manageable. Social workers responding to my research into groupwork practice and experiences (Preston-Shoot, 1986), commenting on reasons for the ineffectiveness of groups, highlighted the difficulties inherent in achieving vague or ambitious aims, and in tackling very wide issues. Where they achieved clear aims and purposes, where the work was clearly defined and focused, groupwork was felt to be more effective.

Effectiveness appears also to be related to the attitudes of significant others, either members of the user's own environment or other agencies. Their willingness to engage in the change process is often essential to a successful outcome (Sainsbury, 1986; Preston-Shoot, 1987b; Corden and Preston-Shoot, 1987).

Finally, an essential prerequisite is that tasks and objectives should be thoroughly discussed and agreed (Sainsbury, 1986). This emphasises the contractual nature of the groupwork encounter. Social workers in my research, commenting on those factors which appeared to facilitate their groups, highlighted clarity of intention, and members' investment in and willingness to work at the concept of their group. Groupworkers found that groups were less likely to achieve their objectives where members and leaders were not in agreement about desired outcomes and where the groupworkers appeared to have failed to communicate effectively their purpose in offering the group. This suggests that the process of negotiation with potential members is particularly important. It suggests that the user's own definition of their problems and the difficulties to which they lead should be elicited. Differences between groupworkers and users should be openly acknowledged and negotiated. It is not simply groupworkers, therefore, who pose and answer the key questions 'what?', 'why?', and 'how?' (Mullender and Ward, 1985). It is rather a process whereby users and groupworkers either mutually agree the objectives or conclude a reciprocal agreement where they have different objectives but where they believe that they can co-operate in helping each other achieve their respective goals (Sheldon, 1986; Corden and Preston-Shoot, 1987).

Indeed, the practice of user participation permeates the entire evaluative approach. Not only are consumers actively included in establishing what the issues are, in deciding the goals of the work and in problem-solving, but their skills and resources are also applied to recording and reviewing progress. Rather than being passive recipients, consumers are active participants. This involvement is an active demonstration that consumers have things to offer. Moreover, it does appear to increase morale, productivity, the reality of the goals and the self-esteem of users.

These findings can be incorporated into the following step-by-step model (Preston-Shoot and Williams, 1987). Depending on the objectives of the group, the steps will be negotiated with individual members and/or with the group as a collective entity. Where the objectives of the group are group-centred, for example in social action groups, the model can be negotiated with the group. Where the objectives are more individual-centred, each member will be involved individually in the application of the model (Corden and Preston-Shoot, 1987).

A model of evaluation

Step one: describe the current situation as precisely as possible.

Step two: describe the broad aim or desired outcome for the work.

Step three: identify feasible objectives, specific goals, the achievement of which will help to accomplish the desired situation.

Step four: describe carefully the intervention designed to achieve the desired situation, including the methods to be used and the resources and time required.

Step five: identify indicators (something observable which tells those involved that change or movement towards or away from an objective is occurring) which will reveal change.

Step six: decide who will record what, how and when.

Step seven: set out the first six steps as a plan for evaluating the effect of the work and implement it.

Step eight: establish and review the results of the intervention prior either to a return to step one or termination and subsequent follow-up. Set review dates at the beginning.

Example 1.

This example, from a group for children, is an application of the model used from the beginning of the group. It is an example where the objectives of the group were primarily individual centred. Accordingly, each member was involved directly in the application of the model but, for reasons of space, only two of the eight children have been included here. Step one describes the problems/issues and how they are experienced by those involved. It could, as a baseline, have added the present level of these problems/issues in terms of effects and frequency. Step three highlights the distinction between mutually agreed objectives (Mark) and reciprocal agreements (Joanna).

THE CURRENT SITUATION.

The group is for eight 10 and 11 year olds referred by teachers or parents because of difficulties at home and/or at school. The children have been referred to the group for different reasons within these broad categories. Each child, the child's parent(s) and teacher have indicated on a rating scale the extent to which these reasons are a problem for them, thereby establishing a baseline. Mark was referred by his teacher because of his withdrawn behaviour in class. Mark does not speak to anyone and rarely works. The teacher believes Mark to be unhappy. Mark is constantly looking out of the window and seems 'in another world.' The teacher and Mark's parents have all rated this problem as most severe on the rating scale. Mark has told the groupworkers that he agrees with this rating.

Joanna was referred by her mother because of constant complaints about her aggression towards other children and adults, particularly teachers. She has also begun to truant. Joanna's mother rated these problems as most severe on the rating scale. Joanna does not agree with this rating, believing that only her truancy is a problem. Joanna's teacher rated the problems as moderately severe.

THE DESIRED SITUATION.

That, by the end of the group, the ratings will chart a reduction in problem severity, and that the frequency of the complained-of behaviours will have decreased. Secondly, that the group will show that children with these types of difficulties can be helped by attending a closed group.

OBJECTIVES.

Teachers, parents and children have identified particular goals for each child as part of the preparation of the group. Thus: Mark would like to become more involved in class and in playing with friends. He would like to feel more confident when with peers and adults.

Joanna would like to feel more confident. Her teachers and parents would like Joanna to be able to talk through difficult or conflictual situations rather than resort to aggression.

The objectives of the group include an expectation that all children attend the group and take an increasing part in planning and running it.

THE INTERVENTION.

The group will run for 28 sessions, with reviews after sessions eight, 16 and 24. Each review will include teachers and parents. Social and therapeutic activities will be organised, based around the members' particular goals. A planning meeting will be held at the beginning of each group. Members will be invited to write the group rules and participate in planning the group.

INDICATORS.

For Mark, that he initiates and responds to contact with the group, peers and teachers; that he asks for help in class and is bullied less; that he is assertive in the group, putting forward his point of view and refusing to be picked on. For Joanna, that there are few outbursts in class and in the group; that she is able to make and retain friendships. For the group, that all members attend regularly; that they are involved in planning and are interested, involved and co-operative with each other in the group; that members resolve differences between themselves; that they write the group rules.

RECORDING.

The opinions of the parents, children and teachers will be sought by questionnaires and interviews before the group, before each review and in a follow-up after three months. This will provide comparisons with the initial baseline. Each meeting will be recorded by groupworkers and members, using a self report format and a checklist of behaviours tailored to the objectives for each child and the group. Rating scales will be used after each group: with Mark, to chart the extent of his involvement in the group and of his confidence in relation to group members and groupworkers; with Joanna, to chart her behaviour towards other group members and her ability to talk through difficult situations arising out of the group.

PLAN.

This plan will be written into a contractual agreement with each child and with the group. It will be reconsidered at each review.

ANALYSIS.

At each review and at the end of the group, the records will be used to establish the degree of movement towards or away from the objectives and, therefore, the extent to which the group has been effective. It is hoped to establish what has been achieved, to what degree, and whether the group has made a difference both to members and to their parents and teachers.

Recording

Having defined the problems or issues to be tackled and the objectives sought, and having written these into the step-by-step model, the next stage in evaluation is data collection and recording. Once again, consumers can be actively involved in this process, the objective of which is to chart the movement between the current and desired situation and to identify the factors which may have produced or obstructed that movement. By means of questionnaires, rating scales and reports, consumers and groupworkers can record changes and developments in individuals and the group, the extent to which the group works cohesively, and the type of interactions between members (Preston-Shoot, 1987b). Rating scales, using clearly defined points, can monitor the extent of the problem at defined intervals; the nature of participants' involvement in sessions; participants' views on the helpfulness of the group. Checklists can be designed to provide information on the frequency or timing of behaviours/activities in the group. Douglas (1976) describes a checklist of types of contribution made by group members, and rating scales on the clarity of the goals, trust in the group and on how decisions were made. Self-reports are appraisals of the group: whether members feel that problems or issues were dealt with satisfactorily; why change did/did not occur; what was helpful or unhelpful. The type of recording undertaken will depend on whether the focus is on outcome, process or both, whether on desired outcomes and/or on those factors which produced or hampered movement towards the desired situation (Preston-Shoot and Williams, 1987). Key questions are, therefore, who will record, 'what', 'when' and 'how'.

Example 2.

This example is from a group for parents and children under five where the broad aims were conceptualised as:

i. to help parents and children play and learn together;
ii. to help parents notice their child's needs and to take pride in their child's progress;
iii. to offer support within the group for parents who are lonely in their community and need a safe space to find out about themselves and their child.

After each session parents completed this questionnaire:

i. What was I helping my child to do today?
ii. What toys did I use to help?
iii. What did I do to help?
iv. What worked best? Why?
v. What did not work? Why?
vi. What do I want to do next week?

A checklist was also completed by parents and groupworkers together for each child:

Hung up coat?	Sat at table?	Went to toilet?
Joined in songs?	Played outside?	'Pretend' play?
Cried or had fit of temper?	Played with parent?	Played alone?
Played with other children?	Used Wendy House?	Used paints?
Used bricks/lego/jigsaws?		

Rating scales, charting the interaction between parents and their children, were completed by groupworkers with each parent. Two examples are illustrated here:

i. Did not play with child at all.
Tried once to play but gave up.
Tried several times but did not persist.
Played with child for several periods in group.
Played with child regularly throughout the group.

ii. Did not respond to child's approaches.
Responded with anger or with aggression.
Responded briefly with attention.
Responded with pleasure and sustained attention.

Reviews

Reviews, the timing of which will have been determined when plans for the group were finalised, are the key to registering the results of the intervention. Once again, consumer involvement is central.

Reviews have two purposes. First, retrospectively, to contrast the initial current and desired situations with any changes that have occurred, to illustrate the evidence for those changes, and to describe the new current situation. The process of specifying the new current situation will enable participants to conclude either that objectives have been achieved well-enough for the group to close or that further work is required either with or without modifying the initial objectives. This part of the analysis is on the work done, identifying the achievements, or the blocks to progress, and the evidence for each. Secondly, prospectively, to identify how much and what type of further work is required to achieve the present objectives, to elaborate the issues to be tackled, and to identify any necessary changes in the methods used. In other words, this part of the review aims to establish the new current and desired situations, what is to be done and further review dates (Preston-Shoot and Williams, 1987). Once again, the process involves negotiating around what consumers want to address and what social workers view as important targets for change.

The process of review is central to the process of evaluation. Both processes are concerned with ensuring that the work is purposeful. Both seek to determine the effectiveness of the work, to appraise the value of the group. The difference between them is that evaluation is the continuing, step-by-step process, whereas reviews are points in the group process where those involved register the extent to which the work has been successful in achieving the desired situation, and confirm or redefine the objectives. Clearly, if reviews are held too frequently, they will interfere with the work of the group. If held too infrequently, the clear focus of the group may give way to imprecision, drift or divergent views about the group's direction and usefulness.

Example 3.

This example comes from a women's group. The questionnaire was used by groupworkers to assess the work done since a previous review and to identify further aims. It combines retrospective and prospective questions (iii. and iv.; v. and vi.). This questionnaire allowed members to identify achievements easily and to express doubts or fears. It was especially important at the point where it was used because the groupworkers felt that the group was 'stuck'. Using this questionnaire opened up new areas for discussion and identified specific tasks to work on which were consistent with the group's overall objectives.

i. I like coming to the group because...
ii. When I came to the group at first I was worried that people would...
iii. The group has helped me become more/less...
iv. I think the group would be better if...
v. I would like to have talked about .... but have felt too shy/frightened/unsure.
vi. It would help me to talk about the above if...
vii. I would like the group to continue for .... weeks.
viii. Before the group ends I would like to...

Follow-up

Follow-up is often neglected but is useful in determining how long the benefits derived from the group experience have endured and the extent to which consumers found the group helpful. Consumers' views may change over time as gains become apparent or familiar patterns return.

Establishing consumers' views is difficult. Statements of satisfaction can be influenced by consumers' knowledge of available services, attitude to the interviewer, psychological defences, educational experience, differential understanding of words used in questionnaires, expectations based on past encounters with social workers and the success or failure of the intervention (Shaw, 1976, 1984). Nonetheless, consumers can be enabled to comment freely on their experiences of groupwork by involving them in defining the questions to be asked.

Example 4.

This questionnaire was compiled as a weekly recording form by the members of a parent and toddler group where the objectives were similar to those described in the second example. At the final group review members rewrote the questionnaire for use in a three month follow-up. Both questionnaires are given here.

Weekly recording form.

i. What I enjoyed most about the group was...
ii. What I did not like about the group was...
iii. What I found most difficult was...
iv. What I found easiest was...
v. What I found most helpful (and why) was...
vi. I have been able to use what I have got from the group in the week by...
vii. It has been difficult to keep this up when...
viii. I intend to use what I have got from today's group by...
ix. Next week in the group I would like to...

Follow-up form.

i. What I enjoyed most about the group was...
ii. What I did not like about the group was...
iii. What I found most helpful (and why) was...
iv. My expectations on joining the group were...
v. What I experienced as a member was...
vi. I have been able to use what I have got from the group by...
vii. It has been difficult to keep this up when...
viii. When I joined the group I was finding...difficult.
ix. When the group finished I was finding...easier/more difficult/the same.
x. Since the group ended I have been finding...easier still/about the same as when the group ended/becoming more difficult/as difficult as when the group began.
xi. If there was another group I would/would not like to join and concentrate on...

Conclusion

The evaluative approach outlined above provides a structure for describing practice, measuring progress and demonstrating effectiveness. The findings can be presented in reports which adopt the format of the step-by-step model. Step eight, analysis, will include the evidence for what happened and why, the influence of factors within and beyond the group, any redefinitions to the original first six steps made at reviews, the final outcome and, most importantly, the implications for groupwork practice. The result will be a cumulative body of knowledge available to practitioners.

The approach has clear similarities with behavioural methods which begin by identifying the problems to be addressed, the changes sought and the intervention programme (Yelloly, 1980). It is the specificity, the clear thinking and the well defined assessment and goals which will lead to improved practice and effectiveness.

Acknowledgements

The author would like to acknowledge the willingness of staff at Camden, Edinburgh and Leeds Family Service Units to share their groupwork practice and experiences when the model described in this paper was in the process of development.

References

Brown, A., Caddick, B., Gardiner, M. and Sleeman, S. (1982) 'Towards a British model of groupwork'. *British Journal of Social Work,* 12 (6), pp 587-603.

Corden, J. and Preston-Shoot, M. (1987) *Contracts in Social Work.* Aldershot: Gower.

Douglas T. (1976) *Groupwork Practice.* London: Tavistock.

Mayer, J. and Timms, N. (1970) *The Client Speaks.* London: RKP.

Mullender, A. and Ward, D. (1985) 'Towards an alternative model of social groupwork'. *British Journal of Social Work,* 15 (2), pp. 155-172.

Preston-Shoot, M. (1985) 'Report on a questionnaire survey of evaluation practice and needs in FSU'. *FSU Quarterly,* 36, pp. 14-20.

Preston-Shoot, M. (1986) 'Co-leadership in groups: Decision or drift?' in Wedge, P. (ed.) *Social Work – Research Into Practice.* Proceedings of the first annual JUC/BASW conference. Birmingham: British Association of Social Workers.

Preston-Shoot, M. (1987a) 'Groupwork presents its challenges – and its rewards – for those with the right initiatives'. *Social Work Today,* 18 (27), pp. 12-13.

Preston-Shoot, M. (1987b) *Effective Groupwork.* London: Macmillan.

Preston-Shoot, M. and Williams, J. (1987) 'Evaluating the effectiveness of practice'. *Practice,* 1 (4), pp.393-405.

Sainsbury, E. (1986) 'The contribution of client studies to social work practice' in Wedge, P. (ed.) *Social Work – Research into Practice.* Birmingham: British Association of Social Workers.

Shaw, I. (1976) 'Consumer opinion and social policy: a research review'. *Journal of Social Policy,* 5 (1), pp. 19-32.

Shaw, I. (1984) 'Literature review: consumer evaluations of the personal social services'. *British Journal of Social Work,* 14 (3), pp. 277–284.

Sheldon, B. (1982) 'A measure of success.' *Social Work Today,* 13 (21), pp.8-11.

Sheldon, B. (1986) 'Social work effectiveness experiments: review and implications'. *British Journal of Social Work,* 16 (2), pp. 223-242.

Yelloly, M. (1980) *Social Work Theory and Psychoanalysis.* Wokingham: Van Nostrand Reinhold.

GROUPWORK (1988) 2, 158–172

GROUPWORK AS THE METHOD OF CHOICE WITH BLACK CHILDREN IN WHITE FOSTER HOMES

AUDREY MULLENDER

Whilst professional child care thinking has rightly moved increasingly towards 'same race' placements as the placements of choice for black children in care, the needs of those young people who are already established in long term transracial foster homes and of their carers have frequently been ignored. The authorities which made these placements in the past have a continuing responsibility in the present to support them, with appropriately targeted intervention. Some of the key advantages of a groupwork response are explored, and the impact of one particular group on the self-image of its young black members is evaluated. The conclusion is reached that the existence of such a group allowed essential black identity work to be commenced at an earlier stage than is normal in one-to-one work. Some of the features of the group itself are critically examined in relation to its overall aims, and a further, complementary groupwork model is put forward. The conclusion is reached that all such efforts must take place within a context of far reaching agency policies which attempt to combat institutional racism. and to offer developmental input to foster carers and social workers as well as to transracially placed young people themselves.

The first impression gained from scanning the literature on transracial placements is of a largely static account of the pros and cons of such placements as they currrently exist. What will be attempted in this article, is to move on from summarising the common criticisms to an illustration of what progress and development may be possible in current practice and, in particular, of the special contribution which can be made by groupwork.

In the longer term, the major improvements which should be looked for in social work practice in this field would certainly be the reduction of the disproportionate number of black children in care, and the recruitment of adequate numbers of black families to provide homes for those who remain (Schroeder *et al.*, 1985). Whilst these constitute crucial ultimate goals, however, they are not yet the whole answer in that their achievement is not imminent. (A detailed consideration of the reasons why lies outside the scope of this paper.) Meanwhile, many black children will remain in transracial placements for the foreseeable future even where further transracial placements are most actively opposed (Small, 1985, p.11) and, elsewhere, black children continue to be placed in white homes (House of Commons Social Services Committee, 1984, p. cxxii).

A large number of black children in white homes will consequently be there for some time to come, and their needs cannot be ignored. The chief area of improved practice to which this paper hopes to contribute, therefore, is that of the quality of care offered by agencies through their existing transracial placements. This should in no way be taken to indicate complacency about either the over representation of black children in care, or the under representation of black families in lists of approved foster and adoptive homes. What it does imply is that substitute carers themselves are not to blame for the past or present policies adopted by the agencies who placed children with them, and that those agencies have a duty to help transracial carers offer the best quality of care possible. Such help needs to encompass direct work with transracially placed children, aimed at developing in them a positive awareness of their cultural and racial origins and of themselves as young black people growing up in a predominantly white, racist society (e.g. Maximé, 1986). It will inevitably take place against a background of criticisms of the placement of black children in white families; these will be briefly outlined before being followed through into the detail of practical intervention.

Criticisms of transracial placements

IDENTITY, SELF-IMAGE AND CULTURAL HERITAGE

Many painful accounts have been written of and by black youngsters in white placements who are unable to accept that they are black and who, for example, try to bleach or scrub themselves white (Ahmed, 1981, pp. 139–40; Adeniji, 1983, p.12). Black foster children with a white self-image are not uncommonly seen as well adjusted by white professionals (as recorded by Maximé, 1986, pp. 102–3) and by researchers (Gill and Jackson, 1983, p. 130). Like Maximé, Ahmed finds this astonishing: *'If your child went round saying, "I'm black", you'd think they were mentally ill – yet if I think I'm white, people think I'm integrated'* (Ahmed quoted in Laurance, 1983, p. 501). Not surprisingly, such children may reject not only their own blackness but other black people, perhaps refusing to see their natural parents (Ahmed, 1981, p. 140), or fighting against the idea of black foster parents (Maximé, 1986, p. 103), unless they can be helped to grow towards a pride in being black (Brunton and Welch, 1983, p. 17; Maximé, 1986, pp. 107–8).

Parr (in Black and In Care Steering Group, 1985, p. 38) discovered that being brought up as if she were a white person did not stand her in good stead as a young adult when she found herself

> ... in the black community and at first felt afraid of black people ... [who]

> couldn't realise why I didn't know of black food and culture such as history and reggae music and West Indian dialects.

ABSWAP (1983, pp. 7–8) also points out that, however white a black-skinned young person feels, he or she will still not be accepted as such by white society and so 'will have to return to the black community' on leaving care. Giving a transracially placed child a knowledge of black cultural heritage through contact with other black people, by means of which a positive black identity may develop, is therefore essential.

SURVIVAL SKILLS

A number of further criticisms are commonly levelled against transracial placements. Notably, white substitute parents are seen as less able than black parents to teach the skills necessary to survive the impact of racist abuse and prejudice (Cheetham, 1981, p. 57, quoting the National Association of Black Social Workers in the USA; James, 1981, pp. 15–16; Children's Legal Centre, 1985, p. 7). White caretakers may tend to dismiss the problem as just a *'chip on the shoulder'* (NFCA, undated leaflet), or as best ignored (White, 1985, p. 16). Black adults, on the other hand, would take such matters seriously, would speak from a shared black experience, and could offer the essential combination of techniques for handling abuse, together with the accompanying strength of black self-esteem and racial identity needed to temper the impact of prejudice and discrimination. While one hears of white foster and adoptive parents who do their very best, for example through role-playing unpleasant incidents, this pre-supposes that their black children will tell them when they have suffered playground or other taunts. Yet Mullender and Miller (1985, p. 34) reported that this often did not happen.

ACCESS AND REHABILITATION

A further advantage which black families may have over white is, as Loftus (1986, p. 26) puts it: *'In the majority of instances black foster parents are not intimidated by the thought of access by the child's natural parents'*, indeed they tend readily to accept the idea of working both with the children and their parents. The House of Commons Social Services Committee (1984, p. cxxi) linked black placements with greater ease both of parental access and of rehabilitation with the child's family.

Supporting existing transracial placements

AN INDIVIDUAL APPROACH

As stated earlier, the chief focus of this article moves us on from these current criticisms of transracial placements to a consideration of ways in which black children's needs can be more appropriately met in their present, long term white placements. An individual approach is one possibility. Indeed, it is also the necessary starting point for any other form of intervention, including groupwork, since initially each child's circumstances will require separate assessment. Individual work is best offered as part of a comprehensive departmental response – for example through routine consideration of racial and cultural matters at reviews, as is the case in Bradford Social Services (Mennell, 1986) – rather than allowing any particular child's situation to deteriorate to the point where a specialist black worker has to be called in on an *ad hoc* basis.

Once practical, cultural, racial and identity needs have been identified for each individual child, one alternative is to retain a focus at the individual level in work with that child and the white caretakers. The responsibilities of Barnardo's project worker, for example, have included

> ... working with a number of white adoptive and foster parents who are caring for black children who have been part of their families for some years – to help them develop an awareness and understanding of their racial origin and of the Afro-Caribbean culture (Fratter, 1986).

Through the Ebony project, a number of black teenagers were helped to consider the same broad range of issues, but using a groupwork rather than an individual approach. (See Miller, 1985; Mullender and Miller, 1985; Mullender, 1988a, for descriptive accounts of the first and second Ebony young people's groups; also Mullender, 1988b, which deals with the Ebony foster parent group.)

A GROUPWORK APPROACH

Selecting a Groupwork Approach

Although nothing exactly like the Ebony groups for young black people in white foster homes has been located elsewhere in the literature, nevertheless, groupwork can generally be said to be a stimulating method to use with young people. It is also more relevant to their normal experience than is intense counselling or other one-to-one intervention, which would inevitably form a major part of any alternative means of tackling identity, cultural, and racial issues. All children, in fact, have current experience of involvement in groups. They are taught in groups, they live in groups, play in groups, and, as Ross and Thorpe (1983, p. 105) point out *'vast numbers'* of them are involved in uniformed groups *'such as scouts, life-boys, guides, marching-bands, teams etc.'* Thus it can seem perfectly natural to a young person to attend an early evening group like Cubs or Brownies, Guides or Scouts, or like Ebony.

In the Ebony project, groupwork was chosen as an effective way to raise levels of black self-awareness and pride, and of cultural and racial knowledge, and also to help develop survival skills against racism. The methods used were discussions, experiential exercises, games, and listening to black guest speakers. This group was clearly very different from the organised groups listed above, although it did share with them the spirit of belonging and being like others, which is often extremely important to children. Thus, Hilary White reports from her small study of transracial adopters, that although none of the adoptive parents personally felt the need for support groups, one couple '*thought that there might be a need for occasional meetings between the children themselves to talk about their similar experiences and hence minimise possible isolation*' (White, 1985, p. 17).

The ten members of Ebony were helped to share their experiences of isolation and prejudice – and their feelings about being black in white homes, white schools, and a predominantly white racist society – in the context of a group in which they also learned a considerable amount about the history of Africa and of the Caribbean, and about black music, black food, and black hair and skin care. In addition to their fellow group members, the children in Ebony could look to the black group leaders as an important role model. The adults also provided an example of survival skills and of positive feelings of black pride and achievement. Overall, a groupwork approach may have been more effective than an individual approach because the emotional strength and credibility of the whole group encouraged attitudinal and behavioural change, as well as changes in self-perception.

Progress in the Group: Black Self-Awareness and Cultural Knowledge

After the second Ebony group had run, the progress of each child was reviewed in terms of black self-awareness and positive self-image, as revealed by the child's attitudes and the terminology they used to refer to themselves.

During the introductory meeting the young people had been asked to say how they wished to be described. This question was posed because the language which is used to refer to black people has more than a purely descriptive value; it tends also to have negative resonances, indicative of our racist society's fascination with the detail of imagined superiority and inferiority. Where black is regarded as inferior, then lighter skin is valued more highly (ABSWAP, 1983, p. 10), particularly if the person concerned may be able, at times, to try and pass as white. Such comparisons are invidious, of course, and they obscure the fact that the experience of racism and of racial stereotyping is held in common by all those who are not seen as white. This includes people of mixed parentage, as were some of the Ebony group members. Hence, '*"black" is one category when race is in question*' (Mullender and Miller, 1985, p. 36). Otherwise, there must be a specific reason to be more precise about an individual's origin. For example, it would have helped to bring the Ebony group to life had the children known not only that they were all of Afro-Caribbean origin, but also their birth parents' islands of origin; but no one responsible for their care appeared to hold this information or to have passed it on. Similarly, a child's mixed parentage should only be referred to when specifically relevant; for all other purposes, there are only black and white children, not black, white and mixed parentage.

ABSWAP (1983, p. 10) explains why the latter term is to be preferred:

> The concept 'mixed parentage' should be used instead of 'mixed race', since the former does not imply the race superior quotient implied by the latter ... We should be constantly aware that when the majority of prospective adopters and some social workers use the term 'mixed race' they do not mean the child of Indian and African parents nor Chinese and a person of African descent.
> They generally mean a 'white' person and any other person who is not white.

The expression 'half caste' is still less acceptable, not only because it *'stems back from slavery meaning half white which is offensive'* (Black and in Care Steering Group, 1985, p. 23), but in addition to these overtones of superiority and inferiority, it is inaccurate, and it makes the child sound incomplete. Other terms which the Black and In Care Steering Group (1985, p. 23) objects to, include 'coloured' and 'olive skinned': *'Firstly, because the words came from white people'* and *'Secondly, white people are not pure "white" but they are not labelled'.* To use words like these, or similarly 'brown' rather than 'black', is to deny both the pride that should be taken in being black and also the shared experience which the child has with all other black people in our racist society.

It is significant, in the light of the above, to reflect on the terminology in which the Ebony group members referred to themselves. When it came to reviewing progress after the group, there had been some movement in the children's descriptions of themselves, but it was clear that a time-limited group could not, on its own, guarantee that these children would achieve a strong black self-awareness. Some children had not altered their preferred view of themselves as, for example, 'white', 'half-caste', 'colourless', or 'just myself'. Only one group member had become able to accept the term 'black' in relation to herself and perhaps it was no coincidence that she was in the process of moving from a white foster home, where she had lived for most of her life, to black foster parents.

Levels of cultural knowledge had also been very low before the group, to the point where some children held false beliefs – including the ideas that West Indians wore no clothes, that they sweated more than white people, that they had holes in their stomachs, or an extra bone in their heels which made them run faster. At least some of these ideas had been communicated by the children's own foster parents, which highlights why the Ebony project encompassed a group for them in parallel to the young people's group which is the subject of this paper. Both groups offered a similar process of new learning at both a factual and an emotional level but, clearly, the foster parent group did this in the context of challenging white racist views, whilst the young people's group was primarily aimed at developing black awareness. When their group presented them with factual information to rectify the strangest of their notions, an encouraging number of the children found this sufficiently interesting to want to supplement it by going to the library between meetings. One or two asked to attend a further Ebony group should one be available.

Some examples will perhaps illustrate the changes which occurred in a number of the children, but also the further work which remains to be undertaken with them. Details have been changed sufficiently to conceal the identities of actual group members without obscuring the impact of the group. The first five young people mentioned below had all been living in their white foster homes for most of their lives.

i. Marguerite constantly refused to admit to any difficulties, fearing that, should she do so, she would be moved from her foster family. She did gain some cultural knowledge during the sessions, and joined in all the games and exercises, but at the end she still perceived herself as 'just Marguerite'.
ii. Ellie was the most negative of all the children towards blackness and hated the idea of being called 'black'. She referred to herself as 'white'. Whilst always eager to participate in group activities, Ellie showed no ideas of her own.
iii. Evette was extremely lively in the group and willing to be first to try everything. At the outset, she had no black identity although she was aware of the positives of living in a black home. At the end of the group, Evette's knowledge of her culture had been increased, but she reiterated that she saw herself as 'colourless'.
iv. Ros was one of the most reserved young people in the group although she participated fully in her own, quiet way. She confided that she had once, as a small child, powdered her skin so that she would be white like her foster sisters. Unfortunately, this had never been discussed with her by her foster parents or by social workers. Of all the group members, Ros showed the most interest in her roots and her heritage, and appeared to be making her own attempts to find and understand her black identity. She was also trying to mix with and relate to black people. At the end of the group, despite her progress, Ros still called herself 'half-caste'.
v. Martha was a lively, attentive girl who asked many questions in the sessions and joined in everything, apart from the role play which she believed would lead to her foster parents being told about what she had

said. During the Ebony group, Martha found the content so fascinating that she went several times to the library to seek more information on various subjects. She had absorbed a number of misapprehensions about black people from her foster parents and appeared to be re-examining these in the light of her new knowledge. Martha was the most enthusiastic about the Ebony group and was eager to attend another one. Despite this, Martha still could not quite bring herself to describe herself as 'black'.

The next two children had either recently left or were about to leave their white foster homes, after placements that had lasted well over ten years.

vi. Edwin's placement had broken down when he tried to establish links with the black community. He presented as a strong, 'streetwise' young person, and was the only member of the group who had managed to make effective links into the black community before attending Ebony. He was very keen to learn about his historical roots and argued that, if he had been placed in a black family, he would naturally have been more aware of his cultural heritage. Edwin enjoyed the group because it gave him the opportunity to express some of the problems of living in a white foster home and also to obtain help and advice from other young people on how to cope with these difficulties. Although he continued to describe himself as 'half-caste', Edwin left the group with greater acceptance of, and pride in, his identity.

vii. A black foster home had been found for Debbie. In the group she was at first introverted and nervous, and would avoid eye contact with other group members. She came with little knowledge of black culture and a negative attitude towards Rastafarians and Africans. As the weeks progressed, Debbie relaxed and began to contribute openly to group sessions. She internalised much of the information presented in the group and was the only member at the end who said she would call herself 'black'.

In considering the differences between group members, it appears that age and personality were factors, as were the existence or lack of any contacts with the black community and, perhaps particularly, the effect the young people thought – or feared – their views and attitudes would have on their caretakers. Thus Debbie, knowing she was moving to a black foster home, could perhaps find the confidence to call herself 'black', whereas Edwin had already learnt the hard way, when his white foster placement broke down, that his wish to find links with the black community was not acceptable to all white people, and so he was perhaps still too ambivalent to arrive at the stage of describing himself as 'black' during the limited life span of the group. Martha's case typifies this confusion of feelings. She drank in all the information she could obtain from the group and from the library, and yet was frightened that her white foster parents (who themselves had mistaken and negative ideas about black people) would learn about her ideas if she took part in a role play. No wonder she could not reach the point of calling herself 'black'.

A number of the young people, such as Evette, gained significantly in knowledge about black culture and heritage through the group, but found it harder to apply that learning to their own circumstances. Ros, being in her late teens and considerably older than Evette, was clearly at an age where she was struggling to find her own adult identity. She used the group to reflect back on her earlier experiences as a black person in a white environment, such as when she had powdered her skin. She also welcomed the opportunity to spend time with other black people and to see herself in an all black context. In view of the progress that Debbie and, to some extent, Edwin – with their experiences of black foster parents and the black community respectively – made in the group, a possible variation to consider for future Ebony groups would be a mixed group of children from both black and white foster homes. Those who were more 'aware', or who had experienced both white and black placements, could then support the others in their development towards greater understanding and a more positive self-image.

It may arguably be seen as a major strength of groupwork as the mode of working with all these young people that it had succeeded in uncovering the level of confusion which existed, both in relation to purely factual information and to self-image. Prior to this, the children's social workers had expressed some concern about how they perceived themselves, but would not have referred them for urgent identity work on an individual basis at that stage. Since it so happened, however, that the team of groupworkers came together to establish the Ebony group at about that time, and these youngsters were seen as likely to benefit from it, they were referred. Individual work with a black worker, on the other hand, tends only to be requested when serious difficulties have already arisen in the young person's placement or if a major event is about to happen, such as a change of placement. This is perhaps because the initiative for referral under those circumstances lies with the child's own social worker, who is often white, whereas the initiative in seeking referrals to a group lies with the groupworkers themselves. Since the groupworkers with the Ebony young people's group were all black, they provided a black perspective on the level of need which the group would potentially be seeking to serve.

Were Ebony to become not only a mainstream provision but a normal requirement of the package of intervention designed for each transracial placement – as all those who have worked directly on the project would want to see happen – then it could offer an essential developmental input to every transracially placed black child, whether or not any problems had been identified or were simmering beneath the surface of the placement. This could constitute an important facet of preventative work, and could perhaps save some children from the worst traumas of desperately longing to be white. They could discover, instead, in the company of others like themselves, that to be black can be to have confidence and pride in oneself and one's cultural heritage.

Alternative Models of Groupwork with Transracially Placed Young People

Brown, Caddick, Gardiner and Sleeman (1982, pp. 588–9) describe in British practice:

> ... a distinct and prevalent form of groupwork ... whose general features include: individual centred aims consistent with meeting client need and carrying out agency function; an eclectic theoretical base; an overall approach which values peer sharing and mutual feedback; the creative use of a range of group techniques; co-leadership; a 'closed' membership of from six to twelve adults (usually strangers initially, but sharing similar problems) and time-limited duration.

Apart from the fact that its members were not adults and that a number of them happened to be related to each other, Ebony shared all these features. So prevalent has this model become in British practice, indeed, that it is commonly adopted without considering whether it is the most appropriate for the task in hand. On reflection, for example, the Ebony groupworkers found that they did not have sufficient time over the eight weeks when the group met to achieve their ambitious aims fully, because almost all the members of the young people's group were at an 'unaware' stage. Hence, a relatively brief and time limited group structure, with its duration fixed in advance, emerged as unrealistic for this type of group.

The co-leadership aspect of the model put forward by Brown *et al.*, was amongst those which emerged as most valid in the Ebony young people's group. The groupworker team of black field and residential workers found that their skills complemented one another. The fieldworkers, for example, were aware of the pressures on the young people in their family settings, while the residential workers felt confident in handling boisterous or difficult behaviour, and were also accustomed to conceptualising each child's needs within the context of what the group could tolerate from the individual, and what the individual could be offered by the strengths of the whole group. The valuing of 'peer-sharing and mutual feedback' (again Brown *et al.*, 1982) was indeed much in evidence in that it was the main tool for change used in the group. Only one exercise was found by the children to go too far into painful memories for them to want to share their experiences with other members. They therefore worked individually with the groupworkers on that single occasion. All the other material dealt with in the group sessions was applied by members to themselves at however profound or shallow a level they could personally manage. Thus some exercises became merely games to the younger children, whilst others drew forth interesting responses from them all.

The 'closed' group, made up of strangers, is typical of what Brown (1979, p. 6) has elsewhere called 'formed groups', or 'groups which have been specially composed for some purpose'. In other words, they have been artificially brought together by social workers, on the basis of referrals meeting pre-determined criteria, and the members would almost certainly not have met had it not been for the group. However, the aims of the Ebony group would also hold good with 'natural', that is pre-existing groupings of young black people in care. Such natural groups could include friendship or sibling groups, or those living in the same group foster home or residential setting. Lee and Pithers (1980, p. 113) provide an example of a pre-existing group in a residential setting, which sounds as if its members' needs could equally well have been met by an Ebony style of approach:

> In another home a group of black children have formed themselves into a special association. They spend a lot of time together, eat at the same table and are involved in what would be called 'consciousness raising' or 'solidarity' groups. They had not heard of such terms until a politically conscious members of staff explained them. This was not a challenge to equality within the home but a recognition of the special needs of some groups who encounter special problems.

The Ebony young person's group itself, had a mixture of therapeutic and educational aims, and was not strictly an example of 'consciousness raising' because it was a worker-led group where the groupworkers largely pre-determined the content, and because it was not aimed at social change (Longres and McLeod, 1980, p. 268 and p. 276). However, it was certainly aimed at raising consciousness about problems wider than the members' own circumstances and which they had not caused (Donnelly, 1986, p. 24; Longres and McLeod, 1980, p. 268), amongst people sharing a life experience of discrimination (Donnelly, 1986, p. 27), and it did have a relatively strong element of peer support (Donnelly, 1986, p. 25).

An alternative model for a group aimed at raising awareness would be one on 'self-directed' lines (Mullender and Ward, 1985, pp. 163–5; see also Burley, 1982; Ward (ed.), 1982; Smith, 1981), with an 'open', that is a fluctuating membership, not selected by a worker, which could at times reach a size much larger than that of formed groups. This model would be closer to the 'Black and In Care' type of group (see Black and In Care Steering Group, 1985), but on a local basis. The group members would choose their own meeting time and place and determine their own aims and procedures, probably with adult help to facilitate group process at first including, for example, the stimulation of initial participation by young people whose views have not normally been sought before (Stein, 1983, p. 98). The aims would include mutual support and the raising of awareness through pooling group members' own experiences and understanding, but would extend into campaigning for external change in directions chosen by the group itself. Typically, these could begin with attempting to alter the negative way in which young black people are perceived and treated in the care system and in wider society (Black and In Care Steering Group, 1985), whereas they actually have an enormous amount to offer once they find mutual strength (Mullender and Ward, 1985, pp. 168–9). Through a national federation of such local groups, their goals might extend into trying to affect social work practice so as to reduce the number of black children entering care (Mullender and Ward, 1985, p. 169) and to give those who are in care a choice as to where they are placed, and whether with black or white caretakers (Black and In Care Steering Group, 1985, p. 25). This type of group would also tend to achieve positive individual change as a 'secondary advantage' (Mullender and Ward, 1985, p. 156), but it would not necessarily be an alternative to the existing model of Ebony young people's groups. Rather, the two could exist side by side, achieving different purposes, and all young black people could be given the opportunity to belong to one or both.

Conclusion

This paper has been based on the assumption that, in the longer term, social work practice in relation to black children in care must change sufficiently to mean that their numbers are less out of proportion to their number in the population at large, and to facilitate the recruitment of adequate numbers of black foster families for those who remain in care. In the meantime, many placements in white families still exist and new ones no doubt continue to be made. The social work profession has a duty towards the black children in these transracial placements and, indeed, to their white substitute parents. The latter may well feel under constant attack in the current climate, and yet their services were no doubt gratefully enough accepted at the time when they were first offered. Social work support, and multi-cultural and anti-racist education for such foster families, should not be reserved for placements at risk of disruption or where the young people are about to move on.

For the young people themselves, groupwork expertise has now reached the stage where it can positively promote a strong black identity and self-image, knowledge of black cultural heritage, and the development of the survival skills necessary to cope with racist abuse and prejudice. It is not sufficient for such intervention to be offered on an *ad hoc* basis. What is needed in every authority which has made transracial foster placements, is a policy sophisticated enough to ensure that those placements are now supported and enhanced to a level that can answer the criticisms which were briefly outlined at the beginning of this paper. This can only be achieved by putting groups such as Ebony onto a permanent footing, with mainstream rather than special project funding, and with sufficient staff time released to undertake all the necessary preparation of social work colleagues, individual young people and their carers; adequate planning by groupworker teams and space to run the groups themselves; together with consultancy and feedback time. Nor can an initiative like the Ebony young people's group be effective in a vacuum. Such a group needs to be accompanied by at least an equal amount of focused input with the transracial foster parents (see Mullender, 1988b), and by training or other learning opportunities for the young people's social workers. Since both can have such a significant influence on the young people, careful work needs to help them to reinforce and not to undermine the positive benefits of attending the group.

Without adequate policies to underpin an initiative like Ebony, the institutionalised racism which has led to the neglect of the needs of black children in care until now, will remain as an obstacle to what could develop into an effective form of support for existing transracial placements.

Acknowledgement

This paper would clearly not have been possible without the innovatory practice of all those from Nottinghamshire Social Services Department who have been involved with the Ebony groups.

References

Adeniji, F. (1983) 'West African fostering: a personal experience'. *Foster Care,* 33, March, pp. 12-13.

Ahmed, S. (1981) 'Children in care: the racial dimension in social work assessment', in Cheetham, J., James, W., Loney, M., Mayor, B. and Prescott, W. (eds.) *Social and Community Work in a Multi-Racial Society: A Reader.* London: Harper and Row.

Association of Black Social Workers and Allied Professions (ABSWAP) (1983) *Black Children in Care: Evidence to the House of Commons Social Services Committee.* London: ABSWAP.

Black and In Care Steering Group (1985), *Black and In Care Conference Report.* London: Children's Legal Centre.

Brown, A. (1979) *Groupwork.* London: Heinemann Educational.

Brown, A., Caddick, B., Gardiner, M. and Sleeman, S. (1982) 'Towards a British model of groupwork'. *British Journal of Social Work,* 12 (6), pp. 587-603.

Brunton, L. and Welch, M. (1983) 'White agency, black community'. *Adoption and Fostering,* 7 (2), pp. 16-18.

Burley, D. (1982) *Starting Blocks: Aspects of Social Education Group Work with Young People*. Leicester: National Youth Bureau.

Cheetham, J. (1981) *Social Work Services for Ethnic Minorities in Britain and the USA*. Oxford: Department of Social and Administrative Studies, University of Oxford.

Children's Legal Centre (1985) 'Placed in a white family – views of young black people'. *Childright*, 22, November/December, pp. 7-10.

Donnelly, A. (1986) *Feminist Social Work with a Women's Group*. Norwich: University of East Anglia, Social Work Monograph 41. Norwich.

Fratter, J. (1986) 'Barnardo's black project worker'. *Foster Care*, 45, March, p. 15.

Gill, O. and Jackson, B. (1983) *Adoption and Race: Black, Asian and Mixed Race Children in White Families*. London: Batsford.

House of Commons Social Services Commitee (1984) *Second Report from the Social Services Committee on Children in Care*, Vol. I. London: House of Commons Papers, Session 1983-4, HMSO.

James, M. (1981) 'Finding the families', *Adoption and Fostering*, 103 (1), pp. 11-16.

Laurance, J. (1983) 'Should white families adopt black children?' *New Society*, 64 (1076), pp. 499-501.

Lee, P. and Pithers, D. (1980) 'Radical residential child care: Trojan horse or non-runner?', in Brake, M. and Bailey, R. (eds.) *Radical Social Work and Practice*. London: Edward Arnold.

Loftus, Y. (1986) 'Black families and parental access'. *Adoption and Fostering*, 10 (4), pp. 26-7.

Longres, J.F. and McLeod, E. (1980) 'Consciousness raising and social work practice'. *Social Casework: The Journal of Contemporary Social Work*, May, pp. 267-276.

Maximé, J.E. (1986) 'Some psychological methods of black self-concept', in Ahmed, S., Cheetham, J. and Small, J. (eds.) *Social Work with Black Children and Their Families*. London: Batsford.

Mennell, M. (1986) 'The experience of Bradford Social Services Department', in Ahmed, S., Cheetham, J. and Small, J. (eds.). *Social Work with Black Children and Their Families*. London: Batsford.

Miller, D. (1985) 'Proud to be black'. *Community Care*, 21 February, pp. 18-19.

Mullender, A. (1988a) 'Groupwork with black children in white foster homes' in Triseliotis, J., (ed.). *Groupwork in Adoption and Foster Care*. London: Batsford.

Mullender, A. (1988b) 'Groupwork with transracial foster parents' in Triseliotis, J. (ed.) *Groupwork in Adoption and Foster Care*. London: Batsford.

Mullender, A. and Miller, D. (1985) 'The Ebony group: black children in white foster homes'. *Adoption and Fostering*, 9 (1), pp. 33-40, p. 49.

Mullender, A. and Ward, D. (1985) 'Towards an alternative model of social groupwork'. *British Journal of Social Work*, 15, pp. 155-172.

National Foster Care Association (undated) *'I Like You White, Do You Like Me Black?'*. London: NFCA.

Ross, S. and Thorpe, A. (1983) 'Groupwork with children', in Lishman, J. ed., *Working with Children*. Research Highlights no..6, Department of Social Work, University of Aberdeen.

Schroeder, H., Lightfoot, D. and Rees, S. (1985) 'Black applicants to Ealing recruitment campaign'. *Adoption and Fostering*, 9 (2), pp. 50-3.

Small, J. (1985) 'Policy and practice in transracial placement', in Nottinghamshire County Council, *Conference Paper on Transracial Fostering and Adoption.* Nott'm: Notts. County Council, West Bridgford.

Smith, M. (1981) *Creators not Consumers: Rediscovering Social Education,* second edition. Leicester: National Association of Youth Clubs.

Stein, M. (1983) 'Protest in Care', in Jordan, B. and Parton, N. (eds.) *The Political Dimensions of Social Work.* Oxford: Basil Blackwell.

Ward, D., ed. (1982) *Give 'Em a Break: Social Action by Young People at Risk and in Trouble.* Leicester: National Youth Bureau.

White, H. (1985) *Black Children, White Adopters: An Exploration in Uncertainty.* Norwich: University of East Anglia, Social Work Monograph 31.

BOOK REVIEWS

The Group Process and Family Therapy: Extensions and Applications of Basic Principles SHEILA THOMPSON AND JACK KAHN 235pp Oxford: Pergamon Price: Paperback £11.00 ISBN 0-08-034286-X

The title of this book immediately caught my attention. How encouraging to come across a volume spanning and linking two spheres of work whose connections so often appear to be forgotten by groupworkers and family therapists alike.

The book starts out at an interesting but frequently neglected point – at the very start of work, when the problem presented by the client to a member of the helping professions is successively shaped and reshaped until a good enough fit is achieved for work to progress. At this early stage a central theme of the book is also introduced – the importance of those professionals being open and flexible in their approach, bringing their training, their professional knowledge and that of their colleagues to bear on their work. As Thompson & Khan say: *'The communication of ideas between professionals is an important theme throughout this book, which is itself a product of interdisciplinary communication.* Clearly it is aimed at a range of professionals, assuming little prior knowledge of group processes or of family therapy.

Three systems of groupwork – psychotherapy, counselling and discussion are fully discussed, with examples from a wide range of settings to illustrate these systems. The authors state their aim as developing the theoretical basis of each system of groupwork by *'. . . indicating where the boundaries of the three systems may be drawn.'* The difficulties they encounter in this – for example, in describing group psychotherapy in a manner which clearly differentiates it from group counselling and group discussion – are not hedged. As they write *'group psychotherapy is that which is practised by group psychotherapists'*. Despite such difficulties, they succeed in broadly outlining each group process without recourse to jargon.

The family as a group is the focus of the latter part of the book. Four chapters together provide an excellent overview of the family as a group, of family functioning and family therapy. The capacity of families to solve problems is illustrated by such everyday examples as how different families might fit their furniture into a new house, making compromises and adjustments along the way. Once again case examples are well used, including an illustration of the relevance of family therapy concepts in a situation where a family is not seeking treatment. The chapter on scapegoating and splitting is particularly good, thoroughly but briefly explaining these processes.

The final section of the book is devoted to the development and application of a psychostructural model of families, in which the authors *'discuss family activities in relation to a notion of a family ego, family superego and family* id'. I struggled with this part, having had no opportunity to put the model to the test. As the authors write: *'If this model has any vailidity, it lies in its function as an additional tool . . .'* However, they succeeded in convincing me of its potential.

Throughout the book, the authors succeed in presenting their concepts in a straightforward style, using language which is free of jargon. Thus they practice what they preach, communicating their ideas in a manner which makes them accessible to professionals from a range of backgrounds. Their belief that *'. . . many*

professional workers who are in no sense family therapists can enrich their professional work with families through a knowledge of the family group processes' is evident throughout. I recommend the book to any such professional worker, qualified or in training. It is not a 'how to' book; it does not set out to be. However it achieves its aim of bringing the family, and family process, within the same framework as other group processes.
Jane Batchelor, Social Worker

Effective Groupwork MICHAEL PRESTON-SHOOT 158pp
Practical Social Work Series. London: Macmillan Education 1987
Price: Paperback £5.95 ISBN 0-333-40988-4

The book aims to focus on *'basic issues'* and to provide a *'practical guide for social workers'* with particular emphasis on co-working and the *'pragmatic and therapeutic potential of co-working and solo working'*.

The first 95 pages are about preparations for groupwork, and the final 38 pages concentrate on supervision and evaluation of the groupworkers' efforts. The intervening pages (Chapter 6) are about 'Working with a group'. The book may therefore be likened to a do-it-yourself guide to motor-cycle maintenance and performance evaluation, without giving much indication of what it is like to actually *ride* the thing! A lot about the rider and the machine, but not much about the thrills and spills of travelling.

Given the above reservations, the book condenses much of current wisdom into a relatively few pages. It skims across a variety of theoretical frameworks, while indicating a commitment to an unashamed eclecticism, and presents concerns around such preparatory matters as aims, types of group, worker values, size and selection etc. It gives strong emphasis to the co-worker issue, devoting some 18 pages to this topic. The writer claims *'the first publication to give detailed consideration to co-working'* yet draws heavily from John Hodge's 33 page publication devoted exclusively to its title *Planning for Co-Leadership. Effective Groupwork* allocates only a couple of paragraphs to the gender aspect of co-worker selection and activity, and no space at all to the issue of race in relation to co-working. Both of considerable current concern to actual and would-be groupworkers and demanding attention in any detailed consideration of co-working.

In the 'Working with a group' chapter there is no more than a selection of group phenomena, including scapegoating, the dominant member, and dependency, and an outline of the stage-formulation of group development à la Tuckman, Garland *et al.*

Stylistically I found the constant use of *'firstly'*, *'secondly'* etc rather irritating, though I appreciate that this 'check-list approach' may be useful as a source of reference. For beginners the sheer number of things to be thought about may be daunting and even off-putting – in the same way that reading a manual of motor-cycle maintenance may put one off going for a ride. It is also a rather wordy book, without illustrations or examples from practice. Describing a sociogram without reference to a diagram is rather like describing a spiral staircase without using gestures – hard work and potentially confusing.

My own preference is for the simple over the complex wherever possible. For a basic book the use of such words as disconfirm, sapiential, contraindicator and that recently-emerged horror 'modality' where there are simpler forms of expression is, I almost wrote, contra-indicated. I found this a strangely unbalanced book, with a great deal on 'before' and 'after' and only glimpses of the 'during' where the effectiveness of groupwork is ultimately demonstrated. This is not intended as a churlish review, but rather one that points up some of the unexpected consequences of a book on *Effective Groupwork* that points the way *towards* such an outcome, but does not address the many problems that limit groupworker effectiveness when in the thick of the action. I was left regarding this book as one of several the groupworker will need on the shelf. Other writers will be needed to convey a sense of enthusiasm, and also help workers' through the interactional problems that arise in the group. Michael Preston-Shoot has provided a handy reference against which to check the workers thinking and action when preparing to begin a group. However, too much emphasis on the groundwork can sometimes frighten off beginners, and this is not a publication to be used as a sole guide to the groupwork galaxy.

Harold Marchant, Independent Trainer and Consultant

Social Group Work: Competence and Values in Practice

EDITED BY JOSEPH LASSNER, KATHLEEN POWELL AND ELAINE FINNEGAN

New York and London: Haworth Press 1987
Price: Hardback £27.50 ISBN 0-86656-643-0

This book comprises 14 papers (the introduction claims there are 15) from Symposium VI for the Advancement of Social Work with Groups held in Chicago in October 1984; it has 23 contributors amongst whom are some of the best known American groupwork authors; it has five separate sections *viz*: groupwork theory; groupwork structure; gender and race issues in groupwork; the use of groups for coping with family issues; groupwork in health settings and one initial paper on social work with oppressed populations. This is an overwhelmingly American text with but three or four scant references to articles on work being done elsewhere. But it contains some good material, though its price will tend to put it out of the direct reach of those who would most benefit except via the library services.

The first paper by Judith Lee is basically a plea for reversing social work's headlong gallop towards therapy and for practitioners to get themselves into *'the midst of transactions between people and systems'*. Detachment, she says, vitiates the basic values of social work. Helen Northen's excellent argument is that we still don't appear to have adequate knowledge about how we determine for whom and under what circumstances a group is the instrument of choice. She lists those kinds of people for whom a group would be most suitable; what kind of group for what kind of problem; the contra indications for the use of groups; and she attempts to introduce some relative clarity into an area of notorious subjectivity. Her reference list is huge and very useful.

'Teaching and learning the practice of social groupwork' presents the group log, group analysis, record of service and approach to practice as four proven tools in instructing students in groupwork. Greenfield and Rothman introduce the concept of 'transformation' into the steps of group development, this being the stage after the group has completed its original task and, rather than disband, it transmutes into a different organism. Various kinds of noted transformations are listed by the authors.

The development of the 'environmental competence' of a group is Moore's theme which in a way is an example of 'transformation' when the group turns from its internal affairs to concern itself with and to use its resources on, intervention in the community of which it is a part.

Galinsky and Schopler's contribution is a very interesting research document on the positive and negative value of 'open ended' groups. The value to the client; the worker; the group and the agency involved in 'open ended' groups is lucidly discussed.

The next two papers are concerned to explore the value and the methodology of single session groups both in hospitals, but one specifically related to diabetic patients in the waiting room. 'Gender and race of leaders' and the effects they have on group behaviour is the remit of another research paper which produces some very interesting conclusions e.g. white male and black female leaders are seen as *'more competent, comfortable and less confused than black males and white females'*. It should be remembered however that these conclusions are from an American context and may not be directly transferable, but the research format itself could certainly be replicated here.

The next two papers are concerned with the establishment of group support systems, one for the 'caregivers' (those caring for elderly relatives) and one specifically for mother/daughter relationships.

Beck's article suffers from a certain obfuscation of language but he is presenting groupwork for individuals who have experienced problems deriving from their relations with members of their family of origin through the collection of data about the family and the presentation of 'genograms' to the group.

Volunteers working in the hospice system and their need of a support group is discussed in the Parry and Schwartz paper and finally groups in which medical teams can explore humanitarian issues during the process of their education are illustrated in the last paper.

There is no index and no overall list of references, but the papers are short enough and the contents pages reasonably adequate as an indication of what the book contains for this to be no real problem for those seeking to discover what is on offer.

I find it fascinating that at last this book gives concrete evidence that American groupworkers have foresworn the verbose descriptive papers of the past and gone for detailed analysis, and specifically designed research projects to increase the amount of substantial data which is made available to practitioners. Illustrative material is offered in plenty, but it is accompanied in most of the papers by a rigorous analysis which while not denying the heart puts the head securely in control of the response.

Tom Douglas, Freelance Consultant

'Once Upon a Group' MICHAEL KINDRED
Publisher: Michael Kindred
Price: £2.50 ISBN 0-9512552-0-7

Michael Kindred's aim in writing and publishing this 80 page revised edition is clearly stated. He writes:

> This book, then, is aimed at providing a light-hearted and amusing approach to a subject which can be quite heavy. I hope it offers an easily digestible way of gaining insights into how groups tick . . .

Mr Kindred succeeds in his aim. Amusingly illustrated with cartoons that invariably enhance the text, this book makes direct and straghtforward statements which the worker, new to leading groups, will find immensely valuable. (I believe it also has much to offer to those whose experience is much greater.)

The book starts with a brief and gentle encouragement to the reader to start to conceptualise their experience of groups before moving to an excellent 20 pages on the basics of 'Setting up groups' with each page covering a particular topic. Starting with 'Purpose and contract' this section ranges through such issues as seating arrangements and breaks. If Mr Kindred's advice on these basic matters was followed more rigorously by all involved in running groups in whatever capacity, I suspect our effectiveness as group leaders would be enhanced.

Subsequent sections in this book give helpful and clear advice on boundary and rule setting followed by a masterly, succinct examination of group development.

I suggest, however, that the new group leader will find the section on 'What goes on in groups' of particular value. Over half the text's 78 pages address events in the group process which all of us involved in groupwork will experience. A readily understandable analysis is offered, linked with advice as to the possible ways forward.

I believe there are many people involved in groupwork and in Mr Kindred's words *'that's all of us'*, who would benefit from this brief work. It is then a sad state of affairs that over 40 publishers failed to recognise its value. It is a credit to Mr Kindred that he had the determination to publish this excellent book himself.

John Hughes, Assistant Chief Probation Officer, Berkshire Probation Service.

Mental Handicap – a practical guide for social workers PETER GILBERT 130pp
Community Care: Business Press International Ltd.,
Quadrant House, The Quadrant, Sutton, Surrey SM1 4QQ 1985
Price: Paperback £3.95

This book should be required reading for all social work practitioners (or would-be practitioners) whether specialists in this field or not. Too often one hears social workers saying that they cannot work out a role for themselves with this client group. This book spells out clearly what can be offered and indeed makes casework an attractive proposition. As well as this, the history of care and present trends is well documented. Mr Gilbert is a specialist social worker of repute in this field and this shows throughout the book.

Quite rightly he questions whether the move towards care in the community is in the best interests of the person with a mental handicap or whether this should be viewed as just another fad or fashion of the planners. Reading his section on past attitudes to care, one can be left in no doubt that something had to be done to improve the quality of life, and whether it was the author's intention or not, he devotes the rest of the book to telling us how a more humane and dignified approach can be achieved.

Much of the information in Chapters 5 and 6 on the effects of disability on both the person concerned and the family, has been said before, but this is reproduced here in a concise, readable form which enhances the value of the work. Reading lists at the end of chapters are extensive and useful to the reader who wants to know more.

If there is a criticism of the book, it is in the presentation. The sequence of chapters could well lose a potential reader's interest insofar as Chapters 1 and 2 on definitions and numbers, while necessary, do little to encourage someone new to the subject to read on. And this would be a pity because perseverance pays.

The many tables in the text are informative and comprehensive, but that these actually interrupt the text is irritating.

Also, through no fault of Mr Gilbert's, the figures in chapter two are now very out of date – perhaps another reason for excluding such figures in the next edition and instead merely noting trends.

The list of useful addresses in Appendix I is indeed useful as is the information on medication in Chapter 14. However, as with the figures in Chapter 2, these will require to be updated from time to time. The passing of the Disabled Persons (Services, Consultation and Representation) Act will have considerable impact on service delivery, so perhaps since the book has been in print for three years, it is now time to consider a revised edition which will take account of the changes in this field since it was first published.

Lotte Mason, Freelance Consultant in mental handicap

SELECTED ABSTRACTS

Each edition we hope to cover a range of publications relevant to the readers of **GROUPWORK**. This will vary from general abstracts to abstracts based around selected themes.

General theoretical articles

'Models of social-groupwork in Britain: A further note' by A. Brown and B. Caddick in *British Journal of Social Work*, Vol. 16 (1), pages 99–103, 1986.

Follow-up to an earlier articles outlining a model of British groupwork and a response to a critique by Mullender and Ward. Outlines why a British model needs to take account of groups with more than just social goals and social change focus and include groups that have a more overt social control function.

'The use of confrontation in group treatment: Attack or challenge?' by K. Reid in *Clinical Social Work Journal*, Vol. 14 (3), pages 224–237, 1986.

Looks at different ways in which confrontation can be used to benefit the group process. Looks at some of the consequences of handling confrontation well or badly.

'Groupwork understandings and skills applied to intervening in personal networks' by D. Whitaker in *Journal of Social Work Practice*, Vol 2 (4), pages 93–113, 1987.

Examines the meanings of social networks in relationship to social work. Using case studies and examples it looks at how social workers can improve networks with which they work.

Self-help groups

'Factors perceived as helpful by the members of self-help groups: An exploratory study' by S. Llewelyn and A. Haslett in *British Journal of Guidance and Counselling*, Vol 14 (3), pages 252–262, 1986.

Looks at three different self-help groups and examines the factors which members saw to be helpful/unhelpful to the group. The groups were for people suffering from depression, from asthma, and for people who had recently been widowed. Uses work of Yalom to develop the factors used in the study. . .

'Compliance and control: Issues in group training for diabetics' by C. Rabin, S. Amir and B. Ovadia in *Health and Social Work*, Vol. 11 (2), pages 141–151, 1986.

Examines a self-help group for nine women with diabetes, focussing in particular on improvements in individual confidence. Discusses how co-operation with medical staff can also be linked with personal assertiveness in a behaviour group model.

'The perils of borrowing: roles of the professional in mutual help groups,' by P. Silverman in *Journal for Specialists in Group Work*, Vol. 11 (2), pages 68-73, 1986.
Looks at the substantive differences between self-help groups and groups that have an assigned leader and argues why they need to be described in different ways.

'Treatment for survivors of incest' by R. Hall, J. Kassees and C. Hoffman in *Journal for Specialists in Group Work*, Vol. 11 (2), pages 85–92, 1986.
Looks at a variety of groups run within the context of a parents anonymous organisation in Delaware.

'Counselors and self-help groups' by R. Riordan and M. Beggs in *Journal of Counseling and Development*, Vol. 65 (8), pages 427–429, 1987.
Brief note which looks at the growth and beneficial characteristics of self-help groups. For a more detailed discussion, see also:

'Self-help groups and professional helpers' by P. Balgopal, P. Ephross and T. Vassil in *Small Group Behaviour*, Vol. 17 (2), pages 123–137, 1986.

Parents' groups

'Developing post-placement services in Lothian' by G. O'Hara in *Fostering and Adoption*, Vol. 10 (4), pages 38–42, 1986.
Describes the range of services developed for adoptive and foster parents who take children with special needs. This includes the development of a mutual support network.

'Results of anger control training for battering couples' by J. Deschner and J. McNeil in *Journal of Family Violence,*, Vol. 1 (2), pages 111–120, 1986.
This article describes a structured group for parents who have experienced violence in their families either as perpetrator or victim. It also reports on a follow-up study to the groups which suggests at six to eight months after completing the group programme 85 per cent of the families remained free from violence.

'Support groups for parents of sexually victimized children' by J. De Voss and B. Newlon in *School Counsellor*, Vol. 34 (1), pages 51–56, 1986.
Describes therapeutic strategies that might be used with parents whose child has been sexually abused by someone other than the parents.

'Group treatment that helps abusive or neglectful parents' by A. Tuszynski in *Social Casework*, Vol. 66 (9), pages 556–562, 1985.
This article concentrates on mothers and their pre-school children. The group on which it is based uses a variety of behavioural techniques designed to change established patterns of mother-child relationships.

Carer/partner/relationship groups

'Gay grief: An examination of its uniqueness brought to life by the AIDS crisis' by S. Klein and W. Fletcher in *Journal of Psychosocial Oncology*, Vol. 4 (3), pages 15–25, 1986.

Looks at a grief recovery group run in Los Angeles, where most of the members had recently lost a partner through AIDS. Examines some of the differences for this group in coping with grief from other peoples' experiences of grief.

'Support groups for family caregivers of patients with Alzheimers disease' by M. Wasow in *Social Work*, Vol 31 (2), 1986.

Considers the consequences of Alzheimers disease for those providing care and the differential needs that such people might have.

'Painting their way out of the blues' by O. Otway and M. Ellis in *Community Care*, No. 655, pages 16–17, 1987.

Looks at an art therapy group for women who are having difficulties with family relationshps and other problems.

Groups for older people

'A support group in a retirement home' by I. Stone and M. Koonin in *Aging*, No. 352, pages 18–19, 1986.

Describes the formation and operation of a support group for older people living in residential accommodation. The group ran for eight weeks and dealt with some of the feelings associated with aging.

In addition to the above edited abstracts readers can also consult *SOCIAL WORK WITH GROUPS* which covers a wide range of articles.

FRENCH SUMMARIES

Preparing the Client for Social Groupwork: An Illustrated Framework

ODED MANOR

Tout en utilisant la transcription d'un jeux de rôle cet écrit explore de quelle manière les assistants sociaux peuvent aider de façon plus adéquate les clients en leur qualité de membre d'un groupe.

Groups for Older People in Residential and Day-Care: The Other Groupworkers

LORRAINE BERNARD, JOHN BURTON, PHYLLIS KYNE AND JUNE SIMON

Cet article, Naît de la participation à un cours local de formation, décrit quatre aspects de pratique de travail en équipe avec les résidents de maisons pour personnes âgées.

'But I Don't Want to Lead a Group!' Some Common Problems of Social Workers

KEN REID

Ken Reid explore certains des mythes et problèmes communs associés à la responsabilité de groupe; ceux-ci comprennent la mauvaise utilisation de techniques ainsi que l'examen de l'attitude favorisée par le responsable. Il apporte quelques suggestions pratiques sur la façon de résoudre ces problèmes.

Programming Skills in Social Groupwork

SUE ROSS AND ANDY THORPE

S'appuyant sur les théories et pratiques développées d'après des programmes de travail en équipe, cet article met en place un modèle d'aide aux travailleurs a l'organisation de leur groupe. Il discute aussi de quelle façon une telle organisation peut aider le processus d'évaluation.

A Model for Evaluating Groupwork

MICHAEL PRESTON-SHOOT

Cet écrit expose l'importance du processus d'évaluation à la pratique de travail en équipe. Il met en avant un modèle de mise en place du processus d'évaluation avec, comme thème central, la participation des membres du groupe.

Groupwork as the Method of Choice with Black Children in White Foster Homes

AUDREY MULLENDER

Lois du debat, sur les besoins des jeunes noirs placés par les services sociaux, ceux des jeunes gens qui font l'objet de placements transraciaux ont souvent été méconnus. Cet article discute à la fois les implications d'un point de vue de politique sociale et de mise en place d'un tel travail en connection avec un groupe spécifique du projet..

GERMAN SUMMARIES

Preparing the Client for Social Groupwork: An Illustrated Framework

ODED MANOR

Anhand der Niederschrift eines Rollenspiels, untersucht dieser Beitrag, in welcher Weise Sozialarbeiter ihre Klienten adequater auf eine Aufnahme in eine Gruppe vorbereiten können.

Groups for Older People in Residential and Day-Care: The Other Groupworkers

LORRAINE BERNARD, JOHN BURTON, PHYLLIS KYNE AND JUNE SIMON

Resultierend aus der Teilnahme an einem regionalen Trainingskursus, beschreibt dieser Artikel vier Exemplare der Gruppenarbeitspraxis mit älteren Heimbewohnern.

'But I Don't Want to Lead a Group!' Some Common Problems of Social Workers

KEN REID

Ken Reid untersucht einige der mit der Gruppenleitung läufigen Mythen und Sachthemen: diese beinhalten den Mißbrauch der Techniken, sowohl als auch eine Untersuchung des Führungsverhaltens von Gruppenleitern. Er macht praktische Vorschläge zur Lösung dieses Problems.

Programming Skills in Social Groupwork

SUE ROSS AND ANDY THORPE

Aufbauend auf die aus den Gruppenarbeitsprogrammen entwickelten Theorien und Praxisvorschlägen, beschreibt dieser Artikel ein Modell, das Sozialarbeitern bei der Plannung ihrer Gruppenarbeit hilft. Er beschreibt ferner wie solche Plannung eine Auswertungshilfe darstellen kann.

A Model for Evaluating Groupwork

MICHAEL PRESTON-SHOOT

Dieser Beitrag beschreibt die zentrale Rolle der Auswertung für die Gruppenarbeitspraxis. Er präsentiert ein Modell für die Praxisauswertung, das als zentralles Thema, das aktive Mitwirken der Gruppenmitglieder hat.

Groupwork as the Method of Choice with Black Children in White Foster Homes

AUDREY MULLENDER

In der Auseinandersetzung über Bedürfnisse junger schwarzer Leute in Pflege, werden die Bedürfnisse derjenigen, die in nichtwießen Familien untergebracht werden, oft außer acht gelassen. Dieser Artikel untersucht sowohl die theoretischen als auch die praktischen Folgen solcher Arbeit auf ein bestimmtes Gruppenprojekt.

Revisiting Open Groups

MICHAEL HENRY

Michael Henry beschreibt die Arbeit mit Gruppen, die keine geschlossene Mitgliedschraft haben und entwickelt ein Modell, das zu einer besseren Arbeit mit solchen Gruppen führt.

NOTES ON CONTRIBUTORS

Lorraine Bernard is currently a worker in a specialist day centre for older mentally infirm people. She has extensive previous experience of working with older people in residential care and nursing, alongside caring for her own family.

John Burton is an independent consultant and trainer who works with many different groups at all levels in social services departments. He has long experience as a practitioner and manager of residential work with older people, children, adolescents, and their families.

Michael Henry is Deputy Project Leader at Lawrence Weston Family Centre (Barnardo's), Bristol, and he has had experience of working with groups in residential, field and day care settings. His article is based on a Personal Social Services Fellowship study at Bristol University.

Phyllis Kane is a night care assistant in a large old people's home where she has worked for ten years, since bringing up her own family and doing various other jobs. She would like to see care staff more involved at the beginning of a resident's stay with encouraging activity in the tasks of daily living.

Oded Manor, PhD, has practised and supervised groupwork and family work in local authorities for many years prior to taking up a teaching post as Senior Lecturer in Social Work, Middlesex Polytechnic. He is the author of a number of papers on groupwork and editor of *Family Work in Action* (Tavistock, 1984). He is a consultant in groupwork and offers training workshops in this country and abroad.

Audrey Mullender is Lecturer in Social Work, University of Nottingham. She acted as one of the consultants to the Ebony project, which forms the basis of her article. Her other key interest in the groupwork field is in relation to the development, jointly with Dave Ward, of a particular model of intervention known as 'self-directed groupwork'. A book in which this model will be expounded in detail is in process of preparation.

Michael Preston-Shoot is Principal Social Worker in Leeds Social Services Department. He is also a family therapist at Leeds University Family Therapy Research Centre and a psychotherapist. Previously he has worked as a social worker, groupworker and mental health specialist. He is author of *Effective Groupworker* (Macmillan, 1987) and co-author with John Corden of *Contracts in Social Work* (Gower, 1987). From September 1988, he will be Senior Lecturer in Social Work, University of Manchester.

Kenneth E. Reid, PhD, is a Professor of Social Work, Western Michigan University, Kalamazoo, Michigan, where he teaches courses on group treatment in the graduate program. Dr Reid has published numerous articles on social work and is the author of the book, *From Character Building to Social Treatment: The History of the Use of Groups in Social Work.*

Sue Ross is an Area Social Work Organiser in a social work office, Fife, Scotland. She is a groupwork practitioner and trainer, and has written articles on groupwork practice, Intermediate Treatment and family work. Her PhD thesis is in systems approaches to child care and she is co-author of a book to be published in autumn 1988 entitled *Social Work Management and Practice – Systems Principles.*

June Simon has recently become an assistant officer in charge, helping to manage a very large Part III home. She has spent many years as a care assistant and in nursing, as well as bringing up her own family, and now looks forward to further training and developing her career in work with older people.

Andy Thorpe runs an Adult Training Centre in Nottinghamshire for people with a mental handicap. He is a groupworker and trainer, with many years of experience with a range of social work clients. He and Sue Ross are co-authors of an article entitled 'Groupwork with children' (Research Highlights: Aberdeen University, 1984).

NOTES FOR CONTRIBUTORS

Potential contributors

Articles are welcome from all who have an interest in work with groups (whether as practitioner, trainer, researcher, user or consultant) and who wish to contribute to the development of groupwork theory and practice.

Types of articles

The journal will publish two main types of articles:

i. practice-based papers
ii. theory-building papers

Although these two types of article will differ in emphasis and perspective, both are seen as equally important. The intention is that the practice papers will draw out general principles and the theoretical papers will indicate their relevance to practice.

i. PRACTICE-BASED PAPERS

These articles will be based directly on groupwork practice experience, but written in a way which is evaluative as well as descriptive. The material will make a direct contribution to practice theory in a way which will enable groupworkers to learn from it, and to develop their practice competence. The journal would like to receive articles from groupworkers from a wide range of settings working in different ways with people having different needs and circumstances. This range includes statutory and voluntary agencies, fieldwork, residential, daycare and hospital settings; members of diverse age, race and gender; and methods varying between discussion, structured activity, therapy and action. We recognise that many practitioners may not be familiar with writing for journals, and we wish to suggest the following guidelines to assist in this process:

(a) A brief summary of the contents of the article (100-150 words), drawing attention to any particular theme or emphasis.

(b) Background to the group, the context, e.g. agency setting, type of group, workers and members; group aims and objectives; and the theoretical/philosophical perspectives i.e. any particular principles or values central to the approach taken.

(c) A brief review of the group, content, methods and process.

(d) Outcome and analysis, specific topics of interest relevant to the focus of the article, e.g. key issues arising from this piece of practice; and evaluation of the group drawing out learning points for other practitioners.

ii. THEORY-BUILDING PAPERS

Each issue will carry several theoretical papers ranging over groupwork concepts, theory, research, issues and values. These papers will have no set format, but contributors are asked to begin with a brief summary of the contents of the article (100-150 words) and to include a section at the end which indicates the specific implications of the theoretical material for groupwork practice. Papers on the following topics would be especially welcomed:

(a) The current 'state of the art' of groupwork.

(b) Papers analysing the significance for the groupwork process of race, gender, class, culture and other social factors.

(c) Papers analysing key group concepts and issues.

(d) Papers from different countries, sharing current developments and theoretical concerns and preoccupations likely to be significant for groupwork practice in Britain and elsewhere.

(e) New sources of research evidence.

(f) Groupwork training and skill development, consultation/supervision.

We recognise that some contributors may wish to write papers which do not fall neatly into one or other of these categories, e.g. papers drawing out general principles from groupwork practice programmes. Such papers will, of course, be just as welcome in the journal.

Length of papers
The normal range will be 2,500-4,000 words, with practice accounts not longer than 3,000 words. Exceptionally, longer articles will be accepted and there will be a place for briefer contributions on new developments, responses to previous articles and other material of special interest.

Form of submission
Articles should be submitted in one of two ways:
i. typed on A4 paper, 3 copies, double-spaced with wide margins
ii. on computer disc. Materials submitted in this way should be for use on either IBM-PCs and compatibles (e.g. Amstrad 1512, Apricot PCs, or Amstrad PCW 8256), and should use either Wordcraft, Wordstar or Smart word-processing packages. Those intending to submit material in other formats should first contact the editors.

References
These should be quoted in the text by giving in brackets the author's name and year of publication. They should then be listed in alphabetical order at the end of the article as follows.

Books – author's surname, initials, date, title of book, place of publication, publisher's name, page if relevant.

Articles – author's surname, initials, date, title of article, title of journal, volume and number. Only those references which occur in the text should be listed. Where appropriate, additional resources may be listed separately as further reading.

N.B. It is important that punctuation and the use of capital letters should accord with the style used in GROUPWORK.

Assessment for publication
Articles submitted will normally be passed to members of the journal's panel of assessors, and decisions as to publication made by the editors in the light of the assessors' comments.

Publication
The journal will be published three times a year, in February, June and October.

Abstracts and information section
Any information for inclusion in this section, e.g. notification of conferences, network meetings, recent groupwork publications of particular interest, should reach the editors not later than two months prior to the publication month of the relevant issue.

Authors
Authors should include brief information – two or three sentences – about themselves and their background.

Enquiries
Any potential authors who would like to discuss their ideas prior to writing or submitting an article are welcome to contact either of the co-editors...

Allan Brown, Dept of Social Work, University of Bristol, 40 Berkeley Square, Bristol BS8 1HY
Tel: 0272-303030, ext. M208

Andrew Kerslake, School of Humanities, University of Bath, Claverton Down, Bath BA2 7AY
Tel: 0225-826826, ext. 5815.

ALL TYPED ARTICLES AND INFORMATION FOR THE ABSTRACTS SHOULD BE SENT TO ALLAN BROWN.

ALL ARTICLES ON COMPUTER DISC AND MATERIAL FOR REVIEW SHOULD BE SENT TO ANDREW KERSLAKE.

NATIONAL INSTITUTE FOR SOCIAL WORK

DIPLOMA COURSES IN STAFF DEVELOPMENT, EDUCATION AND TRAINING

Does your job involve enabling learning and change? Are you looking for opportunities for personal and professional development in this field?

The **Developing Groupwork** course covers work with clients, supervision of groupwork and groupwork training. Day-release over one year from January.

The **Consultancy Skills** course provides training in work with individuals, teams and organisations. Day-release over one year from January.

The **Course in Social Work Education** is a CCETSW approved post-qualifying course. It provides opportunities to link theory and personal skill development, develop means of improving practice using the workplace as a base for learning, and plan how to confront discrimination in and throughout social work. Fee awards may be available. Two days per week for one year from January. *Developing Groupwork* or *Consultancy Skills* can be incorporated in this course.

We also offer a wide range of workshops that can be taken individually or combined with tutorials to comprise **Individually Negotiated Programmes of Advance Study.** Workshops include skills in teaching and learning, helping skills, creative and effective team-work, and management development for women.

Further information from: **Diana Broad, National Institute for Social Work, 5–7 Tavistock Place, London, WC1H 9SS. Tel: 01-387 9681.**

GCT

GROUPWORK CONSULTATION & TRAINING OFFER THE FOLLOWING TRAINING COURSES FOR 1988

SEPTEMBER.

7-9 Models of Groupwork TA, Psychodrama, Gestalt
7-9 Men in the Workplace†††
12-13 Co-Leadership in Groups
14-16 Introduction to Psychodrama
21-23 Basic Groupwork
26-27 Groupwork with Truants
28-30 Groupwork with Young People

OCTOBER.

3-5 Multi-Racial Groupwork
6-7 Introduction to Transactional Analysis
13-14 Groupwork Supervision & Assessment
24-25 Groupwork with Victims of Sexual Abuse: Adults***
26-27 Groupwork with Victims of Sexual Abuse: Children***

NOVEMBER.

1-2 Groupwork Approach to Women as Rape Surviors
9-11 Why Do I Work with Groups?
23-25 Once Upon a Time Use of fairytales as a technique
28-30 Women & Authority***

***Women only courses †††Men only courses.

COST: 2 day workshop £30 3 day workshop £90

THE ADVANCED CERTIFICATE OF TRAINING 1989
ONE YEAR PART-TIME COURSE
at the Greenwich College, London SE10

13 January-27 October 1989, Wednesdays 4.30-8.30 pm.
One residential weekend, 3 days, 26 sessions
The course is divided in three parts: academic, experiential (group processes) and consultancy/supervision.

Consultants: *Dr Tom Douglas, Dr Oded Manor.*
Tutors: *David Warren-Holland, Diana Lam, John Harper*
Applications are invited from staff in multi-disciplinary settings, who have good experience of group-work and wish to build on this.

Cost: £750, *there will be a 10% reduction for those who have attended GCT short courses. A limited number of grant-aided places (up to £250 off the total fee) are available in certain cases.*

Enquiries To: GCT, Greenwich College, Meridian House, Royal Hill, Greenwich, London SE10 8RT
Tel: 01-858-6627

SOCIAL PHILOSOPHY AND POLICY

Edited by Ellen Frankel Paul

Each 192-page issue of **Social Philosophy and Policy** is devoted to a single topic in social or political philosophy, with specially invited papers (and, for designated issues, unsolicited papers) by leading scholars on the most important issues of our time. The topics for Volume 5 are *Equal Opportunities* and *An Examination of David Gauthier's* ***Morals by Agreement.*** Previous issues have focussed on *Distributive Justice, Human Rights, Liberty and Equality, Ethics and Economics, Nuclear Rights/Nuclear Wrongs, Marxism and Liberalism, Philosophy and Law*, and *Beneficence, Philanthropy and the Public Good*, with contributions from such distinguished philosophers as Maurice Cranston, Ronald Dworkin, R. M. Hare, David Gauthier, J. R. Lucas, Amartya Sen, Jon Elster, and G. A. Cohen, among others.

October and April for the Social Philosophy and Policy Center, Bowling Green State University, USA

Subscription to Volume 5, 1988
Individuals: £12.00 (UK) £13.60 (overseas) US$16.35 (N. America)
Institutions: £29.00 (UK) £36.00 (overseas) US$50.00 (N. America)

Please send orders with payment to:

Iris Taylor
Journals Department
Basil Blackwell
108 Cowley Road
Oxford OX4 1JF
England

or to: **Journals Department**
Basil Blackwell
PO Box 1320
Murray Hill Station
NY 10156
USA

Basil Blackwell · Oxford and New York

Social Work Education

SOCIAL WORK EDUCATION is the leading European journal on staff development, education and training for practice in all social work agencies. It provides information and discussion of current issues for practice teachers, training officers, study supervisors and lecturers.

SOCIAL WORK EDUCATION is edited by Daphne Statham, Director of the National Institute for Social Work of the United Kingdom.

Social Work Education. ISSN 0261-5479. Three times per year. A4, average 44 pages per issue.

Subscription rates for Volume VII (First Issue, November 1987):

	UK	Overseas
	£18	$36
Concessionary rate for individuals	£12	£30

(Back numbers for Volumes 1-VI available at £5 per copy)

Details from: The Subscription Manager, Whiting & Birch Ltd, 90 Dartmouth Road, Forest Hill, London SE23 3HZ. (01-699-0914)

CHILDREN AND SOCIETY

A new multi-disciplinary quarterly from
the National Children's Bureau.

★

CHILDREN AND SOCIETY will aim to be
the leading International journal of communication
between all those involved
with children and children's services
—professionals, academics
and policymakers.

★

EDITOR: Peter Riches

★

EDITORIAL BOARD
David Hull (Chair). John Tomlinson,
Don Niak, Margaret Yelloly, Stephen Wolkind,
Shirley Goodwin, Ron Davie

★

Subscription orders and enquiries should be sent to:
The Subscription Manager,
Whiting & Birch Ltd,
90 Dartmouth Road,
London SE23 3HZ.
(TEL: 01-699-0914)

GROUPWORK

Volume 1 Number 3 1988

Editors: Allan Brown and Andrew Kerslake

CONTENTS

EDITORS:
Allan Brown, Andrew Kerslake

EDITORIAL BOARD
Jo Campling, Editorial Adviser
Ken Heap, (International Editorial Advisor), Director, School for Advanced Training, Norwegian Lutheran School of Social Work, Oslo.
Nano McCaughan, Principal Groupworker, Croydon Social Services.
Rick Morgan-Jones, Consultant and Lecturer in Groupwork, National Institute for Social Work.
David Ward, Lecturer in Social Work, University of Nottingham.

ASSESSORS AND ADVISERS, Lucy Ball, Margot Breton, John Burton, Brian Caddick, Derek Carter, Tom Douglas, Sheila Ernst, Eric Ferron, Charles Garvin, George Getzel, John Harper, Peter Hawkins, John Hodge, John Hughes, Norma Lang, Jenny Lumley, Oded Manor, Harold Marchant, Catherine Papell, Michael Preston-Shoot, Sandra Regan, Kenneth Reid, Dudley Roach, Beulah Rothman, Paul Senior, Lawrence Shulman, Peter Smith, Theo Sowa, Christine Stones, Ann Walford, Dorothy Whitaker.

SUBSCRIPTION, ADVERTISING AND OTHER BUSINESS ENQUIRIES
should be addressed to the publishers, Whiting & Birch Ltd, 90 Dartmouth Road, Forest Hill, London SE23 3HZ. Telephone 01-699-0914 (Int'l +441 699-0914). Telex 8950511 ONEONE G. Quote Mailbox 39000001.

SUBSCRIPTION RATES
British Isles £29.00: Elsewhere US$65
Special reduced rates apply as follows:
Individuals to private address: £16.00 British Isles: $35 Elsewhere
Groupwork is published three times per year.
Two and three year, and multiple copy rates on application to the publishers.

PAYMENT
Should accompany order. Cheque or banker's draft (made payable to Whiting & Birch Ltd) may be in any convertible currency to the relevant amount. Direct transfer can be made to either our Girobank account (no. 5440564), or bank account (Midland Bank, 20 Wimbledon Hill Road, London SW19 7BX, sort code 40-07-30, account number 91109693 78). The following credit cards are also accepted: Access/Mastercard, Visa, Diners Club, American Express. Quote card number, expiry date and give cardholder's name and address if different from delivery address.

REPRODUCTION OF ARTICLES
© Whiting & Birch Ltd. All copyright reserved by Whiting & Birch Ltd. Enquiries regarding rights of reproduction should be addressed to the Publishers in the first instance.

PUBLISHED BY WHITING & BIRCH LTD, LONDON **ISSN 0951-824X**
Printed by Antony Rowe Ltd, Chippenham.

GROUPWORK (1988) 3, 195–196

EDITORIAL

We are delighted to include in this issue an article by our colleagues from Norway, Gerd Kramm Engebrigtsen and Ken Heap. It is not only a deeply moving account of groupwork in the unbelievably painful, protracted circumstances of 'chronic sorrow', but also a classic demonstration of how to relate theory and practice, thought and feelings. A complementary contribution is found in Anne Badger's piece on a 'brothers and sisters' group. The author and her colleagues recognised the peculiar deprivations which are often experienced by the siblings of children with special needs, in this case physical disabilities, and offered the group as some compensation for these children. These articles also raise issues about the relationship between family groups and peer groups for members of different families who share similar individual experiences.

'Social action' groupwork, an approach in the social goals tradition, is attracting interest among practitioners and theoreticians in Britain at the present time. Mullender and Ward (1985) outlined the model in a paper in the *British Journal of Social Work*, and it is explicated in two very different articles in this issue. The first, by Eamonn Keenan and John Pinkerton, takes the issue of member dependency on the groupworker as the focus for an elegant conceptual exploration of the '... *contradiction within practice committed to empowerment*'. This is done through the medium of a one-to-one consultation relationship sharing the same social action values framework. The second is a practice account of an inter-agency approach to the needs of young people on a large housing estate in Nottingham. Bill Badham, Michael Bente and Pauline Hall describe and analyse their work designed to enable young people to gain more control over their own lives and resources. We hope to include further articles on social action groupwork, and would encourage contributions from readers who may wish to share their views and experience, and develop discussion of this approach.

We are also particularly pleased to publish articles on the rather neglected groupwork topic of 'open groups'. Michael Henry reminds us that open groups are widely used, and are found in many different guises from 'drop-in' to quasi-closed. He opens up many of the theoretical and practice issues, which we hope will stimulate other contributions to our understanding of how to make the best possible use of this practice mode.

How often do members of staff groups, particularly in day and residential settings, find that issues in their own staff group relations get in the way of offering an effective groupwork programme to users? In another 'consultation' article, John Taylor, Di Miles and John Eastgate, all experienced in groupwork with adolescents, reflect on their first attempt at applying their groupwork skills to a team development exercise for staff in a residential home for children.

Finally, we also include the first of what we hope will be a series of specialist abstracts, this time on work with adolescents. We are grateful to Alison Skinner, of the National Youth Bureau, for bringing this information together.

This third issue of the journal marks the end of the first year of publication. For ourselves, as co-editors, it has been a stimulating experience, and we are learning all the time! We look forward to continuing what we believe to be the unique feature of this journal: the bringing together of theory and practice in the development of groupwork as an effective and enabling method of practice. We shall, however, continue to be entirely dependent on you, the readers, contributors and subscribers, for the future good health of GROUPWORK.

Allan Brown and Andrew Kerslake

Reference

Mullender, A. and Ward, D. (1985) 'Towards an alternative model of social groupwork'. *British Journal of Social Work*, Vol 15 (2).

Apology

The Editorial in Volume 1, Issue 2 mentioned the inclusion in that volume of an article by Michael Henry. This was incorrect, Michael Henry's article appears in this issue. The publishers apologise for their error.

GROUPWORK (1988) 3, 197–214

SHORT TERM GROUPWORK IN THE TREATMENT OF CHRONIC SORROW

A Norwegian Experience

GERD KRAMM ENGEBRIGTSEN and KEN HEAP

This article describes the use of short term groupwork in supporting parents of children with a congenital progressive terminal disease. Both content and group process are exemplified and they provide a basis for exploring the needs of persons suffering chronic sorrow. It is suggested that short term groupwork may both support and extend members' ways of coping.

We discuss an experience of short term supportive groupwork with parents of children and young adults suffering from a rare, chronic disease which is an inherited, incurable and progressive condition.* This raises issues concerning the possibilities and limitations of short term groups, the range of viable aims for such groups and the possibility of their providing support for families in states of chronic sorrow.

The agency

Frambu Health Centre is a short term residential agency in wooded lake country some miles south of Oslo. It serves the whole of Norway. Since 1975, it has admitted groups of children who are severely handicapped, and their families, for periods of two weeks, during which a range of services are offered. As each intake of children suffers the same condition, much service consists of collectively given medical information, experiences, lectures, films, introductions to new techniques and aids, experimenting with play and teaching materials, and so on. The patients and their families also have individual physical assessment and some counselling. There is an intensive social activity among residents, many of whom otherwise live in considerable isolation and very rarely, if ever, have contact with fellow sufferers except at Frambu.

As one means of supporting and expanding parental coping, groupwork is established as a permanent feature of the stay at the centre. Parents participate in either three or four group sessions during their stay. Typical sessions are of one and a half hours duration. The first and final sessions are placed as near as possible to admission and departure respectively.

Typically, the children admitted suffer from serious handicaps and rare and sometimes progressive diseases. There are a few exceptions to this, such as dwarfism and conditions which may be treated and ameliorated with time, such as analatresia and oesophagusatresia which leave residual problems. Throughout the year, children pass through the centre who suffer from spina bifida, congenital heart disease, osteogenesis imperfecta, Batten's disease, haemophilia, cerebral palsy, cystic fibrosis, immune deficiencies, Prader Willi's syndrome, congenital deaf-blindness and other conditions. Every year children who suffer from one of these conditions, spend two weeks at the centre with their parents and sometimes siblings.

The disease

At present there are about 30 young people in Norway who suffer this particular condition. It is an inherited incurable progressive disease. Its first symptom is usually the onset of blindness at the age of five or six years, followed sometimes by epilepsy and marked behavioural and emotional changes. The children usually become disturbed and have psychotic periods. The organic brain impairment causing the disease progresses in such a way that the children first stagnate intellectually and then become reduced to a state of profound mental deficiency. Speech becomes less clear and gradually disappears. Muscular tensions and loss of muscular control seriously interfere with movement. Over time they become totally paralysed. By their late teens they are blind, mute, defective and immobile. Death usually occurs in the late twenties. There are cases of more than one patient in a family.

We are discussing a remorseless and irreversible process of destruction. It devastates the child, subjects the parents and healthy siblings to horror, fear and prolonged grief. The demand for parental coping through the long years of care is very great indeed.

Literature

We have found little material on the psycho-social impact of this specific condition on the family. Our Norwegian sources are Brandsborg (1987) and Ingstad and Sommerschild (1984). Other chronic conditions which make heavy demands upon the family's coping are, however, more extensively reported. Sources which have increased our understanding of the impact of chronic childhood disease on the family include: Dvoretsky, 1982 (progressive muscular disease); Binger *et al.*, 1969; Kaplan *et al.*, 1973 (leukaemia); Chodoff *et al.*, 1964 (cancer); Burnette, 1975 (cystic fibrosis); Freeston, 1971 (spina bifida); and Korsch *et al.* 1971 (renal disease). Shapiro (1983) provides an extensive and helpful review on this subject. The notion of chronic sorrow — a continuing theme — is clearly and movingly discussed by Olshanky (1962) and by Jackson (1974).

There is a wealth of clinical literature on the use of group methods in this area, though, again, not specifically with these families. Groupwork with chronically ill children is represented by Hughes, 1981 (rheumatoid arthritis, orthopaedic problems); Sheridan, 1975; and Geist, 1979. (Both Sheridan and Geist address a broad range of conditions).

Groupwork with the parents of chronically ill children is abundantly reported. Clearly many professionals have perceived the supportive potential of groupwork for parents in these situations of protracted grief, burdened as they also commonly are with physical exhaustion and intense, painful and often conflicting feelings. Kornfeld and Siegel (1979) describe groupwork with parents of children with Duchenne muscular dystrophy. West *et al.* (1979) present a model of groupwork with parents of children suffering William's elfin faces syndrome. Ross (1979) describes groupwork with parents whose children have terminal cancer. Parents of leukemic children have worked in groups described by Knapp and Hansen (1973), Heffron *et al.* (1973) and Kartha and Ertel (1976) among others. David and Donovan (1975) discuss groupwork with parents of severely multi-handicapped children. Mothers of children with renal disease, involving both dialysis and transplantation, attended groups described by Glass and Hickerson (1976).

Whilst the groupwork approach utilised at Frambu partly reflects the thinking and formulation of one of the present authors (Heap, 1979; 1985), we have also been influenced by Ingstad and Sommerschild's (1984) ideas on coping, and by Lebow (1976) on anticipatory mourning. Finally, in the ongoing method development at the centre we are continually exercised by the issue of time. In this regard Alissi and Casper's (1985) special issue of *Social Work with Groups* has been particularly helpful.

Experiences in groups

Themes recur throughout the groupwork at Frambu, some of which are common to the problems of chronic sorrow and progressive disease. The particularly devastating nature of this disease, however, brings some of these into especially sharp focus, exacerbating as it does both the remorseless inescapability of degeneration, and the lonely and sometimes eroding intradependence of each damaged family, struggling to survive both despair and the increasing demands upon coping.

In the following we shall describe some of these recurrent themes and will refer separately to *themes in the group content* and *themes in the group process.* The material presented is drawn from the content of eight meetings which were process-recorded soon after the close of each session. Four of these meetings were with a group of parents with young sufferers at earlier stages of the disease, who were attending Frambu for the first time in 1985. Four others were from another group attending for a second time after a gap of a year.

Themes in the group content

While we have not aimed at precision here, the sequence in which these themes follow reflects our impression of their relative frequency and intensity.

THEME: IMPACT ON FAMILY CULTURE AND ORGANIZATION

Following the initial shock of diagnosis and the brutal truth of the child's prognosis, the family begins a process of change. This process is not a closed and finite reorganisation, but involves continual readjustment as the child's illness and dependence increases and the demands upon the family's coping ability become progressively severe. In some of the families yet another child manifests the disease. Each in their turn suffers increasingly and yet more demands are made on the family system. All parents with younger children live with the threat of these also becoming afflicted.

The aims of this continual readjustment are several. It is primarily aimed at seeking ways of ensuring maximum care of the child while family members' resources are also invested in ensuring economic survival. Role distribution and sharing are often very carefully thought through, members of the family — parents in particular — often making major adjustments in their work situation. These adjustments inevitably involve losses, compromises and resentment as well as affording some satisfaction and relief. This may accumulate, with the continual pain of living with the child's devastation, to create a singularly intense emotional climate.

Group members focus with great frequency on this theme. Our impression is that in doing so, they gain relief from emotional pressure and they experience group recognition of both sacrifice and achievement and a rare opportunity to think aloud and exchange ideas about alternative practical solutions.

Example 1

During the introductory round of a first meeting where members were free to decide what they presented, material relating to family reorganisation was very common.

Worker: ... and you? Mr. and Mrs. E.?

Mrs.E. (on behalf of both): We live in a valley near the Swedish border. He (Mr. E.) was in the Navy, but gave it up two years ago. Lene became so heavy and passive, so I just couldn't lift her any more by myself. Now he works behind the counter at the Co-op.

Worker (to Mr. E.): Well, that sounds like a big change ... how is it working out?

Mr E.: Not much choice, really. I realised that my wife could not manage alone any more, but I miss the sea ... It had become my life in a way.

Worker: Yes ... I hear from what most of you have said that there are all kinds of changes and painful losses in addition to the overriding problem with your children.

Mr. B.: Take us, for instance. We come from a small island off the South coast. Two of our children have the disease. Bjørn is 15 and Tone is 13. We also have two healthy children, they are older. I have a joinery business, producing handmade furniture. Our oldest son now works here, and until this happened, Mrs B ran the whole office side of things. A real family business.

Mrs. B.: But now I'm at home 24 hours a day. Two very sick and helpless youngsters to look after takes all my strength and time, although my husband and our healthy children help all they can.

Worker: How difficult it must be for you all, living in such an isolated and small community with such sick children. Is there medical or nursing help down there?

Mrs. B.: Not for many miles. First we have to get the boat going, hope the sea isn't too rough, or we have to wait for the medical emergency team to get to us. But we've always managed so far. If the worse gets to the worst, there is a helicopter ambulance.

Mr. B. (sighs, resigned): Yes, one day at a time, one crisis at a time, but we have managed. As things change, we change.

THEME: WAYS OF COPING

Just as each family finds its own pattern of readjustment, so must each parent find a functional way of coping. Sometimes there seems to be a family consensus on ways of dealing both with the many practical problems of caring, and with the chronic sorrow. Sometimes parents differ, however, and experience the further burden of divergence on a vital family issue, for instance on sharing knowledge with the child or communicating their grief to the child.

Example 2 (from a second meeting, about half-way)

Mr. B (response to worker): Well, I think it would be better to pretend that it is going to be all right. To say that she can come here and get treatment or something . . .

Mrs. D: Well, I wouldn't do it like that. In fact, in a way I'm glad that I was the one who told Bent, so that I could take his despair and those awful tears when they came.

Mrs. B: It is a dreadful thing to have to tell them . . . but it would probably have been better . . . but the time never seemed to be right for it — which was really an excuse, we just couldn't bear to do it —

Mr. B: No, I never agreed with you there. It is right to protect them from as much of it as possible. They have worries enough.

Mrs. E: But then we would have to try not to think about it ourselves. We have tried that at times, in fact. It didn't work.

(Reflective silence, at first comfortable, then more uneasy).

Worker: The group was just talking about concealing this problem from the children and from yourselves . . . how much I wish for you that you could, that it would just go away. But it won't. And it would surprise me if you could manage to 'forget it' for more than, perhaps, a very short time. Is that so?

Mrs. E: No, I have it with me all the time. I always think that each day could be his last. Peter and I have talked about death, and it was he who took it up with me, not the other way around. He didn't say too much about the disease, though, but he did say that it is unfair and unjust. He had read the booklet too. That was some time ago when we accidentally left it lying about.

Worker: You are telling us that Peter in a way does know very much about it, but somehow makes you understand that there is a limit to how much he can cope with at a time.

Mrs. A: Something like that, yes I think. It is really hard to know what they know . . . and how much they ought to know.

Mr. B: That pamphlet! We got rid of that long ago! Reading that can't do anybody any good.

Mrs. E: No, and it even says that they, at best, can only live till they are 30.

(Silence).

Mr. F: I think — we think, that it is best to take each day as it comes and not go too far into the future. There is a lot of pleasure — of joy — in each day if only we can see it.
Worker: And your wife — you have explained why she is not here today — can she see this the same way as you do?
Mr. F: No, she is just sad all the time.
Worker: That must be difficult — to have such different ways of looking at something so important for you — I wonder if others in the group are in similar situations?
Mrs. F: Well, yes, we talk about this rather a lot. My husband says I take it too lightly. I say he makes things even worse.
Mr. A: It is exactly the same with us! I say the same to my wife, but she says that I'm hung up on it and worry too much.
Worker: I think it is often like this, that husbands and wives are at different stages in their grief. It would be strange if it were otherwise in something which stretches over so many years. And then of course, as several of you have just said, husbands and wives may deal differently with painful feelings all the time — I have the impression that several of you here are struggling with that — on top of everything else.
Mrs. E: So true. My husband just doesn't understand me. But I'm the one who has most to do with Arne and the one Arne is most attached to . So it is not so strange really.
Mr. E: Yes, but I've had much more contact with Arne this last year. It is mostly I who help him with his training and who reads to him.
(The group continued for some minutes, both exchanging divergent views about coping and recounting their particular contributions to the family's coping).
Worker: I don't think anyone is going to find *the* right way to be a family, whether or not people have such problems and pain to struggle with as you all do. Perhaps the most important thing, if you parents can't agree on how best to cope, is to keep the issue open as something which can always be discussed, where one is always learning, and where changes with the children will in any case compel changes in the way you cope — and make one or the other of you change his or her mind about something. Meanwhile I feel that I want to say how impressive it is to hear how each of you, whether in agreement or not, does the things you can do and complement each other in the overall care of your children. The caring has so many aspects as the children grow older and become more handicapped, that it is perhaps quite all right that you have slightly different points of view. The most important thing is that you share in it, somehow or

other, and what I hear in the group indicates impressively that you do share.

THEME: THE LONELINESS OF CARING

Members frequently exchange accounts and comments about the demands on their life situation. This is only exceptionally in a bitter or self pitying way. It occurs more commonly as factual statement, seeking not so much sympathy as recognition of commonality — the assertion that 'we here, we and only we, really know what our everyday life is like'. These exchanges are supportive in the sense both that the extent of the burden is recognised and that the achievement of coping with it is acknowledged. A more complaining and critical note on this theme is, however, commonly heard when lack of supportive services is discussed — particularly the feeling of being 'written off' by their social and health services, or their experiences of the insensitivity shown by the services. This increases the feeling of isolation and helplessness engendered by the children's chronic condition.

Example 3

Mrs. A: ... we might have managed differently if we had been told about it differently ... if only they had understood a little more of our reactions. We were horrified and in shock, couldn't grasp it and were no doubt very difficult to deal with. But the people at the hospital simply became defensive and angry. We became enemies, adversaries. They saw us as hysterical parents and we saw them as cold and rejecting. Either they didn't know what we were going to be facing, or they didn't want to know. We lost confidence and have never regained it. So we feel very alone with it all.

Mr. F: It was the same with us. The first time we came to the doctor and he gave us the diagnosis, he said the best thing would be to leave the child behind. He said there was no way that we were going to be able to cope with her at home, over time. My wife was so furious that she took the child's hand and marched out. The shock that time made us very sceptical towards doctors, although we've had many good experiences since.

Mr. C: It was dreadful for us too. Birgit is the first of these children they've seen at our hospital. The doctors and nurses actually avoided us after the diagnosis. — Looking back, it must have been difficult for them too, but the way they dealt with it, made it even worse for us — we felt completely alone.

THEME: UNCERTAINTY

While the relentless course of this disease is well known to the parents, its tempo with each child is not. The age of death may vary by as much as ten years and the preceding losses of function and contact may vary correspondingly. Thus an abiding uncertainty further agitates existing tensions and grief and continually threatens the stability of the re-organisation and coping which has been achieved by the family at any time.

Example 4

Mrs. D: The uncertainty is the worst of all. Knowing for sure that we shall lose them, but never 'when'. And I shall lose two, first Constance and then Bent. In a sense I have already lost Constance, and so I hold even tighter to Bent. But I'll lose him just the same, but as I said I don't know when.

THEME: THE FRAMBU EXPERIENCE

The 14 days and nights of the stay at Frambu involve powerful experiences. From their normally isolated position the families are suddenly surrounded almost exclusively by others 'in the same boat'. The experience of commonality and fellowship inhibits the feeling of deviance, of being chosen by a malignant fate, which burdens families like these in their home surroundings. This is often referred to. Equally, however, the visibility of the common problem sweeps away any possible escape into defences against recognising its intransigence and its remorseless course.

This combination of support through identification and inescapable confrontation provides a recurrent theme in the groups. Though this is often painful, it is central to members' work in finding ways of managing and surviving.

Example 5

Mr. E: It was dreadful the first time we came here. Seeing so many very sick children — especially the older ones. It sort of told us very clearly what our own children were going to be like a year or two down the road.

Mr. C: God, yes, it was frightening. Alf, for instance, do you remember him?

Mrs. E: Yes, and Gro ... she died last year ... did you know that?

Mrs. A: Yes, I knew. Her mother wrote to me at Christmas. I had to tell Petter about it, because he had expected to meet her here this time too. Telling him was dreadful. He was in absolute despair, and I could find no way to comfort him at all ... Since then it has been difficult to get him to think about coming here this time, because the two of them found so much pleasure in each other's company, also with Bent and Tone (from families D and B).

Mrs. D: We didn't know about Gro's death before we came here. I do wish we had. The first thing Bent did when he came this time, was to ask if Gro was here. It was such a shock for him, so painful. Then, as we got up to our room at bedtime yesterday, he said to me: '*Mummy, perhaps I'll be the one who doesn't come next time*' ... What could I say? How should I have answered? It was awful.

Mr. F: But Bent is in good shape. He is not much worse than he was three years ago.

Worker: I can see how very painful this kind of situation must be for all of you. You all know each other and each others' children so well after having been together here before. But it is not only the death of children whom you know; it's also dealing both with your own child's reaction to those deaths and with your own feeling about it happening to yourselves and your own children sooner or later ... I can understand that this must be a very hard part of being here.

(Silence).

Worker: You know, a few minutes ago Mrs. D raised a question that was not answered. Perhaps the group could come back to her question. We could think of and discuss different ways she could have answered Bent, and in doing so might get a few things clearer for ourselves at the same time ... Shall we do that? ...

THEME: AMBIVALENCE TOWARDS THE SICK CHILD

From time to time, members bring out their feelings towards the sick child. This includes, notably, ambivalence and sporadic aggression and rejection which they experience as irrational and unjust and which is thus a source of guilt and shame. There is relief in discovering in the group that this is a common experience.

Example 6

Mrs. D: At times I am just so furious with them because of the continual agony which they cause us parents. But then I get very upset afterwards — it is so wrong and unfair. They have not asked to be the way they are ... Oddly enough, sometimes I think Bent understands me in a way, it is as if he tries to comfort me at times. Am I the only one like this? You, Mrs. D, don't you ever feel angry and bitter?

Mrs. B: (nodded, began to speak, and struggled to overcome tears).
Mrs. B: We are never angry with Lene. It's not her fault. (Looked anxiously around the group). If it's anyone's fault it is ours.
Mrs. C: Yes, I agree.
Worker: I'd like to come in at this point. I hear some of you expressing worry and guilt about feeling angry at times. Others find it important to assert that you never are angry . . . . There is something here which is very important to talk about ... There are mixed feelings between *all* people who live together in families. Loving and being fed up with, caring and wishing at times to be rid of ... these things are as common as breathing.
(Continued by inviting discussions of anger and ambivalence towards healthy children and spouses and reasons for this). ... how even more understandable ... is anger and periodic rejection of children whose infirmity demands one's whole attention and energy and who, in time, will bring steadily increasing demands and grief.

Themes in the group process

Despite the painful nature of the common problem and of the intense feelings of grief and protest pervading members' lives, these groups rarely behave dramatically. This, we believe, is less because of the cultural phlegmatism of Norway than of members' gradually acquired adjustment to chronic sorrow. Long experience has taught that whatever explosions of emotionality occur today, the child remains there to be helped and held or carried tomorrow. The disease will progress and become worse each year. Strong reactions exhaust and reduce the reserves available for the steadily more demanding coping. There is a pragmatism and a realism in this, yet this approach to chronic sorrow also brings sufferers closer to the edge of resignation and depression or, alternatively, invites recourse to denial defences which impoverish the whole family.

In our view, treatment of chronic sorrow should never attack the 'good enough' coping mechanism which families have developed. It is, however, very important that members remain in touch with their strong and conflicting feelings and continue to react reflectively and flexibly to the changing situation. It is precisely for this reason that groupwork is so well suited as a means of help. Controls are supported but feelings recognized. Ways of coping are acknowledged and supported. The fact of isolation is asserted, but close fellowship runs through the group experience. The themes of the group process reflect these needs and contrasts, and in an almost classic sense show the group process itself functioning as the main means of treatment.

THEME: SUPPORT THROUGH MUTUAL IDENTIFICATION

Group members evidence close interest in others' accounts of their experiences and problems. Members may often speak at length without losing others' attention. Members question each other a good deal and both seek and proffer details about their lives and ways of coping back home. This active *'search for commonality'*, in Sarri and Galinsky's terms (1975), leads to a mutual identification which is a rich supportive resource. This support takes many forms.

Typical exchanges and responses include signs of understanding of what has been described, acknowledgement of underlying pain and conflict, and assertion of close or partial similarity to the speaker's situation. Suggestions are made and advice given. Sympathy and admiration are shown. Differences of opinion and of coping practices are admissable; they are articulated, but in our experience this has not led to conflict. It is as if members' common awareness of the extent of each others' chronic distress permits much wider normative latitude than we are accustomed to see.

The support which emerges from this strong group bond may at times be expressed in spontaneous physical ways, reflecting closeness and warmth.

Example 7

> In *example 4* we heard Mrs. D grieve, having virtually lost her daughter already, and describe how she desperately held on to her son whose illness was not yet so developed ... At this point she began to cry. Mr. F. immediately crossed the group and folded his arms around her and rocked her. The group at this point were all very moved.

THEME: GROUP IDENTITY AND COHESION

A specific aspect of group support as a theme in process is the way in which members sporadically assert the meaning and value of the group itself (and indeed the entire agency) to them. On more than one occasion this has followed some painful exchange, so we speculate that these sporadic assertions of group identity were also collective assurances or reassurances to the worker that the group is not damaged by the admission of pain.

Example 8

(This from the first meeting of a second year group. The group had been discussing their experiences of the first meeting one year previously).

Worker: ... so you make very clear to me that whilst there was also something good about it, it was a painful — I think one of you said, a 'shocking', experience.
Mr. C: Yes, but in a way, coming here is the best thing that has happened to us since all this began.
Mr. B: ... and we all have such fine contact with each other now. We have been writing and telephoning and helping each other throughout these two years. It's so important to keep contact with others who know what's going on. It's good to know that we have each other.
(Others nod in agreement and support).

THEME: VENTILATION AND SELF CONFRONTATION

A number of the examples already quoted reflect members' use of the group process as a facilitator of ventilation and self-confrontation. Away from the agency they are isolated family units at vast distances from each other. Throughout the year they cope and suffer, they defend themselves and they survive. No doubt innumerable small devices are used to make this life situation more acceptable. It would be inhuman to expect anything other than some reliance on defences over the years.

The group bond, however, clearly gives sufficient support to enable members to reassert for each other the pervading pain of their common situation and to give expression to at least some of their feelings about it. In this sense the group process acts as an ego-support, holding up the mirror of reality and reinforcing members' ability to think effectively, to feel appropriately and to confront the continuing need to make decisions and choices. (This ego-strengthening potential of group process is further delineated in Heap, 1985). This processual theme is poignantly exemplified in one group discussion of 'time'.

Example 9

Mrs. N: In a way, he binds me even more than necessary. He makes it clear that he feels alone and frightened if I once in a while manage to get out. And then I feel bad about being out, so I might as well have stayed at home ... (some tears). And I don't know how much longer we'll have him. He is 18 already and in a very bad way. We've no time to lose in upsetting each other.
(Silence some moments)
Worker: What about this question of 'time'? Is that something others are occupied with? To use the time best — there is none to lose? And what is 'best' and so on? ... Shall we talk about that?
Mr. O: Just a certain, limited amount of time. We all feel that.

Mr. F: But every human being, all of us, have only a certain limited time to live.
Mr. O: But that is not the same, is it Mr. F? I can see you hate to face it. We all do, and it makes it a bit easier sometimes to say 'all people die'. But this is not the same as maybe dying at 50 or 60 or 70. These are children. Our children. And they are, with certainty, dying now ... We all know it.

THEME: REALITY MAINTENANCE

One product of the intermingling of defensive coping strategies in daily life and the continuing need to deal with each day of grief and practical caring, is that some aspects of reality become blurred in the service of defence. A function of the group process which impressed us, was its use in checking and correcting members' perceptions of reality. This is a very important function indeed in groups whose over-riding aim is support of adequate coping in situations of prolonged stress.

This is exemplified already in the group's rejection of Mr. F's invitation to share a denial defence. We see it again in the sequel to *example 3*. The dissatisfaction and criticism felt towards hospital staff could have compacted into a collective projective defence. This might have damaged their future co-operation with the doctors and home nurses on whom they were so dependent, as well as alienating them from their own real feelings. The group process led, however, to an affirmation of rational criticism accompanied by a withdrawal of displacements and projections, representing such 'reality maintenance' as we are discussing here.

Example 10
Mr. B: The second time was even worse. By then we knew what the disease really meant. We got the diagnosis for Tone just at the time Bjørn was becoming epileptic. The first time we didn't know anything, nobody knew anything. I think the doctor just wanted to get us out of there.
Mrs. A: I'd like to say that I think I have been very fortunate. We were at X hospital (a major teaching hospital). The doctor we had was just fantastic. He sat with us for more than an hour. He said several times that we could come back and talk with him anytime we needed to ... That was very important, because we were in shock and it was weeks before we even knew what we wanted to ask ... But my point really is — that doctors also vary — both in their knowledge and in their ability to be helpful. On the whole, if we are honest, we must admit that they are giving us a lot of help and a lot of caring ...

But the whole disease is so awful that we have to be allowed to get angry at *somebody* — and the doctors will do very nicely, thank you.

Discussion

We have already stated our position that 'good enough' coping mechanisms should not be attacked in the treatment of chronic sorrow. Nor should defences which enable day-to-day survival be gratuitously questioned in the service of more 'appropriate' feelings in the face of ongoing and pervading distress. The groupwork, as part of the agency provision, is a support to coping, not to an alternative reorganisation of the family.

The dilemma, however, is that the workers repeatedly observe coping patterns which function at a survival level, but which clearly also involve some suppression of members' feelings, and thus both impoverishment of relationships and loss of authenticity. The worker may then wish to intervene with a view to expanding coping styles by facilitating more open expression of ambivalent feelings and of forbidden wishes and fantasies. In this regard the issue of the groups' brief duration is important. Awareness of the limited time framework helps the worker to avoid overambitious and intrusive aims for the group. At the same time, we are aware that the families are in a process of continuing change as the disease runs its course, as new challenges and losses occur, and a readjustment of coping is necessitated. With this in mind, the workers' interventions in the groups — while not attacking present coping — are intended to legitimate the widest possible range of coping and responses, as well as asserting the assumption that change in coping may well be developed in the situation.

Earlier, in the groupwork at Frambu, we were concerned about the hazard of 'opening up', of confronting areas and degrees of pain or ambivalence which could not be adequately dealt with in the limited time. This issue now appears to be resolved. The workers' interventions, as exemplified, are never aimed at increasing exposure beyond the limits set by members' initiatives. Responses are limited to clarification, generalisation and acceptance. In addition to this, the supportive and permissive nature of the group process, as seen so far, is usually free of the familiar pressures to adopt particular approved positions. Individual members feel thus encouraged in their ways of coping, and only the most tentative questioning occurs (as in *example 9*). The intention is that parents take with them both satisfaction with their present coping and a less rigid commitment to it, permitting the consideration of alternative styles and the admission of other feelings. To the extent that the group provides a referent in its absence — the 'invisible committee' of the reference group — it is hoped that experience will aid the families in their evolving situations to modify and extend their coping in appropriate ways. A useful means for this is, as in all groupwork, the increased availability of thoughts and concepts which have been raised during group discussion. Chronic sorrow weighs heavily upon the parents, and reduces both their flexibility in meeting change and their ability to grasp or to construct opportunities for periods of pleasure or distraction — no matter how brief they may be. It is hoped that the invisible committee of the group supports such adaptability, as well as enabling members to permit themselves roles other than that of suffering parent.

The groups also function as referents in other ways. They have become a supportive network. Members correspond periodically and telephone in crises or to discuss decisions.

Parents report how often their exchanges include reference to something which happened or was said in their group. This, too, encourages us to believe that the group experience, despite its brevity, is an important source of support even for those people who are continually burdened with chronic and irresolvable grief.

Note

*In accordance with the wishes of the agency and of the families concerned, the authors are not able to specify the disease precisely. It is so rare that no attempt to disguise the identity of the families could succeed, should we name the condition, in a country with so small a population.

References

Alissi, A. and Casper, M. (eds.) (1985) *Time as a Factor in Groupwork: Time-Limited Group Experiences, Special Issue; Social Work with Groups.* New York: Howarth Press.

Binger, C.M., Albin, A.R. *et al.* (1969) 'Childhood leukaemia: emotional impact on patient and family'. *New England Journal of Medicine*, 280, February, pp. 414–418.

Brandsborg, K. (1987) 'Psykiske reaksjoner og psykologiske behov hos familier med barn som har en progredierende sykdom'. *Tidsskrift for Norsk Psykologforening*, 24, s. 20–27.

Burnette, B.A. (1975) 'Family adjustment to cystic fibrosis'. *American Journal of Nursing*, 75, pp. 1986–1989.

Chodoff, P., Friedmann, S.B. and Hamburg, D.A. (1964) 'Stress, defences and coping behaviour: observations in parents of children with malignant disease'. *American Journal of Psychiatry*, 120, pp. 743–749.

David, A.C. and Donovan, E.H. (1975) 'Initiating group-process with parents of multihandicapped children'. *Social Work in Health Care*, 1 (2), pp. 177–183.

Dvoretsky, B. (1983) 'Reaksjoner hos foresldre med barn med progredierende muskelsykdommer'. *Muskelsyk*, 4, s. 4–6.

Epstein, D.J. (1975) *Genetic Counselling: Present Status and Future Prospects.* Leiden University Press.

Foss. L. (1981) 'Når familien får beskjed om arvelig sykdom'. *Sosionomen*, 8, s. 2–8.

Freeston, B.M. (1971) 'An enquiry into the effect of a spina bifida child upon family life'. *Dev. Med. Child. Neuro.*, 13, pp. 456–461.

Geist, R. (1979) 'Onset of chronic illness in children and adolescents: psychotherapeutic and consultative intervention'. *American Journal of Orthopsychiatry*, 29 (1), pp. 4–23.

Glass, L. and Hickerson, M.D. (1976) 'Dialysis and transplantation: a mothers' group'. *Social Work in Health Care*, 1 (3), (Spring), pp. 287–296.

Hamilton, A.K. and Noble, D.N. (1983) 'Assisting families through genetic counselling'. *Social Casework*, 64 (1), pp. 18–25.

Heap, K. (1979) *Process and Action in Work with Groups: The Preconditions for Treatment and Growth.* Oxford: Pergamon Press.

Heap, K. (1985) *The Practice of Social Work with Groups* London: Allen & Unwin.

Heffron, W.A., Bommelaære, K. and Masters, K. (1973) 'Group discussions with the parents of luekemeic children' *Pediatrics*, 52 (6), pp. 831–840.

Hughes, M.C. (1981) 'Chronically ill children in groups: recurrent issues and adaptations'. *American Journal of Orthopsychiatry*, 54 (4), pp. 704–711.

Ingstad, B. og Sommerschild, H. (1984) *Familien med det Funksjonshemmede Barnet.* Oslo: Tanum-Norli.

Jackson, B. (1974) 'Chronic grief'. *American Journal of Nursing*, s7, pp. 1288–1291.

Kaplan, D.M., Smith, A., Grobstein, R. and Fischamn, S.E. (1973) 'Family, education and stress'. *Social Work*, 18 (4), pp. 60–69.

Kartha, M. and Ertel, I.J. (1976) 'Short-term group therapy for mothers of leukemic children'. *Clinical Pediatrics*, 15 (9), pp. 803–806.

Knapp. V. and Hansen, H. (1973) 'Helping the parents of children with leukemia'. *Social Work*, 18 (4), pp. 70–75.

Kornfeld, M.S. and Siegel, I.M. (1979) 'Parental group therapy in the management of a fatal childhood disease'. *Health and Social Work*, 4 (3), pp. 100–117.

Korsch, B.M., Fine R.N., Gruskin, C.M. and Megrete, V.F. (1971) 'Experiences with children and their families during extended hemodialysis and kidney transplantations'. *Peds. Clin. N. Amer.*, 18, pp. 625–37.

Lebow, G. (1976) 'Facilitating adaptation in anticipatory mourning'. *Social Casework*, 57, pp. 458–468.

Olshanky, S. (1962) 'Chronic sorrow: A response to having a mentally defected

child'. *Social Casework*, 43 (4), pp. 190–193.
Ross, J.W. (1979) 'Coping with childhood cancer: group intervention as an aid to parents in crisis'. *Social Work in Health Care*, 4 (4), pp. 381–391.
Sarri, R. and Galinsky, M. (1975) '*A conceptual framework for group development*', in Glasser, P., Sarri, R. and Vinter, R. (eds.) *Individual Change Through Small Groups* New York: Free Press.
Shapiro, J. (1983) 'Family reactions and coping strategies in response to the physically ill or handicapped child: a review'. *Soc. Sci. Med.*, 17 (14), pp. 913-–931.
Sheridan, M.S. (1975) 'Talk-time with hospitalised children'. *Social Work*, 20 (1), pp. 40–44.
Voje, G.I. (1985) '*Familiens situasjon når et barn blir alvorlig'. langvarig syk.*
Weiss, J.O. (1976) 'Social Work and genetic counselling' *Social Work in Health Care*, 2 (1), pp. 5–12.
West, M. McIlvaine, R. and Sellis, C.J. (1979) 'An interdisciplinary health care setting's experience with groups for parents of children with specific disabilities'. *Social Work in Health Care*. 4 (3), pp. 287–298.

GROUPWORK (1988) 3, 215–228

REVISITING OPEN GROUPS

MICHAEL HENRY

Open groups represent a substantial part of the everyday practice of groupworkers, yet comparatively few contributions exist to conceptualise this form of groupwork. This paper reviews the literature on open groups and begins to identify the major themes. Several definitions and contexts are given as examples of open groups, and the question, 'why do it this way?' is explored. Open group process is discussed — group cohesion, and member entry and exit, feature as important elements.

Based on these ideas, and with practice insights, a profile and a basic typology are presented and used to illustrate further understanding of open group structures and processes. The paper concludes with some key questions for practice.

We all hold simultaneous membership of a variety of groups and groupings. Some are more clearly defined than others. For example, having a clearly defined 'beginning' and 'end' to the association; who 'is' and who 'is not' a member; the permeability of the group in terms of a visible exchange with the environment; how cohesive the group is and how easy it is to become a member; the purpose of the group, and whether goals are predetermined by the agency, are group-created, or directed towards encompassing individual aims.

The open group is frequently a method of choice in settings which involve groupwork approaches. In these groups, members come and go depending on individual needs, or after a set period of attendance. This fluidity creates reconstitutions of membership as the group progresses. Open groups do not always fit neatly into prescribed models of groupwork, commonly based on 'closed group' designs. They challenge many of our traditional orientations, yet it may be possible to view these groups as an important practice alternative rooted in groupwork traditions.

Definitions of open groups in the literature are based primarily on membership change, a feature which links these groups conceptually, and differentiates them from closed groups. For example:

> The terms open and closed refer to groups which do or do not add members once the group has convened in its initial sessions (Hartford, 1971).
> 'open-ended' refers to a group in which the membership is continually changing (Shulman, 1984).

> Groups open in terms of membership are those in which members enter and leave the group at their own pace of growth and change (Henry, 1981).

These definitions illustrate different aspects of the open group based on the single variable of membership change. Hence, the *intention* to change membership, the *rate* of this change, and the *criteria* for change, emerge as specific concerns.

Examples of open groups

The literature indicates that these groups are managed in various ways, in terms of members' affiliation with the group, and the associated patterns of membership-change. This is illustrated by three contrasting examples:

i. A multiple family therapy group which helped cancer victims and their families on an 'as needed' basis. Families attended for anything from one session up to the entire eleven months of the group's existence (Wellisch, 1978).
ii. At a child mental health centre, there was weekly intake, for purposes of assessment. Members finished after six weeks of attendance, and could then be filtered into other services at the centre such as individual, group and family therapy (Todd and Barcome, 1980).
iii. Whitaker (1975) discusses 'short-term transition' groups, in which ten or twelve persons initially meet twice weekly for a set period of ten weeks. At the end of this time, a reorganisation produces a new group consisting of some of the remaining members plus a complement of new members. In this way each group has time to develop and the 'disruption' of new intake recurs once every ten weeks.

Why do it this way?

Generally, open groups exist for service delivery reasons and because practitioners wish to offer more appropriate and better received services. Only scattered references are made to therapeutic benefits like the idea that it may be useful to have a group consisting of people at relatively different stages of personal achievement. For example, newcomers can see that change is possible by looking at the examples of successful members; more long-standing members can help new members through their 'denial' of the problem, and get further gratification from sharing their experience (Henry, 1981; Freese, 1972; Heap, 1985).

Groups may be 'open' because of:

i. The rapid turnover of users of a larger system, i.e. a maternity home (Shulman, 1984) or a hospital (Bloom and Lynch, 1979; Yalom, 1983) in which members are frequently entering and leaving an institution at unpredictable times.
ii. The natural short term goal of the group, i.e. assessment or screening groups (Todd and Barcome, 1980).
iii. The service providers taking account of individual abilities to change and grow at different rates. As some members achieve their aims sooner than others, new members are needed to maintain the group.
iv. The user's needs for urgent and temporary help, for example in crisis situations. Caplan (1961) proposes that a crisis is resolved, for better or worse, within five or six weeks. Hence, members enter the group as and when they need it, and stay for up to a maximum time period. In crisis intervention there is a need to offer 'timely' and immediate help, and often users cannot wait for a new group to commence. A 'rolling' group offers early entry to the service (Brown and Seymour, 1983), and further reduces the problem of waiting lists.
v. The need to offer continuing help. An 'open-ended' group can provide the opportunity for re-entry and intermittent membership (Brabender, 1985).
vi. The need to be directly responsive to users' needs and wishes. In traditional approaches, users may not take up a service because they feel they may not be able to achieve the required time commitment and regular attendance (Breton, 1985). There may be further concern about the *intensity* of group member relationships, and more flexible approaches may be more appropriate for inexperienced people.

A frequent criticism of open groups is that they are unable to 'develop'. This depends on the aims of the group. A 'drop in' group may meet the requirements of accessibility to the service and achieve basic socialising aims, as intended. Indeed, one example of a 'drop in' group for suicidal people, actively discouraged group cohesiveness, preferring to instil a 'no commitment, use it if you wish' approach, and avoiding a sense of obligation to the group (Farberow and Marmor, in Rosenbaum, 1983, p. 344).

An examination of the literature indicates that most, but by no means all of the published material on open groups is to be found in American journals and texts. Among these sources, two recent articles by Schopler and Galinsky (1984, 1985) provide valuable material.

They draw attention to extensive practice examples of groupwork using 'open-ended' approaches and serving a variety of agency and user needs. Their analysis of a survey of 66 open groups in the USA has identified a possible classification in terms of purpose:

i. helping clients cope with transitions and crises;
ii. providing other types of short and long term therapy;
iii. offering support to clients with common problems;
iv. assessing and screening clients;
v. orienting and educating clients;
vi. training and supervising staff and students;
vii. facilitating outreach efforts.

Interesting findings from this survey indicate that multiple purposes are frequently addressed in open groups, and that a dominant purpose is '*helping clients cope with transitions and crises*' (Schopler and Galinsky, 1984, p. 5.

The authors mention that open-ended approaches may be a useful model for coping with transitions which can '*enhance each member's capacity for responding to external stress*' (p. 6) as members enter and leave the group.

Open group processes

Given that these groups have particular value — we should examine how they work. Open groups can be contrasted with closed groups in terms of process, and here some interesting ideas exist.

Ziller (1965) provided a cornerstone for much of the subsequent conceptualisation of open groups, by establishing four differentiating characteristics:

i. *Time perspective.* The transiency of membership means that for group members the present dominates.
ii. *Equilibrium.* Open groups develop procedures to minimise the disruption of change — minimising 'disequilibrium'.
iii. *Frame of reference.* An expanded frame of reference exists. Open groups consist of a wide variety of people who enter the group, thus increasing the potential for comparing oneself against a set of others.

iv. *Membership change.* Discussed in terms of 'planned changes' in the group structure. Power relationships alter, based on the group's perceived need for newcomers, and the ability of the newcomers to disrupt the group by early departure.

Sue Henry (1981) views the open group as a 'pass-through system' — in its structure, but not necessarily in its process. Members may come and go through the system, but a central 'core or essence' of the group remains to represent continuity. The core is composed of the continuing goal (or initial purpose); the existing normative structure in relation to that purpose; the group's history or tradition and culture; and the worker (p. 308).

Most accounts of open groups are concerned with aspects of group stability, so that goals can be achieved. The emphasis is on continuity in terms of the 'group essence', or a 'core' membership to carry traditions over time and through change of membership (see Douglas, 1979).

It is noted that 'cohesion' in open groups is low, '. . . *so that new members can enter and old ones leave without destroying the group*' (Hartford, 1971, p. 251). Alternatively, cohesion can be viewed as a developmental phenomenon. It can therefore be dependent on the ability to negotiate the timing of entry and exit in relation to the stages of the group's development, so as to cause minimal disruption and to allow cohesion to develop. Also, as cohesion is relative to the sort of group members want to belong to, there may be a contradiction between the group naturally becoming cohesive and then exclusive, whilst trying to maintain the ability to accept newcomers.

There is some question as to whether open groups move beyond addressing formative issues, because of the need to address issues of new arrivals and departures continually. Research has found positive development in open groups despite rapid turnover. The level of cohesiveness develops as group norms and values are passed from generation to generation, either via the leader, or directly between members (Bailis *et al.*, 1978). Another study found that a continuation effect exists, so that a subsequent 'generation' of the group will start at a higher level of integration than previously existing group compositions (Hill and Gruner, 1973).

Some attempts have been made to understand open group development in terms of sequential stages of development. Henry (1981) sees the group as 're-cycling' through re-enactments of earlier stages as new members enter and old members leave. As a new member enters, the group re-enacts earlier convening and conflict stages. As the new member is 'absorbed', the group reaches a maintenance stage level (seen as the most integrated group form). Henry argues that it is possibly unwise to admit newcomers to periods of 'family quarrel', e.g. during the conflict stage when 'power and control' issues are being sorted out. The 'initial' and maintenance stages are seen to be potentially more accepting stages.

Other variables will probably affect the assimilation of newcomers such as: how the group treats the newcomer; whether the group is used to membership change; and how much the group needs new members (Crandall, 1978).

Orientation procedures ease member entry and exit, and increase group stability. These procedures are developed to minimise the energy directed to maintaining stability — easing the flow of members and signalling transitions; from one composition to the next, and from one stage of development to the next. Galinsky and Schopler (1985) state that procedures should address new arrivals and departures, as well as the need for the group to re-integrate following member change.

Procedures act as markers or rituals which become part of the normative behaviour of the group, and are important boundaries to group process in more 'fluid' open group situations. Rituals serve to consolidate progress, share an otherwise unshared history with newcomers, or mark a change in group composition. Rituals operate as 'safety' generators in that they signal a change and help to manage transitions.

A profile and basic typology of open groups

Based on the preceding ideas about the characteristics of open groups, a profile and basic typology are proposed, which take account of the major variables of open groups, i.e. membership change, and time.

A PROFILE

Open groups are linked conceptually by the *intention* to take in new membership while the group is in progress, implying a change in composition (of members or workers) during the association of any one member with the system. In terms of process, this further implies that the '*essence*' of the group will be maintained *across* transitions of group composition by a *core* of membership. This core will consist of member(s), or members and workers.

The core membership represents the possibility of continuity and group functioning, despite disruptions caused by member change. This continuity will generally serve an economic function in the group, reducing the need to re-negotiate continually the rules on which the group operates.

Where the group is used as a 'context' for worker-member interactions, continuity will not be as important, in contrast to using the group as a 'means' of achieving identified goals and individual change. In the latter model, the group must reach a level of maturity, requiring cohesion between members, and an acquired stage of development in which identified goals are able to be worked on through group interaction.

A BASIC TYPOLOGY

It is possible to develop a simple classification of open groups based on these variables of membership change and time boundaries (see Figure 1).

The *'drop-in' ('drop out')* model is characterised by a flexible approach to who 'is' and who 'is not' a member. Membership is self selecting, and entry criteria very broad or assumed (i.e. a category of people such as mothers and toddlers, local residents, etc.). Members attend as and when they wish for an indefinite period, with the possibility of re-entry at a later stage. The composition of the group will be unpredictable on any given day, and there will be no defined limit to group size.

The *replacement* model will typically have a fixed upper limit of members, so group size remains compatible with purpose. There will be a selection procedure to regulate entry and exit. There will be contracted length of stay, so that as one member leaves, a 'vacancy' is created for a newcomer. Member change may occur very frequently, or once a year. Potentially there will be times of disruption and times of relative stability, almost resembling a 'closed group'.

The *re-formed* model is a way of increasing the predictability of membership by use of time boundaries. Members contract for a set period of time, during which no new members are added, although members may drop out. At the end of that time a new group is re-formed, as in a new school term, consisting of some old and some new members. The purpose of the group is able to change 'naturally' with each reformation, and problems of re-integration happen less frequently.

Developing ideas about the basic typology and major variables

THE MEMBERSHIP VARIABLE

Assuming that these three types of open groups can exist in their 'pure' states, the re-formed and replacement models could be seen as

Figure 1.

'Drop in' ('Drop out')

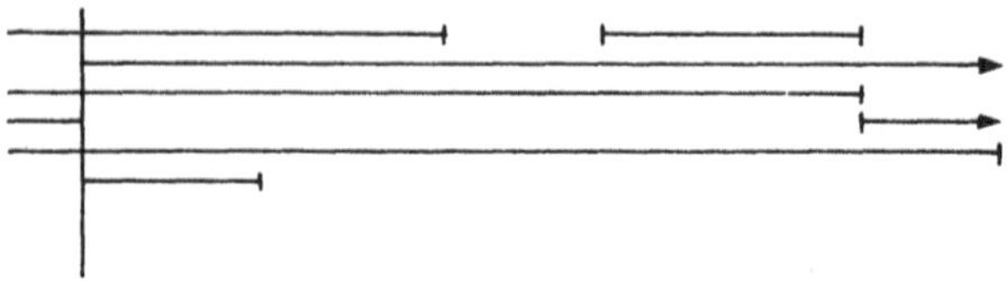

Replacement

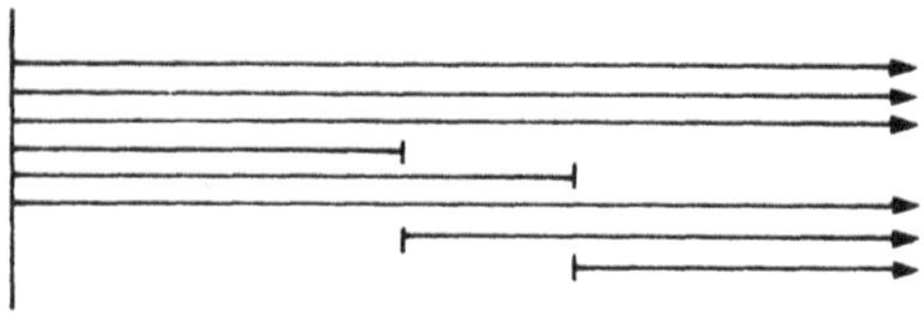

Re-formed

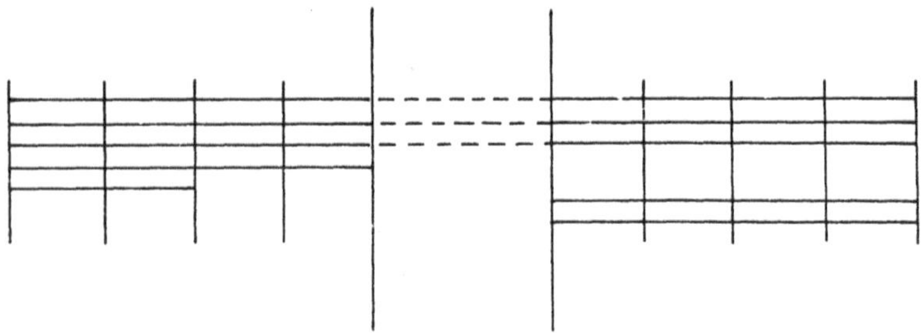

In the diagrams — each single horizontal line represents individual member-attendance. The vertical lines represent time demarcations, i.e. sessions or significant change.

'worker controlled'; the 'drop in' as a 'user controlled' model.

User control is differentiated from worker control by the ability of *users* to decide whether they fit broad entry criteria and exactly how often and when they wish to attend the group, and for how long. More worker-controlled models will tend to place demands on entry requirements and attendance.

In practice, however, there are some similarities between the three proposed models. Each has a core membership existing through reconstitutions in membership, and in each model the rate of member change will affect group stability. Also, patterns of member change may be quite similar, as evidenced by accretions, decretions, replacements, and times of relative stability and instability.

A *replacement* group may resemble a 'drop in', if the composition of people present is different at each session. Here, as in the re-formed group, the distinction lies in the boundary of membership being defined. Fluctuations in membership will be seen as 'absent' members who may not always be present, similar to a closed group.

In the '*drop in*' group, there may be broad criteria of 'eligibility', and yet users group together naturally to create membership boundaries. This can be seen in the tendency for sub-groups to develop and become exclusive cliques. The 'core' may develop its own sub-culture, or secondary goals; possibly incompatible with the original purposes of the group. Group size will be an important element in the potential disruption caused by natural groupings. The smaller the group, the more apparent and influential those sub-groups become. Where the intentions of 'cliques' become incompatible with primary aims, these members may be encouraged to change their role within the group, e.g. to address problems of acceptance and integration of new members; or to start a fresh group, more identified in structure and purpose with their emerging requirements.

Where there are no contracts of exit, groups designed to offer timely, acceptable help, may become 'clogged up' with members who choose to remain, altering the service to something resembling a closed group. Where no imposed limits to group size exist, the group may naturally develop a self regulating maximum membership. This may depend on the physical space available; or the numbers required to achieve the tasks of the group, or to establish the 'group model' required to satisfy members' needs.

This idea of *completion* (the optimum size or group model required) is evident in open group formats where there are:

i. *Accretions* — the group will be constantly reforming with each new introduction, or where members anticipate a full complement (up to a fixed ceiling of membership); they may well wait until that time before beginning their 'work' properly. In this case the group may never get off the ground as members constantly wait for the 'ideal' conditions to exist before investing totally in the group.

ii. *Decretions* — may cause existing members to panic about the group's survival. Also decreased group size may be perceived as a 'second best' to previous group functioning based on more optimal group compositions. Some members of course may prefer the intimacy afforded by decreased group size.

The *re-formed* model creates one solution; putting boundaries around member change for specific time periods. Ideally, members form with a defined set of others, and the group can develop the cohesion and trust necessary to work towards identified goals whilst allowing a 'second term' for those people who have not reached satisfactory achievements. Here, an 'expected' break occurs based on a 'group as a whole' beginning, end, and review, as opposed to a replacement model, in which members individually contract and finish at different times. This kind of total group finish may be desirable where unhelpful group norms have developed. Alternatively, some useful group structures may be disrupted. There may also be issues around 'who decides' whether an individual has achieved an expected level of achievement, and therefore does not warrant an extra 'term'. For example, do individuals, the group, or workers decide the measurement criteria for success? This problem will exist in other open group models unless exit criteria are established.

THE TIME VARIABLE

In each of these models, the use of time is significant in the conceptual boundaries we impose, and has specific implications for the 'programme'.

'Time limited' closed groups generally have a well defined beginning and end. On this basis, the *re-formed* model may seem to be a series of closed groups in which no new members are added until the next series of sessions. However, the core membership, *across demarcations of time*, constitutes the ability of successive groups to carry on traditions based on previous formations. The anticipation that this will happen links these otherwise isolated programmes.

There may also be an optimum gap between 'terms'. This is difficult to prescribe and depends on the state of the preceding group. Too large a gap (i.e. weeks/months) may incite resentment in remaining members that the group has been withdrawn. With too short a gap, (i.e. days/one or two weeks), the core of remaining members may continue and develop previous group purposes and structures within the reconstituted group formation, resulting in new members dropping out, leaving the dominant core of previous, more experienced members.

Similarly, '*drop-in*' formats may either be treated as a series of discrete single sessions, or as a 'succession' of linked and developing sessions. Treated as *single 'one-off' sessions*, the programme may be either changed or replicated each session. The methods used by the workers may be different to maximise the limited time available (e.g. perhaps preferring a more directive role to negotiate contracts of content where this is desirable — and then guarding this contract as a focus throughout the session). Alternatively users may be encouraged to take control of the content of each session or continuity between sessions.

With limited time, the intensity of the group may increase, as it does with a sudden reduction in group size, and will affect group members. Higher intensity can be seen as, '*The coping strategy for relatively limited or reduced time with a group if substantial goals are to be reached*' (Gero, 1984, in Alissi and Casper, 1985, p. 11). Of course, the expectations of members attending the group will determine how the group is used, i.e. to address longer term social needs, or to assist an immediate issue.

The *replacement* open group is a useful illustration of the variable nature of open groups. Potentially membership can change each session, which if treated as 'single sessions' are viable, otherwise they appear as fragmented parts of an obscure 'whole'. Alternatively, periods of stability may occur in which there will be continuous development over time, and an opportunity to sustain continuity of programme.

Questions for practice

In this paper, the 'open group' has been discussed as an alternative to time-limited closed group approaches. A basic typology has been presented which distinguishes three open group designs — based on the key variables of member change, and time.

The following points will be important ones for practitioners to tackle when establishing and working with open groups.

WHY OPEN GROUPS?

Is the group designed as a solution to service delivery questions? Group services often require flexible structures, better suited to an individual's ability to accept the service and remain eligible to partake and contribute.

Is there some therapeutic value to the designs, i.e. as a model for helping deal with stress caused by transitions and crises; or by virtue of the group composition in which members are at different stages of individual development?

ACCESS TO THE GROUP

Who is eligible to become a member, and who decides? Is the group open to anyone, or are there exclusion criteria? Are there physical limitations on whether a person can join a group? (i.e. some institutions and community projects do not have sufficient space to offer unrestricted choices to people who enter the building). Also, can people decide 'not' to join the group when they enter the building? For example, is there a neutral area from which people can choose to join the group or not?

EXIT CRITERIA

Are there established rules about length of affiliation to the group? For example, is there a pre-determined time contract, or is the group available until an individual has achieved identifiable goals? Are there structures for deciding fulfilment of goals — does the individual member decide, or is there a review process? Is there the possibility of re-entry to the group at a later stage? Does the whole group finish together, or do individual members contract an individual length of stay?

OPEN GROUP PROCESSES AND BOUNDARIES

It seems preferable to start with a clear structure. Boundaries of entry and exit will help to clarify the group's identity, and its process (e.g. through transitions); and will offer *predictability* for those associated with the group. Boundaries may be originated by gate-keepers or derived through group negotiation. Having established these boundaries it is possible to be flexible in their use according to practice demands. Where there are unclear boundaries, the system may develop an alternative, covert set of rules which may contradict original intentions.

Most of the questions around group process, are about the ability to create and sustain cohesion (for the group to develop and work despite disruptions created by member change). Where this is desirable, how is it possible to maintain a core of membership to pass on traditions and group norms from generation to generation? Have we adequate procedures to ease transitions (i.e. rituals, markers, reintegration procedures)?

TIME

Conceptually, we can consider open groups as a series of single sessions. However, the ability to maintain a 'core' membership should carry norms and traditions across demarcations of time, and link these otherwise isolated programmes. Time may also be significant when members believe they have limited time together to achieve goals — that is where achievement of goals is dependent on group functioning.

PROGRAMME

How will the reconstitution of membership affect the development of a programme in open groups? Programme can be used as a succession of discrete events or developed around individual members' contracts which are not as dependent on member continuity. Certainly, the programme must be flexible over time and be responsive to times of relative stability and instability.

THE ROLE OF THE WORKER(S)

By comparison with closed groups, the worker(s) may be relied on more heavily to offer continuity, particularly at times of membership instability and turnover. Workers will need to anticipate fluctuations between relative levels of group cohesion and stability. They will need to respond to sudden changes in group composition, and programme. The worker's role within the group will require manoeuvrability — to compensate intermittently, for decreased group functioning and to alter approach in response to the changing needs of group members.

Research (Schopler and Galinsky, 1984) indicates the widespread use of open groups in the USA. Whilst there does not appear to be any comparable information about British practice, experience suggests that open groups are being widely used as a method of choice; in their various formats and to meet a variety of user and contextual needs.

It is now time to concentrate practice and research efforts towards furthering our understandings of this valuable approach.

References

Alissi, A. and Casper, M. (eds.) (1985) *'Time as a factor in groupwork', Social Work with Groups*, 8(2). Special Issue.

Bailis, S., Lambert, S. and Bernstein, S. (1978) The legacy of the group: a study of group therapy with a transient membership, *Social Work in Health Care*, 3(4), pp. 405–418.

Bloom, N.D. and Lynch, J.G. (1979) 'Group work in a hospital waiting room', *Health and Social Work*, 4(3), pp. 48–63.

Brabender, V.M. (1985) 'Time limited inpatient group therapy: a developmental model', *International Journal of Group Psychotherapy*, 35(3), pp. 373–390.

Breton, M. (1985) 'Reaching and engaging people: issues and practice principles', *Social Work with Groups*, 8(3).

Brown, A. and Seymour, B. (eds.) (1983) *Intake Groups for Clients: A Probation Innovation*, Bristol University, SAUS.

Caplan, G. (1961) *An Approach to Community Mental Health*. Tavistock Publications.

Crandall, R. (1978) 'The assimilation of newcomers into groups', *Small Group Behaviour*, 9, pp. 331–336.

Douglas, T. (1979) *Group Processes in Social Work*. John Wiley.

Freese, A. (1972) 'Group therapy with exhibitionists and voyeurs', *Social Work*, 17(2) pp. 44–52.

Galinsky, M. and Schopler, J. (1985) 'Patterns of entry and exit in open-ended groups', *Social Work with Groups*, 8(2), pp. 67–79.

Gero, A. (1984) *A Group Resource Model*. Paper presented at the Annual Program Meeting of the CSWE, Detroit, Michigan.

Hartford, M. (1971) *Groups in Social Work: Applications of Small Group Theory and Research to Social Work Practice*. New York: Columbia University.

Heap, K.(1985) *The Practice of Social Work with Groups*. London: George, Allen & Unwin.

Henry, S. (1981) *Group Skills in Social Work*. Peacock.

Hill, W.F. and Gruner, L. (1973) 'A study of development in open and closed groups', *Small Group Behaviour*, 4(3), pp. 355–381.

Rosenbaum, M. (ed.). (1983) *Handbook of Short-Term Therapy Groups*. McGraw-Hill.

Schopler, J. and Galinsky, M. (1984) 'Meeting practice needs: conceptualising the open-ended group', *Social Work with Groups*, 7(2), pp. 3–21.

Shulman, L. (1984) *The Skills of Helping: Individuals and Groups*. Peacock.

Todd, T. and Barcome, J. (1980) 'Use of groups at intake', *Social Work with Groups*, 3(3).

Wellisch *et al.* (1978) 'Management of family emotion stress: Family group therapy in a private oncology practice', *International Journal of Group Psychotherapy*, 28, pp. 225–231.

Whitaker, D. (1975) 'Some conditions for effective work with groups', *British Journal of Social Work*, 5(4), pp. 423–39.

Yalom, I. (1983) *Inpatient Group Psychotherapy*. New York: Basic Books.

Ziller, R. (1965) 'Toward a theory of open and closed groups', *Psychological Bulletin*, LXIII.

GROUPWORK (1988) 3, 229–238

SOCIAL ACTION GROUPWORK AS NEGOTIATION: CONTRADICTIONS IN THE PROCESS OF EMPOWERMENT

EAMONN KEENAN and JOHN PINKERTON

This paper is about the process and outcomes to date of a series of discussions between a social action worker and a social work lecturer in Belfast. The central theme of the paper is contradiction within practice committed to empowerment. It is an attempt to take our discussion and theorising further by bringing it to a wider audience. Our aim is to contribute to defining the nature of social action groupwork and to identify appropriate forms of support.

> You must assume responsibility for your own professional growth and evolution. No one can develop your practice for you. You must do the work yourself. But at times it can be a painful and difficult experience and you will need support, guidance and encouragement. So assuming responsibility for your professional growth involves setting up a support system which will contain you while you question and examine your practice. (Jarlath Benson, 1987, p. 244)

This article is a statement by and about two actors in just such a support system: one a member of Save the Children Fund's (SCF) Belfast based Youth Unit and an experienced social action groupworker, the other a social work lecturer, with a special interest in practice strategies which resource members of families to work on needs they identify as their own.

The 'times' that prompted Eamonn to set up his support system, and include John in it, are times of change. In Northern Ireland, as elsewhere, SCF is in the process of realigning its work — a realignment neatly summed up in the title of the Division's youth work strategy paper 'Challenges to Powerlessness'. Change is disconcerting. Even for a worker like Eamonn, with a social action perspective, the newly explicit commitment by SCF to empowerment threw up its challenges. Finding a way of articulating the experience of this challenge was the business of a series of monthly meetings we have been having. This paper is about the process and outcome of those meetings to date and thereby, we hope, a contribution to defining the nature of social action groupwork and to identifying forms of support appropriate for those engaged in it.

Getting started

As the starting point for our meetings, we had Eamonn's concern to make sense of and define his role in relation to the opportunity and demands SCF was making on him by re-designating him the primary social action worker for the Belfast Youth Unit. We judge 'concern' to be the appropriate term here because what we are referring to is Eamonn's lived, felt, sense of challenge about the possibilities and pitfalls of his situation; the felt need that had led him, with encouragement from his agency, to set up a support system that included outsiders such as John.

To Eamonn's concern we added what we identified as John's motivation for agreeing to join the support network; his concern about how to develop and check out ideas about practice now that he only experienced it in a very occasional and limited fashion. Through describing and discussing our concerns with each other we generated a set of issues that we could share. We reckoned that we could do limited, focused work on these issues. In addition we expected spin-offs for each of us in other work we wanted to do on the concerns that we had identified. We recognised that work as being our own separate, more personally immediate business.

In this way, we negotiated a shared task, from which we hoped to gain both shared and separate things. We regard terms such as supervision, consultancy or support as too loose and tending to suggest a one up status for the supervisor, consultant or support person.

We agreed on four issues to work on together over a six month period. Each of them we saw as an area of particular challenge and fraught with tensions. The areas were:

i. personal practice ideology;
ii. the relationships between service workers and users;
iii. operationalising agency objectives as tasks;
iv. the role of the voluntary sector

As so often with agenda setting we were overly ambitious. We have only managed to do work of any significance in relation to the first two areas. This is reflected in what follows.

Practice grounding

As we were both concerned, albeit in different ways, with practice, our next step was to explore the relationship between the issues we had identified and Eamonn's practice. We had the issues, so what we needed next was the practice to relate them to. We opted to do this retrospectively by identifying an incident which had involved one of the groups Eamonn was working with.

The group consisted of six young women, aged between 17 and 18. They are a natural peer group all from the same area; a large modern housing estate on the outskirts of Catholic West Belfast, where socio-economic deprivation and the 'troubles' are part of every day life. Eamonn's stated commitment from the outset of his work with this group was to use a social action approach. In addition to this being his preferred style of work, he perceived it as appropriate to the young women's situation. His intention was to facilitate the group in addressing issues that they had identified as important to them. Reflecting this, his approach was to address issues within the group which were clearly located within their own life experience. Their issues were about their feelings of containment, abuse and control. These were experienced within relationships in the home, the neighbourhood and at work.

Coincidental with the beginning stage of the group, Eamonn received notification of a residential weekend being organised for young women to discuss their needs. The information indicated that only two women would be accepted from any one project. Eamonn brought the material he had received to the group for discussion. Two of the group had prior commitments for the weekend in question but the other four were all keen to attend. They asked Eamonn to telephone the organisers and try for the two extra places they wanted. This he agreed to do and was successful in getting the additional places. As transport posed a major difficulty for the young women, he also agreed to drive them to and from the residential venue.

Many youth workers will identify with this fairly typical chain of events. What made Eamonn choose it for our discussion was that it had left him, a social action worker, attempting to empower the group with a nagging feeling that he had failed to match his practice to his theory. The information about the residential weekend came to him, the adult, male worker; he gave the information to the group; he telephoned and negotiated the four places; he supplied the transport. The dependency of the group members on the worker was clearly reasserted at each step. But even worse in his view was the way that he had lost a string of opportunities to engage the young women in understanding what was happening.

Of course, Eamonn knew he could justify what happened on the basis of the reality constraints he was working with. The information came to him as part of a routine mailing to organisations working with young people. The group was only in its infancy and its members had not yet established themselves in taking responsibility for this sort of situation. Telephones and transport were not readily available to group members. The limits of time demanded an immediate response or the places might have been taken. Certainly, opportunities had been lost for group members to gain skills such as negotiating over the telephone, but really that was secondary to the chance being offered by the weekend for learning at a more in-depth and intensive level.

But identifying these 'realities' did not help. Eamonn continued to be nagged by what he saw as the 'facts' that the group was dependent on him for information, it had handed over responsibility for its own activities so easily, and that by acting as he had, he had maintained an unequal relationship that had removed from the group opportunities for developing its autonomy. In Eamonn's view, what he aspired to as a social action groupworker, and what he actually had done, were in conflict. Yet he still could not see what other options there were for him which could have resolved the conflict. Refusing to have done these things for the group, and thereby losing the opportunity provided by the weekend, would have been just as clear a statement of dependency; but a repressive rather than a benign dependency.

Towards an analysis

Having identified this practice incident and Eamonn's views and feelings about it our next step was to relate it to our list of issues. Personal practice ideology was top of our list.

By personal practice ideology, we mean the set of ideas that all workers carry around inside their heads with which they think their every day work experience. This set of ideas form a framework of reference points by which workers can describe and evaluate and thereby engage with the situations they find themselves facing. It is these conceptual frameworks that allow workers to make sense of a practice situation; as it is, as it ideally might be, and as realistically it might be made to become.

By way of this conceptual framework, or practice ideology as we prefer to call it, options are identified and choices made inside the head of the worker. Practice ideology provides and furnishes the conceptual space in which a worker manoeuvres prior to opting for any particular course of action. The outcome of the action that results from this thinking work, conceptual manoeuvring, may be perceived as success or failure, but either way it creates a new experience for the worker's ideology to make sense of. The new experience will either reinforce or challenge the practice ideology that prompted the choice of the particular course of action that resulted in the experience. It seemed to us that Eamonn's practice experience with his group was an example of a challenge to a worker's practice ideology. So as our next step we turned to trying to spell out Eamonn's implicit practice ideology so that we could be clear about what it was that was being challenged.

Personal practice ideology

Eamonn felt it relevant to begin by identifying some of the broad underpinnings of his personal ideology. First was a sense of class identity. Like the young women in the group he came from a background of socio-economic deprivation, lack of educational achievement at school and the experience of interventions by statutory agencies that were generally ineffective. Linked to this class identity was a rejection of the inequality and restricted life chances it represented. This rejection had led him to study as a mature student and from there into youth and community work. On the way he incorporated Freire's notion of 'conscientisation' into his personal ideology. From the ideological reference points he already had he could engage with Freire's ideas:

> ... discovering myself oppressed I know that I will be liberated only if I try to transform the oppressing situation in which I find myself (Adult Learning Project).

> Those who work for liberation must not take advantage of the emotional dependence of the oppressed. ... Using their dependence to create still greater dependence is an oppressor tactic (Freire, 1980, p. 42).

As for ideas specifically about youth and community work he found that what Smith (1981) and Davies (1981) were arguing for synchronised with his basic ideology. They defined an agenda for work with young people in a way that Eamonn was ideologically disposed to value. Davies' assertion that state social policy towards young people is aimed at gaining:

> ... young people's containment, and if possible their uncomplaining adjustment to the often personally demeaning demands of a reconstructed economy and political order under growing stress (p. 14)

was a description that is in line with Eamonn's idea of class oppression. When Smith suggested that there were strategies and professional skills that could help young people:

> ... gain for themselves the necessary knowledge, understanding and develop the feelings, attitudes and values to be able to think and act in ways that will increase their control over their own lives and their ability to speak for themselves,

he legitimised both Eamonn's continued identification with his class background and his educational and occupational movement away from it. Within this ideological framework he could understand his becoming a qualified youth and community worker as a way of gaining something to offer others like himself in their struggle against oppression.

For illustration of what this approach meant in practice, Eamonn looked to the Nottingham Young Volunteers. The practice principles by which that project worked combined descriptive and prescriptive aspects in line with the practice ideology he had developed. As part of its prescription for empowering young people it emphasised the power of groupwork. As Ward put it quite clearly:

> The key task is to create opportunities for choice which mean something to the young people themselves.... The achievement of the task will entail such young people achieving and exercising power in order to bring about changes. This is best achieved collectively (Ward, 1982, p. 6)

Spotting the contradiction

Having set out Eamonn's practice ideology in this way, we were then in a position to try and tease out what it was within his experience of the incident involving the group that had challenged his ideology and set up his nagging sense of dissatisfaction. We aimed to make explicit the way in which his practice experience had provided a critique of his personal practice ideology. In this way we hoped to develop that same ideology. He had not been prepared to compromise and change his personal practice ideology in order to accommodate the incident. At the same time he also had not been prepared to dismiss the self criticism his personal ideology was insisting on in relation to the incident. The result of this was his feeling of failure to match practice to theory noted earlier.

It seemed to us that at the very heart of Eamonn's practice ideology was the idea of a dichotomy; to be powerless/to be empowered.

The young women in his group were either dependent on him or they were independent of him. He received the notification of the residential weekend or they received it. Yet in direct contradiction to that idea of dichotomy, to be powerless/to be disempowered, stood his own biography and experience of work with young working class men and women. Both of these demonstrated that the experience of deprivation and inequality, whether socio-economic, cultural or emotional, is never passive. People respond. They may adapt, challenge, or collapse, but whichever, they make some form of response to their situation. How that response is seen, active or passive, acceptable or unacceptable is a matter of judgement. It was Eamonn, by way of his practice ideology with its core dichotomy, who had judged his provision of services to the group unacceptably active and the group's actions unacceptably passive.

Thus, it appeared to us that Eamonn's practice ideology, despite its central concern with power, failed in any useful way to actually register the power differential that generated the group incident. As the older, male worker, any exhibition of Eamonn's power that asserted the inequality between him and the young women in the group was oppressive and, therefore, was not ideologically acceptable. As for the young, female group members, any use, and thereby acknowledgement, they made of the power differential was dependency. It was, therefore, an unacceptable source of frustration to Eamonn.

Thus we spotted at the centre of Eamonn's practice ideology the contradiction between his idea of powerlessness as passivity and what he knew about the capacity of deprived and oppressed individuals and groups to respond to their situation. It was this contradiction that was giving him his problem with that hoary old groupwork process issue — leadership. Leadership, the exercise of differential power, was experienced as particularly acute within Eamonn's social action practice ideology as it was precisely the exercise of power inequality which was its target for change. We concluded that any useful development of Eamonn's practice ideology would have to find a way of incorporating such inequality as a means of change in addition to being a target for change.

Towards social action as negotiation

Through our discussions it had become clear to us that, just as we had entered into a relationship with different concerns, so too the relationship between social action groupworker and group members had to be based on differences. This was a direct challenge to a basic element in Eamonn's ideology which emphasised identification, lack of difference between himself and those he worked with. We had come together seeing our difference as holding out the opportunity of gaining from each other, and thereby contributing to each other. The difference, as we now see it, between Eamonn as worker and the young women group members was one of access to resources; notification of certain events, experience in telephone negotiation, transport. Therefore, far from being a block to the process of empowerment, negotiation around access to resources as expressed in the incident was inevitably the basis for a social action intervention.

Negotiation has been identified by Payne (1986) as one of the practice skills required for community social work.

> Negotiation is appropriate, then, where there is disagreement between two or more parties about something that is relevant to them, and there is discretion among the parties about the action they can take, and potential power to achieve a result satisfactory to both sides (p. 51)

By replacing 'disagreement' in the first line of the quote with 'difference', negotiation as defined by Payne gives the addition we required to Ward's practice principles. By using it, it is possible to extend Eamonn's practice ideology to bring into its frame of reference the differences between worker and group members and how these can be collectively addressed. What exactly the implications of this would have been for the group incident we focused on, is open to speculation and further work by us. However, some general ground rules are clear if once again we return to the process of our meetings. We had started with different agendas, reflecting our independent concerns, and then negotiated an agreed agenda of issues which have focused our discussions. So too for the social action worker and group members, the starting point must be to identify the different concerns that have brought them together and relate these in a way that allows for an agreed agenda. In this way differences are not resolved but can be more effectively addressed.

This may be a painful process for the worker as it involves disentangling personal practice ideology in a way that confronts closely held assumptions.

Empowerment, the key element in social action as a practice ideology for group workers, is no longer seen as something that only happens to group members. The worker too gets his/her 'piece of the action' — is empowered. It becomes possible to acknowledge that the social action worker is looking for a gain in terms of personal satisfaction, professional recognition, meeting agency aims or whatever. Thus the worker can explicitly bring his/her own agenda to the negotiation that we now see as central to the business of empowerment.

Conclusion

In summary, what we think we have learnt about social action groupwork, and the support which workers involved in it require, is this.

Firstly, workers need to include in their support network at least one contact which gets them out of the quagmire of personal introspection, group process, and agency pressure, so as to work on clarifying and modifying their sense of direction; their personal practice ideology. This work should consciously be based on the same model of social action as workers are bringing to their groupwork. This includes recognition of the differences in personal/practice ideologies between the contact person and the worker. These exist prior to their work together, and are also generated during the course of their creative dialogue.

Secondly, we think that any model of social action must start with a recognition of differences, particularly inequalities in power, and regard group process as the most potent way of working the creative tension within these differences. Social action groupworkers need to accept that they cannot know where the working of this creative tension will lead. Perhaps then the most they can aim for is clarity about their own power base and their own agendas and how these are changing as part of negotiations with group members.

Our advocacy of extra support for social groupworkers to enable recognition of the manner in which their groups are beyond their control may be disconcerting for some; particularly in these days of limited resources and 'output measurement'. But that is what we advocate and we see it as no more than the application and realisation of what Bill Schwartz once said: that as groupworkers we must be '*secure in our own ignorance*'.

References

Adult Learning Project, *Definitions of Key Concepts of Freire, Some Notes.* Edinburgh.

Benson, J.F. (1987) *Working More Creatively with Groups,* Tavistock: London.

Davies, B. (1981) *Restructuring Youth Policies in Britain. The State We're In.* Occasional Paper No. 21 Leicester: Leicester National Youth Bureau.

Freire, P. (1980) *Pedagogy of the Oppressed.* Harmondsworth: Penguin.

Payne, M. (1986) *Social Care in the Community.* Basingstoke: BASW/ Macmillan.

Smith, M. (1981) *Creators Not Consumers.* Leicester: National Association of Youth Clubs.

Ward, D. (ed.) (1982) *Give 'Em a Break.* Leicester: National Youth Bureau

GROUPWORK (1988) 3, 239–251

'NOWT TO DO AND ALWAYS GETTING INTO TROUBLE' The Bulwell Neighbourhood Project: A Social Action Response

BILL BADHAM, MICHAEL BENTE
and PAULINE HALL

This paper describes an inter-disciplinary response to young people at risk of offending, and having difficulties, whether at school, home or with the law. The work undertaken involved Social Services, the Youth Service, Probation and two voluntary sector projects'.[1] The young people concerned belonged to two neighbourhoods in the Bulwell area of the City of Nottingham. The work started in the summer of 1984 and ended in the spring of 1988.
The article discusses:

i. the background to the neighbourhood work: its origins, the proposal, and social action principles;
ii. the neighbourhood work undertaken: working with young people, their issues and concerns, and action taken;
iii. implications for agency practice: inter-agency meetings and consequences.

Background

ORIGINS

There is a firm tradition of neighbourhood work in the Bulwell area, making it a suitable breeding ground for the Neighbourhood Project for three reasons:

i. In the agencies, there was some familiarity with concepts of neighbourhood work and social action (described below), and a broad remit to question current agency practice and to develop appropriate alternatives.
ii. Some inter-team initiatives had been tried, and there was a willingness to talk with other agencies.
iii. In late 1984 a number of workers from the Youth, Social and Probation Services were able to pool their experience and ideas, with the advantage of some having worked together before and been on local inter-disciplinary social action training events together.

When representatives of the statutory agencies met to discuss concerns over offending and young people, and the possible need to work across agency boundaries, two actions resulted. First the area intermediate treatment worker recorded the patterns of young people's offending, using the police referral forms which are sent to Probation and Social Services. This pointed to groupings of young offenders in two areas, Bulwell Hall and Highbury Vale. Second, a street survey of local young people was done by Social Services over several weeks. It highlighted groups who did not use local facilities, but who wanted places to meet. The young people talked to also spoke of conflict with the local police and other adults, and of racial tension in Bulwell.

PROPOSAL

Arising from the monitoring of police referrals and the street survey, the area intermediate treatment worker, a social worker, two youth workers and a probation officer (referred to hereafter as 'the worker team') met to discuss the findings and explore the relevance of neighbourhood work in Bulwell Hall and Highbury Vale. As potential co-workers, we began by clarifying our own values and principles, described below. We then put a written proposal to the local statutory agencies, and attended team meetings to discuss the reasons for wanting to work with these young people.

The written proposal highlighted the natural groups of young people at risk in Bulwell, where there were high levels of individual and joint offending and the statutory involvement of more than one agency. Two aims were put forward: first, to work with young people, at risk and in trouble in their own neighbourhoods, in natural groupings, on issues and concerns they would identify: second, to work within an inter-agency context to discuss issues of agency practice and policy, arising from the groupwork process, as well as to check on the progress of the neighbourhood work itself.

The proposed groupwork was to be based neither on activities nor the social skills model. Rather, the term 'social action' was used to suggest that the workers would be examining with the young people, the concerns and difficulties they experienced, the issues they faced and the ways in which they felt that they could both understand their situations better and take action for themselves. The proposal said:

> The workers seek to maximise young people's control over their own lives by increasing their confidence to act on their own ideas, to use resources available to them and to make their needs known to those who have power over resources.

It was proposed that the work should be reviewed regularly on a joint basis by local agencies, and that each worker team should have the help of weekly planning sessions with a consultant.

PRINCIPLES OF THE NEIGHBOURHOOD PROJECT

By the summer of 1985, the worker team had permission to begin the project. Having worked hard to get to this point, we were eager to 'get started' and meet the young people directly. We agreed, however, that we must first do our own groundwork. Why work with the young people? What are the failings of current, traditional agency responses which seem of limited value to the young people? How can we develop a more relevant response?

The worker team explored these issues, starting with our own dissatisfaction with both current provision and views expressed by colleagues. For example, the youth club leader said that young people need a structure set by adults, need to be provided for, and don't have the ability to take responsibility and action for themselves. Within the probation team, there was resistance to questioning the efficacy of one to one casework, even when the young people themselves expressed dissatisfaction with the service given, and when recent statistics seen by the team pointed to the nature and extent of group offending on Highbury Vale.

Our criticisms were informed by radical social work writers such as Bailey and Brake (1980), Corrigan (1979), and Walker and Beaumont (1981). Agency responses to young people were individualised, and treatment or activity oriented. In consequence the worker's role was generally controlling, setting the agenda and being seen as the expert. Collective issues and concerns were hidden by this divide and rule approach. We acknowledged some new developments but thought these were largely 'old wine in new bottles' (Wilson, 1977). For example, in social skills, the values and methods of the groupwork still focus on an individual's problems, and can be used by course leaders to reinforce feelings of personal inadequacy in group members. 'The wine has been fortified' (Walker and Beaumont, 1981, p. 84).

In contrast, the worker team agreed on some basic principles and values that have continually informed our practice. These are based in part on Freire (1970; 1972), as applied and developed in Nottingham under the term 'social action' (Ward, 1982).

The main principles of 'social action' are as follows:

i. A positive view of young people; young people do have skills, understanding and ability.

ii. Young people should be heard. They have a right to define their own issues and take action on them.
iii. Young people acting collectively can be powerful.
iv. Young people's difficulties are not generally a result of 'personal inadequacies'. Social policy, environmental and economic factors, racism and sexism are major forces contributing to young people's problems. Practice should reflect this understanding.
v. The problems that young people face are complex and responses to them need to cross disciplinary and organisational boundaries.
vi. Methods of work should reflect principles: practice what you preach.

These principles have been the foundation of our work. Overall, they held firm and informed our practice throughout the life of the project.

The neighbourhood work with the young people

AIMS AND APPROACH

The aims of the work on the Neighbourhood Project, based on the above principles, were as follows:

i. To work with natural groups in their own areas.
ii. To work with the young people at their own pace on concerns that they identify as important to them.
iii. To work in partnership with the young people, rather than being seen as 'expert' or 'provider' and doing things for/to them.
iv. Through our understanding of the nature of oppression, to develop anti-racist and anti-sexist practice and to challenge racism and sexism among the worker team, the young people and the agencies involved.
v. Believing our agencies' policies and practices to be part of the problem facing the young people, to raise issues and concerns arising from the groupwork, as a means of improving current policy and practice.
vi. For ourselves to reflect critically on the work being undertaken, through regular support, sharing and planning with a consultant (see Ward and Burley, 1982).

By Autumn 1985 we were ready to begin contacting the young people. Our social action approach can be seen as a five stage process:

i. *What* are the concerns and difficulties faced?

ii. *Why* do these concerns exist?
iii. *How* can change be brought about? What information, skills and resources are needed?
iv. Forming a plan, and *action* for implementation
v. *Reflection* on what has happened: review action, evaluate, raise new questions and make further plans.

WORK UNDERTAKEN

This section offers an overview of the work with the young people from October 1985 until early 1988. It highlights the issues and concerns they raised, and action taken.

While some of them were known to some of the workers, we wanted our initial contact to be as much on their terms as possible. So, instead of using our contacts to pre-arrange a meeting, both worker teams (the team of five was divided to cover the two estates in the project) began getting to know young people on the streets, where we found they spent much of their time.

Bulwell Hall (MOB)[2]

In the first worker team there were the two sessional youth workers and one local authority social worker. The consultant was also from the Social Services Department. In Autumn 1985, links were developed with a group of young people on the streets in Bulwell Hall. There was discussion about what concerned them, especially the lack of facilities and resources on the estate. They wanted somewhere permanent to meet. Workers tried to be clear that they could not 'provide', but would be willing to help the young people look at their concerns in more detail and help them think through what might be done and what action they could take.

The only possible venue was a small hall, attached to a warden aided old people's complex. Many of them were banned from this hall, but, they looked at the issue, planned, and negotiated with the caretaker themselves. The result was permission to use the hall every Friday evening. It still provides the only indoor meeting place for the young people of Bulwell Hall. In the Spring, having achieved their main objective of gaining a place to go on the estate, they sought to develop the facility by trying to get funds and equipment. They arranged and planned a visit by an influential member of the Leisure Services Department. This person met them one evening and promises were made, but not kept.

Although these failed promises, and school holidays coinciding with a spate of offending, saw a decline in involvement over the summer, numbers again increased in Autumn 1986. The young people showed great commitment to the Friday night group they had established. They dealt themselves with occasional conflict with the caretaker that arose from them using the hall. They invited other young people to come, swelling numbers to 20 or more. They put on a jumble sale that raised over £30. There was much concern also at this time over pending court appearances, and so a probation worker was invited to talk with them about some of their worries arising from the court process. When reports were requested, there were contributions from the project workers, putting the offending in context. They also designed, produced and distributed a leaflet, entitled *M.O.B*[2] raising their needs and concerns in the neighbourhood.

During the first part of 1987, this general direction continued and grant applications were made successfully to Probation and Social Services. Some of the young people ably represented their views and concerns at two open meetings between the City Council and the Bulwell Community. Renewed efforts were made to get a grant and a permanent worker from Leisure Services. However, by the Autumn, after the expected Summer lull, the nature of the group began changing. First, some moved away and others, being that bit older, found other interests. There were also four on remand in custody, and others facing court appearances. Helped by the consultant, the workers and young people thought about these developments over a number of meetings. They agreed that the social action focus had shifted. It was, therefore, agreed to stop the weekly meetings, but to continue offering support to those in custody, and that the young people would approach the probation worker, were any new initiatives to arise.

Highbury Vale (TOLO)[2]

The other team was the area intermediate treatment worker and the probation officer. The senior probation officer helped in the planning of the work. When first looking around the area one evening, the workers were seen by some young men known to the probation officer. They were in a house belonging to an adult woman friend and we, the workers, were immediately asked in. The welcome was overwhelming and there was much enthusiasm at our wish to be involved on the estate. These young people had access to the attic of the friend's house, which became our meeting place for a short time. They were very clear about their disillusionment with adults, both workers and residents. Previous initiatives had left them high and dry, they said. The workers encouraged the group to look at what troubled them, and they wrote up on a flip chart the following:

Nowt to do
Complaints when we do do
Nowhere to do it
No-one backs you up
When people do back you up they give up after a bit
Always getting into trouble
Whatever we do we get into trouble for it.

The concerns included the agencies, such as Probation and Social Services, solicitors and the courts. The Youth Training Scheme was seen as not being a proper job, boring, and the college as providing nothing. When asked "what do you want?" they talked mainly about wanting to be listened to and taken seriously. Youth facilities in the area were also mentioned.

These young people had a clear understanding of *what* concerns and difficulties they faced. As to *why* these existed, they had experience of adults not delivering the goods and making decisions on their behalf that came to nothing. This realism also caused disillusionment about *how* to bring about change. This may also reflect the fact that they were slightly older than the Bulwell Hall group and increasingly had other things to do, found work or were on schemes, and were more interested in their partners. During the first part of 1986 there was a lull which caused the workers to review progress and go back to the group to look at what had happened, and not happened, and whether they wished to continue meeting. Consistency was crucial if we too were not to confirm 'when people do back you they give up after a bit'.

Staying in touch has borne fruit. Some specific matters were taken forward, such as raising concerns that the young people had about a club held once a week at a school in the neighbourhood. They felt this facility was limited and run inappropriately to their needs. Also two or three young men started looking to an 'off the road' facility for driving. Consistent contact has been maintained with these young people ever since. We agreed with them to stop our weekly meetings, because they repeatedly said there was no action they wished to follow up. Yet, the workers have continued to offer support in times of difficulty, including being involved in the preparation of reports, keeping in touch when in prison, and helping friends to visit.

Other Issues

The above two accounts have indicated some of the 'products' of the work. Yet, the young people and the workers feel that some of the most important fruits of our involvement together have arisen from the way of working. This is best illustrated by some examples.

Firstly, at Bulwell Hall, the young people gained access to the hall on Friday nights. That was the product. But the process, or the way this happened, was equally crucial. The workers did not hire the hall. It was the young people who had to look at what their needs were and what they could do about it. They had to overcome the barrier of having been banned at the hall before. They had to plan what they would say, who they would say it to, what they wanted and how it would be paid for. Later on, when the group's high spirits have threatened the continuing use of the hall, or when numbers have been depleted and the group disillusioned, this belief in it being their hall and their place to meet has been crucial for their sense of achievement, responsibility and purpose.

Secondly, the leaflet used to publicise the needs of the young people of Bulwell Hall is eye catching and well produced. What is impressive is the manner of its production. If the workers had 'done it for them', then would it not have been adults again speaking on young people's behalf? — one of the very problems they talk about. Helped by the workers, they stated their concern at not being listened to, their need for money and publicity. They decided on using the leaflet and worked out the wording. They wrote to a cartoonist, asking for use of one of his cartoons. They produced the draft leaflet. Then, later, some went to a local advice and resource centre where they were shown how to use the machinery for the leaflet's production. It is not surprising that this episode remains important to the group.

Thirdly, both groups often talked about issues of race and sex, either in general discussion, or through derogatory remarks. Both estates are predominantly white, reflected in the membership of the groups; in Bulwell Hall, particularly, there have at times been a large number of young women involved. When the young people made what was seen by the workers as racist or sexist remarks, the workers' response was to challange this in the context of how it affected the young people and was relevant to them. While this can cause friction — 'people like you think you're perfect' — it not only avoids collusion, but is consistent with the principles behind the way of working.

In Bulwell Hall, there had always been at least one black worker, initially causing comments like 'you're okay Michael, but Paki's are different'. The group themselves began to question and challenge such views and there is evidence of a lot of learning and a reduction in prejudice and racism. They think through more carefully what they are saying. For example, 'we never used to go to the youth club because of black people; no that's wrong it was because of the drugs around and white people have drugs too'.

A similar process happened with sexism. Comments about what women are only good for often got direct reaction from the group: 'would you say that about your mother or sister? you're talking about people not objects'. In Bulwell Hall, when the young men have tended to dominate, the workers have encouraged the whole group to look at this behaviour. In turn, the young people sought to counter it by, for example, ensuring that one of the signatories to the bank account was a young woman. They have also instituted a 'no violence' rule.

Fourthly, whether there have been specific 'products' or not, both groups have repeatedly said they have found our involvement important because 'you see us as we are'. But, 'In the office you sit in the big chair and we sit in the small chair'. Trust has developed, and the workers have some understanding of the neighbourhood and the nature of the young people's concerns, including their offending. They say they like being listened to and taken seriously by adults, getting the confidence to take decisions and responsibilities.

IMPLICATIONS AND EVALUATION

An important aim of the Neighbourhood Project has been to evaluate the work through meetings of relevant agencies, raising practice issues arising from the neighbourhood work. For the project workers, this has been a key, but very demanding element. It has involved three write-ups of the work, and planning and chairing four inter-agency meetings. One worker, on behalf of the project, has linked with a voluntary housing project to discuss establishing a group for ex-residents, based on similar principles to our work. These links are crucial, if the groupwork is to avoid becoming an end in itself, and for evaluation and accountability.

Implications within the project

If the Neighbourhood Project has been of continuing relevance for more than two years to the young people concerned and to the agencies involved, we feel three factors have played their part:

i. Careful preparation, clear planning, the establishing of accepted principles of practice among the worker team, and gaining agreement among the agencies to the proposals.
ii. The commitment to regular weekly planning by the worker teams, using the help of a consultant.
iii. The need for good feedback to teams and the inter-agency forum; write-ups of the work and making sure accurate notes of meetings and decisions are taken and circulated.

Two other points should be considered.

Reoffending. One of the starting points for our work was that groups of young people were offending and at risk of custody. Some have continued getting into trouble, others have stopped. Some have said our involvement directly reduced the amount of their offending (for example, on Friday nights in Bulwell Hall).

Whatever the effect of the groupwork on offending, it was never a specific aim or expectation to reduce offending. However, the young people's concerns frequently included getting into trouble and its consequences. They often talked with the workers about their group or individual difficulties . On their own territory and on their own terms, they have been open about the nature and cause of offending; boredom, lack of money, no jobs ... ... Unlike the labelling and scapegoating comments that characterise the individualised pleading of some social enquiry reports, they did not tend to blame someone else or say they were 'easily led'. Rather, personal responsibility was accepted, but, for example, in the context of limited opportunities, heavy police presence on the estates etc. . . .

It is hard to see how continued offending could undermine the value of the project (unless there was a colossal increase!). There is a risk of testing community action approaches more rigorously in this regard than casework, intermediate treatment or social skills. Unlike these orthodoxies, by working in partnership with people and encouraging collective action on issues they identify to effect change in their communities, social action does acknowledge, and seek to help challenge, the structural causes of much offending. Our work has also helped develop trust and make the 'caring agencies' more accessible, encouraging young people to make demands and get a better deal from their probation or social worker.

Evaluation. While evaluation of the neighbourhood work may not be easily quantified by, for example, looking at offending figures, critical reflection on practice is an essential part of the social action approach. It is not open-ended in time, or lacking boundaries. Within the project, evaluation occurred at three levels:

i. By the workers and young people discussing, learning, planning, taking action, reflecting on outcomes, making new plans. Some sessions would specifically brainstorm 'what's good, what's bad and what could be better about the group.' When the focus was slipping the workers reappraised with the young people the nature of their involvement.

ii. By workers meeting regularly (often weekly) with the consultant. This is essential to air conflicts and successes in the work, set objectives, plan, offer on-going evaluation, assessment and support.

iii. By holding reviews within the relevant teams and having occasional inter-agency forums, involving both main grade staff and management.

Implications for agencies

Whatever the implications for mainstream agency practice, the main reason behind the neighbourhood project, arising out of concern about traditional agency responses to young people, has been to offer a more consistent and coherent response through working with them on their own concerns and issues, in their own neighbourhoods. The inter-agency meetings were seen as a crucial forum in which to evaluate the work and to learn lessons from the groupwork process. Attendance was not only from the three statutory agencies, but also from relevant voluntary sector workers. It was agreed that the emphasis of such meetings was to look critically at agency policy and practice and not to see how X or Y was doing in a group, or to represent particular issues on behalf of the young people. Good side effects included greater mutual understanding, effective working together, and raising the profile of the needs of the estates.

A more principled practice. Discussions at inter-agency meetings have pointed to the need for clear principles of practice with all people, including young people. We feel strongly that the values behind the groupwork approach are equally valid in traditional youth club settings and the one to one casework model. They have implications, for example, for how workers share information, make decisions, prepare reports, write and give access to records. Do we work with people, or do we tell people what to do, trying to resolve individual problems out of their social and economic context? And what messages do we give by sitting in the big 'flashy' chair and hiding behind the security of a solid desk, rather than meeting people in their own environments and on their own terms?

Court reports. A sub-group of the inter-agency meetings looked at the purpose and contents of reports, with special regard to a community perspective and a better understanding of the context of offending. The neighbourhood work with the young people informed our thinking about the importance of the way reports are written: how easy are they to understand; do we share the report with the defendant; do we go to court to support that person, and do we show some understanding of the neighbourhood. Some reports have begun to include a section on the neighbourhood, such as:

> Through this project, we have come to see the occasional periods of offending by the young people in the context of an isolated and under-resourced estate, with no youth facilities, few employment prospects and a history of limited interest being shown in them.

Further, addenda have been written by the project workers themselves, in consultation with the young people, highlighting the nature of their group and many positive aspects of what they have done.

Youth facilities. The young people have repeatedly raised concerns about the inadequacies for them of centralised youth facilities, based on a youth club that focuses on structured leisure pursuits. Also, when they tried to get funding from the Youth and Community Division of the County Council, they were required to have management structures fitted to adult control and decision making. The inter-agency forum has taken this issue forward with relevant senior management. The local youth club leader has tried, so far unsuccessfully, to gain acceptance for proposals for using an auxiliary worker to resource one of the groups, without taking control of it.

Conclusion

The neighbourhood work took nine months careful planning and development, and it lasted two and a half years. It began by a number of workers questioning the neat agency compartments that were felt to manage and contain, rather than listen and respond to young people and their concerns and difficulties. As one senior social worker said, "*we expect young people to adapt to our structures; yet we must adapt to theirs.*"

It is hoped the work described above will give encouragement to do just that:

i. to challenge current practice and agency constraints;
ii. to reflect critically on present provision for youth, be it treatment and cure, or structured leisure pursuits;
iii. to explore in partnership alternative responses, based on principles that do not label the individual or group, or hide behind the power of the professional;

iv. to develop practice, whether individual or groupwork, with people whose difficulties are more likely to be structurally rooted than due to personal inadequacy; who have understanding and ability and a right to be heard; and who can be encouraged to work together to good effect on the issues and concerns they identify.

Notes

(1) The two voluntary sector projects are: Family First, Young People's Project, 30 Waterloo Road, Nottingham and Nottingham Young Volunteers, 33 Mansfield Road, Nottingham.

(2) MOB (Members of Bulwell Hall) and Tolo (short for Tollerton Green in Highbury Vale) came to be the names the two groups gave themselves.

References

Bailey, R. and Brake, M. (eds.) (1980) *Radical Social Work Practice.* Edward Arnold.

Corrigan, P. (1979) *Schooling the Smash Street Kids.* Macmillan

Freire, P. (1970) *Cultural Action for Freedom.* Penguin

Freire, P. (1972) *Pedagogy of the Oppressed.* Penguin

Walker, H and Beaumont, B. (1981): *Probation Work; Critical Theory and Socialist Practice.* Basil Blackwell

Ward, D. and Burley, D. (1982) *Starting Blocks.* National Youth Bureau

Wilson, E (1977) *Women and the Welfare State,* quoted in Walker and Beaumont (1981), p. 82.

For further information about Social Action Training, contact SAT, 33 Mansfield Road, Nottingham. Tel: 0602 476714

GROUPWORK (1988) 3, 252–261

A TEAM DEVELOPMENT EXERCISE

JOHN TAYLOR, DI MILES
and JOHN EASTGATE

This article describes the efforts of three authors to assist the staff of a large children's home. The exercise attempted to offer an understanding of how behaviour as a group affects the ability of staff to do their jobs and how they might develop ways of using those group processes to their advantage.

The children's home concerned was a 16 bed unit for young people aged 12–18 years. Expansion was due to take place increasing the number of beds to 30. Young people are placed there for a wide range of reasons including remand, beyond parental control and school refusal, and the home offers long and short term placement. There are 13 staff of which about half are male. The staff group are all white, as is the majority of residents.

In April 1987, interest was expressed via the head of home in the idea of staff gaining knowledge of groupwork methods in order that they might use them in their work at the home. It was agreed that a way of responding positively should be found since recognition of the importance of groups would be worth promoting. In a further meeting with the head of home additional concerns were expressed:

i. The staff group is very large, shifts change, as do the children living in the home. The result is that group processes within the unit are very complicated and could be used constructively only if the staff were able to focus their attention on them, without the hindrance of interpersonal issues.
ii. We were aware of difficulties within the staff group, and these were probably exacerbated by many staff having received no professional training; many staff being very young and inexperienced — in some instances, staff have responsibility for children only 4–5 years younger than themselves; the vulnerability of staff because of the nature of their work, e.g. it is easy to criticise what they do, both from within the Department of Social Services and without. The net result of such vulnerability is perhaps that staff spend much of their time 'covering' themselves and not supporting each other.

iii. Whilst the head of home was keen to pursue the proposal, there was no finance available from within the Social Services Department to employ outside consultants. The idea was then put forward that such an exercise could be designed from within the Child Guidance Service, for which two of us worked. However, if we were to do this we made it clear that we would want a firm commitment from the entire staff. The head of home was left to explore the matter further with the staff group.

The response came within a couple of weeks — that the staff group recognised the value of a team development exercise and were willing to take part.

Objectives of the exercise

As far as the staff group was concerned, there was some evidence that problems in interpersonal relationships were an issue and that such problems had developed because there had been only limited opportunity to acknowledge how the group was functioning. Examples of these problems included:

i. The growth of subgroups and rivalry between them. (The composition of groups was often determined solely by who worked which shifts).
ii. The failure of some staff members to confront colleagues whose behaviour they regarded as unsatisfactory. More likely, was the tendency to grumble to a colleague about the 'offender' which might offer some short term gain but which certainly did nothing to resolve the original problem. It also meant that often the 'offender' didn't know he/she had done anything wrong. As a direct consequence, levels of friction, frustration and unresolved anger were often high amongst the staff group members.
iii. It was easy for staff members to lose touch with each other. Due to shift work they may only see each other infrequently and it was possible for some staff to remain as strangers to one another.

In acknowledgement of these problems, the primary objectives of the exercise were seen as changing the processes which had led to the problems developing.

Specifically, the objectives were as follows:

i. to enable the members to find out more about each other both in terms of their attitudes and skills in their work and their personal qualities;

ii. to enable group members to develop a much greater degree of trust in each other;

iii. to encourage awareness and acknowledgement amongst the group of the skills and positive contributions made by individuals to the work of the home;

iv. to enable the staff group to devise their own support system in order that they would go on being able to address the kinds of issues which had arisen and which would be likely to arise again;

v. to introduce the staff group to processes which take place in groups and to develop awareness of how they might be used constructively both within the staff group and in their work with the young people in the home.

Leadership

For all three group leaders, the task of leading a team development exercise was new — our previous groupwork experience, although considerable was almost exclusively with adolescents. However, we regarded our general knowledge of how groups functioned as providing a sound basis on which an exercise could be built. Further, one of us had previously acted as consultant to the staff when they required specialist assessments of the children in their care.

That three leaders were to be involved might be seen as likely to generate problems. However, it is important to acknowledge that the size of the staff group — 13 members — would be certain to present complexities which would require careful management. Time was spent on ensuring that we were 'in tune' with each other and about what we were setting out to achieve and the methods we planned to use. We also thought it was important to present the leaders as having equal authority and status — partly because of the 'higher status' held by a psychiatrist. To achieve this, we each took the role of leading exercises throughout the programme. Further, we adopted a pattern of working, which often involved two leaders acting as facilitators whilst the third took the role of observer.

One other consideration was the need to have regular opportunities to consult outside the group. With this in mind, each day was planned to have four separate components, with breaks in between sessions.

In preparing the content we were mindful of our entry into an unfamiliar area of work and some of the differences and similarities between this kind of group and the adolescent groups with which we had previously worked. Given this, we sought to use material which we felt was both appropriate and familiar to us.

The team development exercise

Taking into account our pre-knowledge of the group we divided the programme into three sections:

i. assessing and building trust between group members;
ii. identification of relevant issues, both overt and covert, within the group;
iii. examination of how identified issues could be dealt with and how gains made, could be maintained.

Rather than give a 'blow by blow' account of how individual parts of the exercise progressed (a list of structured exercises used is contained in Appendix 1), it seems more useful to look at the events we felt were most significant in influencing the way the group developed.

Day one

> The higher the trust, the more stable the co-operation and the more effective the communication. A group member will more openly express his thoughts, feelings, reactions, opinions, information and ideas when the trust level is high. When the trust level is low, group members will be evasive, dishonest and inconsiderate in their communications (Johnson and Johnson, 1987).

It is important to note that before the exercise, the staff had acknowledged that there was a lack of trust within the group. However, on day one, throughout the exercises used to assess and develop trust, the group members' behaviour tended to suggest that 'all in the garden was rosy'! Group members were able to participate fully in the exercises and although there were some who verbalised their anxieties, the general pattern was for all to express their trust in one another.

The first exercise to provide counter-indications of some of the issues which influenced the group in their work was 'positive statements'. This required each member to make a positive statement about the neighbour on his/her right. The exercise was repeated twice after seating positions had been changed. What emerged from this was that group members were surprised by comments which were made and clearly were not used to receiving positive feedback about themselves. Comments like 'Do you really think that?' or 'I never realised you noticed me' were made on many occasions. However, other statements were somewhat superficial and perhaps, reflected how little some group members knew one another.

Later on, 'Paper tower' (based on Johnson and Johnson, 1987) led to more issues emerging. The exercise requires the group to build a five foot tower from a limited amount of newspaper and adhesive tape. The tower has to be capable of supporting a cup or mug and the group is allowed 20 minutes to complete the task. Because of the size of the group, it was split into two. Although both groups completed the task, several important incidents were noted which bore relevance to the way the group might operate in the children's home.

i. The head of home abdicated responsibility for the task saying *'I'm not very good at this sort of thing — just tell me what to do!'*.
ii. Some group members, whilst not actively excluded, were only just involved in the exercise, and no-one seemed to take any responsibility for drawing them in.
iii. Although the exercise was not planned as a competition between the groups, it rapidly became one. A great deal of interest was shown by the groups in each other's tower, and there was also banter between them about the quality of what they were doing. Any disasters or failings by one group were capitalised on by the other.

Discussion which followed highlighted the importance of all three issues since the group was able to acknowledge that they occurred in day-to-day running of the home, particularly staff being 'left out' and inter-group rivalry.

Day two

Most headway in facilitating open acknowledgement of how the group operated was made on day two with 'Clay island'. (Brandes and Philips, 1986). The leaders set out to cause the group some specific problems 'on the island' — they contaminated the water supply, placed the only food (wild turkeys) on one person's land, and placed two creatures *'mutated by radioactivity'* on the island. At no time was there any mention that these creatures were dangerous to humans but assumptions were made that they were, and this became a central issue throughout the whole exercise — should the mutants be killed? This resulted in one group member becoming isolated from the rest and actually removing herself, physically, from the group. Sub-groups were formed and reformed, arguments abounded and many ran to the head of home for safety (although he wasn't taking any particular leadership role in the exercise). Three people stated in the feedback that they did not even know what 'mutants' were, but did not like to ask. They merely assumed, because of the reaction of the others, that they must be dangerous. The task — to form an island council — was not even started, let alone completed.

After lunch we discussed what had gone on during 'Clay island', people's feelings concerning the exercise, and how events which had taken place matched what normally took place during the day-to-day working of the team. It became apparent that it accurately reflected interpersonal relationships and group dynamics within the team.

The next part of the day was given over to group members expressing their feelings about being part of the staff group by 'individual sculpting' and 'brainstorming'. In the first exercise most people openly indicated feelings towards the group whilst remaining slightly threatened. The brainstorm, recorded on flipcharts, did produce more positive statements than negative ones, but was quite a painful exercise. This recorded material was not looked at until the following day. Instead the day ended in a more positive vein using the computer game (Dearling, 1980). Although we were careful to select only reasonably positive statements for the cards, some were not always viewed in this light, possibly because there was still some tension around.

Day three

We began the day by each of us saying a little about how we were feeling about being there. On the whole everyone was feeling sorry that it was the last day. The remainder of the time until morning coffee was spent discussing staff relationships as identified over the last couple of days, particularly during the brainstorming session.

After coffee we played 'Dare, double dare' (Dearling, 1980). One reason for this was to break up the day with an exercise to provide some light relief. However, it was also to demonstrate an exercise which could easily be used with adolescents to show that it is alright to take risks (and be very silly) without losing face.

Over lunch we asked everyone to look at the brainstorm of statements about staff relationships and to indicate on both the positive and negative lists the five statements which they considered to be most important.

The afternoon was used to encourage the group to examine ways of holding on to the gains made throughout the exercise. Many ideas were forthcoming and those finally chosen were listed on a flipchart to be taken away. Examples of the ideas which were accepted including checking how staff felt at shift changeovers and at staff meetings and not relying on the head of home to resolve conflicts between staff.

Finally, we felt it was important that people took something positive away from the group. Everyone, including the three leaders, had a postcard stuck on their back. Everyone was asked to write one positive word on each person's postcard, which said what they felt about that person.

Evaluation

A team development exercise is, inevitably, expensive. In this particular case it took the entire staff of the children's home away from their place of work for three working days. It also occupied the time of the three leaders for a great deal more than this. Therefore it was important to make some assessment as to whether this was an effective use of time and resources.

SETTING OF AIMS

Preliminary discussions were held with the head of home, and a single meeting was held with the whole team. The three group leaders also visited the children's home on one occasion, but although this visit gave some feel of the building and nature of the set up, it was inevitably rather artificial and, perhaps, not helpful as a result. The head of home felt his aims included developing a cohesive team, improving direct communications between staff, and reducing indirect communications, such as when he was used as a 'go-between'. Whilst it was possible that the group would help staff improve their own ability to work with the children's group, this was not seen as a major priority.

IMMEDIATE FEEDBACK

Some of the group activities were obviously more immediately effective than others and these have been referred to above. Certain exercises were able to demonstrate immediately to the whole group such processes as splitting, making of presumptions, scapegoating, failures of listening, and tendencies to concentrate on the negative aspects of group functioning. Whether these and other identified problems of functioning would lead to more permanent changes is hard to say. In one of the final sessions, the staff group listed areas of concern, and proposals on how to improve functioning and maintain perceived gains during the three day event. These were taken back to the home, and used in staff meetings thereafter.

SHORT TERM APPRAISAL

All staff attending the group were asked to complete a brief appraisal form, covering such areas as objectives set both by the individuals and group during the programme, whether or not these objectives were achieved; ways, if any, in which the individual's view of the staff group has changed, most useful and least useful parts of the programme, omissions, and general comments.

Again there was a uniformity of responses; the aims of the staff group were to achieve a better understanding of each other, being far more open and honest with each other, and recognising the importance of the individuals within the group. The individual's aims were largely to do with getting a better understanding of colleagues and getting to know one's own position within the group through other people's responses. As to whether these various objectives were achieved, answers ranged from 'to a certain extent', 'have come away with ideas to help act on (achieving the objectives set)', 'I hope so, it's a little early to tell', 'felt I could speak out more freely at the end of the programme', to 'definitely'. Although it seems natural that many staff were reluctant to decide whether or not the objectives had been achieved until they returned to their work setting, no person stated their objectives had not been achieved. As for ways in which the staff group had changed, comments included more gentleness, affection, feeling more positive, feeling more involved, more trusting, feeling safer, and more thoughtful.

The majority of the group found the activity sessions the most helpful part, although members also identified the sharing of positive feedback, and openly discussing feelings as useful. It was perhaps reassuring that the majority of the group identified no parts of the three days as being least useful, although three members specifically mentioned the personal space activity as being unhelpful and/or difficult. Again, the majority of people felt that they could think of nothing which should have been included and was not; one or two mentioned the use of more time, or perhaps a residential setting as being preferable, and a couple of people specifically felt that role plays would be a valuable additional technique.

LONGER TERM APPRAISAL

The three leaders met the staff group to consider the benefits of the programme, approximately two months after the event.

The difficult conditions under which the care staff worked at that time were immediately obvious. The building was being rebuilt around the occupants, and after part of a gable end collapsed half the children and half the staff were lodging in another children's home some miles away. Despite these difficulties, five benefits were identified by the group as a whole. These are not in any order of priority:

i. People were talking directly to one another.
ii. The programme had provided an enjoyable break, with an increase in group cohesiveness.
iii. Staff felt they had developed more, and new, group work skills.
iv. Staff felt they were increasingly recognising the importance of each other's individual skills.
v. Members of the staff group were supporting each other.

Conclusion

Subjectively, it would appear that this exercise has been of value to the head of home, to the staff as a group, and by implication, one would expect, of general benefit to the children. In addition, the staff were trying out some of the activities they themselves experienced with the young people. They have also expressed interest in further developing their individual groupwork skills, and one of the side benefits of this exercise is that a programme for further training in groupwork with young people is to be organised.

Acknowledgement

We wish to acknowledge our debt to the participants in this exercise, and colleagues for their support and encouragement.

Appendix 1
Programme details and structured exercises used

Neck/massage
Name game
Restatement of objectives
Web game
Discussion of feelings about being in the group — (in pairs, feedback to the whole group)

Trust game
Bodyspace game
Trust questionnaire
Positive statements
Paper tower
Indian thumper

Day 2 Clay island (also with a feedback session)
Individual sculpting
Brainstorm on interpersonal relationships
Computer game
Fruit bowl

Day 3 Exercise and discussion of feelings about being there
Dare, double dare
Discussion about support and ways to improve relationships
Feedback forms
Paper on the back

References

Brandes, Donna and Phillips, H. (1986) *Gamesters Handbook.* London: Hutchinson Education.

Dearling, A. and Armstrong, H. (1980) *The Youth Games Book.* Intermediate Treatment Resource Centre, Bridge of Weir, Renfrewshire, PA11 3SA.

Johnson, D.W. and Johnson, F.P. (1987) *Joining Together, Group Theory and Group Skills* (3rd Edition). London: Prentice Hall International.

GROUPWORK (1988) 3, 262–268

'THE BROTHERS AND SISTERS GROUP'
A Group for Siblings of Children with Physical Disabilities.

ANNE BADGER

The group was created for the brothers and sisters of the disabled child in a family. The idea came from a growing recognition of the fact that social work resources are usually directed to the family member with the disability. Often the needs of the brothers and sisters are overlooked, and in most cases they face high expectations from their parents. The plan for this particular group was also influenced by the fact that two of the group leaders had disabled members in their families.

The group was designed to give the children something for themselves, which they could attend without their disabled brother or sister; something which was reliable and consistent. A play environment was created in which the child could play and talk in large and small groups. It was also an environment in which feelings — sometimes hidden feelings — could be acknowledged and responded to.

> The normal children within a family who has a handicapped child are often neglected, not through choice, but human nature. The handicapped child receives most of the attention, their demands and needs are obviously far greater than the normal child.

The above quote was written by a parent of three children, one of whom is disabled with cerebral palsy. The disabled child's elder sister was a member of a group set up in an attempt to focus on the needs of siblings of physically disabled children.

The belief that a group for these children was needed came from all three original group leaders, two of whom have a disabled family member. Whilst working as a social worker attached to an Inner London Education Authority (ILEA) primary school for children with physical disabilities, I found parents would often discuss their worries and concerns about their non-disabled children. As well as feeling guilty about not being able to give the other children as much attention, parents tended to have higher expectations and hopes for the 'normal' child in the family.

Another group leader, a psychologist working with children, first became aware of the needs of the siblings of children when visiting families with children who had a mental handicap. She was struck by the number of quite young children who either carried specific responsibilities in the household, or simply seemed 'mature beyond their years'. Children with handicapped siblings were also over-represented in the number referred for help to a child psychiatry service. Presenting problems ranged from learning difficulties, enuresis, soiling and regressed behaviour, to emotional disturbance and delinquent behaviour in adolescents.

The third leader, a day care adviser for under-fives, was particularly interested in the needs of families with disabled children.

Aims

In developing the aims of the group we tried:

i. to give the children something for themselves which they could attend without their brother or sister — something which would be reliable and consistent and, above all, fun, involving activities in which they might not otherwise have much opportunity to participate, such as swimming or playing in the adventure playground.
ii. to acknowledge the reality of their siblings' handicap, answering questions, providing concrete information where necessary, and enabling the children to learn from each other about common experiences.
iii. to provide an environment in which feelings — sometimes difficult, hidden feelings — could be acknowledged and responded to, using different play techniques: e.g. drawing, painting, acting, talking. Above all, to try to understand and contain the children's feelings, and help them to express themselves.

Referrals

I identified eight possible referrals for the group from families on my caseload whose disabled children were attending the ILEA school. The children, three boys and five girls, were aged between 5½ and 7½ years.

Before the group started we held a parents' meeting to outline our aims and ideas. This was followed up with home visits to meet the children, and at least two of the leaders were included on each visit. Only one boy refused to come to the group, because his disabled brother could not accompany him.

Planning

In order to create an environment in which we could fulfil these aims, we needed to ensure consistency in the setting, timing, adults and children involved, and routine. We wanted a setting in which the children could play, talk — in the large group and in smaller groups, be free to run around, and be able to act out if necessary. This required a large, divisible space with firm boundaries and no interruptions. We were lucky in having the use of two nursery group rooms, together with outdoor space which was secluded and spacious.

The physical setting enabled us to have two separate activities going on simultaneously, or to take a small group of children out of the larger group, perhaps into a quiet corner with cushions. The space was large enough for the whole group to run around together. We were well equipped with play materials, paints, clay, toys and felt tip pens, and we were able to make use of recording and video equipment.

The group met weekly for two hours after school. It was a closed group and efforts were made to ensure that children attended every week. As it is often difficult for families with a handicapped child, particularly single parent families, to take the siblings to after-school activities, transport was a priority for which the group leaders took responsibility.

As co-leaders, our roles developed as the group progressed. Initially my role was more that of a co-ordinator, but we shared the responsibility for planning the sessions, and other tasks. The high staff ratio, particularly when we were joined by a student (our only male leader), meant we were able to give individual attention to the children as appropriate. We were careful throughout the course of the group to meet regularly, outside supervision times, to plan sessions and check out differing styles of leadership and approaches.

Consultancy

From the outset, it was crucial that we, as group leaders, had outside supervision of our work. We met fortnightly with a senior clinical psychologist, took with us the children's drawings, and recounted anecdotes of our previous sessions. We found this supervision added an extra dimension to our sessions with the children, helping us to explore what they might be trying to tell us and how we might best respond.

Method

In describing the setting and the parameters of the group, one concept occurs repeatedly, that of containment. This idea perhaps best sums up our approach to the group sessions, and what we felt we were trying to offer the children. Our way of working was neither didactic nor interpretative in the psychodynamic sense.

Because of the ages of the children, we decided to focus on activities as our main method of working, and these varied from games, use of clay, painting, to visits to the local adventure playground and swimming pool.

Our first session, which set the pattern for the remaining weeks, involved introductory games with the whole group, free play which encouraged individual attention, and eating a meal together. This mealtime became the time for exchanging news and airing problems. The children very quickly identified that they were coming to the group because their sibling was disabled and attended the same school. This immediate acknowledgement of their commonality surprised all of us, and from the first session the group was referred to as the 'brothers and sisters group'.

Summary of group/evaluation

Although each session had planned activities, the children, too, had strong ideas of how they wanted to use the group and they would bring their own ideas for games and activities. One boy suggested we make our own puppets and put on a puppet show. The same boy, who found it difficult to verbalise his sadness, then proceeded to use his puppet 'Plonker the Rabbit' to let us know what he wanted and how he felt.

We used a lot of fantasy in our play together and through this the children were given the opportunity to express feelings of fear, worry, want and need.

As the group progressed, we did a lot of myth dispelling about their siblings' disabilities. One girl's explanation for her brother's inability to sit up unsupported — in fact caused by a form of muscular atrophy — was that he was lifted up too much as a small baby. Similarly, two of the other children could not understand why their elder brother's feet were smaller than theirs. Certain group members wanted their siblings to be able to do things they could and a favourite theme was that of a magic carpet where it didn't matter if your legs didn't work.

The children were all very caring to each other and to us adults —

they would listen to each other's difficulties and offer advice. When one child was being bullied and teased at school about having a disabled brother or if someone was absent due to illness, this was always noted and discussed.

Following the Christmas break, one boy failed to return to the group. At the previous session, he had hit the other boy in the group, his 'mate'. The 'mate', along with all the group, was very upset he had failed to return, and the children decided that a delegation, consisting of the leader who had dealt with the upset and the 'mate', should visit the boy at home and convey the wishes of the group that he should return. This proved to be successful and strengthened the cohesiveness of the group.

The group ran for seven months, from October 1985 to May 1986, with one or two breaks during school holidays. Ending the group was very difficult for all involved, and in spite of efforts made by the group leaders, over several weeks, to focus on the group ending, the children avoided the issue until the penultimate session when feelings of anger at the group's impending close were at their height.

As leaders, we felt we were able to address the original aims of the group, and in particular were able to provide a safe environment for each of these children to be themselves. They were able to display their anxieties and concerns, not only about their disabled sibling, but also about themselves, with the knowledge these would be accepted and contained.

We were struck by how readily the children accepted each other's idiosyncratic behaviour. As the group developed and became safe, all the children began to display individual feelings and needs of their own, as children in their own right. One girl, who obviously felt under pressure at home to be good and helpful to her mother, a single parent, gradually changed from being tense and withdrawn to being naughty and as noisy and cheeky as the others.

The children's perceptions were highlighted in a session when we introduced a series of demons to be coloured in — a lonely demon, an angry demon and so on. The children very quickly chose a demon appropriate for themselves, each other and for us adults too. It was perhaps interesting that the children never referred to us as grown-ups or adults, only '*the big ones*'. One particular child, outwardly the most sensible, practical 'little mother' of the group, surprised us all by choosing the messy demon to be '*her*'. Until then, we were unaware that she was enuretic and soiled in the daytime. We were then able to introduce some very messy play sessions with finger painting and clay which gave her obvious pleasure.

By attending weekly, the children clearly indicated to us that this group was something special for them.

To help the children view the group as a place where they could feel free to talk and act as they needed, we chose to keep involvement of parents to a minimum. Parents did not usually bring or collect their child, and although there was a certain amount of contact when the children were taken home, we discouraged parents from asking for a report on their child and instead encouraged the child to share with their parents any aspects of the group they chose. Support for the group from the parents increased significantly during the time the group ran. Another parents' meeting was held shortly before the group ended, inviting parents' comments. These were mostly very positive, and expressed the view that the group had given their child a chance to be 'special'. Parents recognised the value of the group to their child, expressed concern and dismay when the group finally ended, and emphasised the need for similar groups to be set up in the future. One parent also commented that she had been given an insight into things she had never thought about, and said:

> The group provides the brothers and sisters with the ability to understand they are not the only ones who carry the burden of being the normal one. Being able to express themselves to others outside the family becomes a natural and healthy part of their development. How many of us can relate and talk freely to our parents?

Conclusions

From the experience of our group, and following a brief review of the existing studies on siblings of children with disabilities (Gath *et al.*, 1972; Sullivan, 1979; Grossman, 1972; Tew and Lawrence, 1973), we think that these children are, in comparison with others:

i. more likely to have to forego opportunities or restrict activities (because they are unsuitable for their handicapped brother or sister);
ii. more likely to be victims of teasing or bullying, and less likely to discuss it with their parents.
iii. more likely to experience feelings of guilt and resentment, in relation to their handicapped sibling;
iv. more likely to be at risk of developing psychological difficulties or symptomatology and problem behaviour;

They are also more likely to be ill-informed about the nature of their sibling's handicap, its course and prognosis.

Additionally, they are:

i. unlikely to talk to other people, even their parents, perhaps for fear of burdening them, or because their parents believe (or need to believe) that the sibling is unaffected, thus rarely giving the child's feelings a chance of expression;
ii. seldom likely to have the opportunity to meet with, or talk to, other children in a similar situation.

The decision to write about this group was made with the hope that other professionals involved with families who have a child with a disability, and parents too, will recognise and become more aware of the brothers and sisters.

References

Gath, A. *et al.* (1972) 'The school age sibling of mongol children', *British Journal of Psychiatry*, 123, pp. 161–167.
Grossman, F.K. (1972) *Brothers and Sisters of Retarded Children.* Syracuse, NY: Syracuse University Press.
Sullivan, R.C. (1979) 'Siblings of autistic children', *Journal of Autism and Developmental Disorders*, 9, pp. 287–295.
Tew, B. and Lawrence, K.M. (1973) 'Mothers, brothers and sisters of patients with Spina Bifida', *Developmental Medicine and Child Neurology*, 15, pp. 69–74.

GROUPWORK (1988) 3, 269–277

GROUPWORK WITH ADOLESCENTS: ABSTRACTS

ALISON SKINNER

Groupwork theory

'Why groupwork?' by John Baldwin in *Social Work Today*, Vol. 8 (19), 15 February 1977, pages 7–9.

Describes the basic elements of the groupwork model of IT and, in the light of delinquency research, analyses ways in which it can offer positive non-deviant roles and meet certain basic needs previously linked with offending. Among these are relations with adults without labelling, opportunities for reward and status, mutual help and the development of new skills.

'Where the real work is done' by Ian Butler in *Community Care*, 445, 13 January 1983, pages 14–16.

Draws a distinction between two different models of groupwork: the group as instrument and the group in context. Suggests that the latter approach has considerable benefits in working with young people on IT projects and outlines a specimen programme on offending, making use of outside speakers, role play and cartooning as methods.

'Groupwork with adolescents' by A.S. Kerslake in *Social Work with Adolescents*, Jones, R. and Pritchard C. (eds.) pages 138–164. Routledge & Kegan Paul, 1980, ISBN 0 7100 0633 0.

Reviews the literature on groupwork as a method of social work with adolescents. Describes its development in Britain, particularly through IT, and discusses issues arising in preparing and forming groups, leadership roles, and the content of groupwork programmes.

'Leadership in low intensity intermediate treatment groups' by A.S. Kerslake *Journal of Adolescence*, 6 (1) 1983, pages 27–41.

Discusses the problems involved in low-intensity groupwork with adolescents and identifies four areas of preparation which leaders need to undertake prior to starting groups. Sets out models of leadership style and stages of group development relevant to 'one-night-a-week' IT groups.

One Night a Week? Aspects of Groupwork in Intermediate Treatment by Trevor Locke (ed.), National Youth Bureau, 1981, 20pp, ISBN 0 86155 029 3.

Contains three papers on the theme of the planning and programming of IT groups. The first, by Mike Anderson, covers aims, goals and contracts: the second, by Brian Heritage and Vic Vivian, sets out the planning stages that group leaders need to undertake and includes detailed checklists of action required at each stage; and the third by Alan Caygill and Colin Barker, briefly describes activities which can be used by groups. Includes flow charts and a guide to further reading.

'Playing the game' by Sue Ross and Andy Bilson in *Community Care*, 320, 31 July 1980, pages 15–17.
Examines the use of games in developmental groupwork and the ways in which they can help to move groups through their development stages. Using examples from IT groups, it discusses how games were used to help groups come to terms with their needs for inclusion, control and affection and to increase trust.

'The sacred cow of IT' by Sue Ross in *Community Care*, 499, 16 February 1984, pages 24–26.
Article challenging the pre-eminence of groupwork as an IT method. Considers the emergence of other, individual models of work with young people such as befriending, linking and tracking schemes and the correctional curriculum.

'Groupwork in intermediate treatment' by John Waterhouse in *British Journal of Social Work*, 8 (2), 1978, pages 127–144.
Provides an account of the operation of two evening IT groups over a six-month period and makes use of the data to discuss issues in the practice of groupwork by social workers with young adolescents. Analyses group processes, member participation and leadership styles and distinguishes between different types of activity and focused discussion as groupwork methods.

Groupwork with solvent abusers

'The heart of the matter' by Colin Beech and Jenny Grice in *Community Care*, 449, 16 February 1984, pages 21–24.
Detailed account of a ten-week programme organised by IT workers in Rochdale for a natural group of young people referred for truancy, glue sniffing and offending. The focus of the intervention was on school non-attendance and a system of financial and other incentives was introduced to encourage children to attend regularly, which was ultimately successful in breaking the association of truancy with glue sniffing and offending. The group produced a video about their experiences which was shown to their parents at a special session.

'Old skills applied – new lessons learned' by William Francis in *Community Care*, 578, 5 September 1985, pages 19–21.
Description of a group for young offenders with glue sniffing problems organised by IT workers at the Rotherham Adolescent Project. Used a groupwork approach and a token economy system. Discusses the issues involved in responding to solvent abuse as an issue.

'Solvent misuse in context' by Richard Ives, (ed.) National Children's Bureau, 1986, 74 pp, ISBN 0-902817-24-8.

Collection of readings on solvent abuse looking at theory and practice in different contexts and settings. Includes a chapter on IT work with solvent misusers which discusses a group work approach.
Available from: National Children's Bureau, 8 Wakley Street, London EC1V 7QE.

'Sudden Impact' A Groupwork Approach to Solvent Abuse by David Mann and Grant Blackwell. Rotherham Adolescent Project, 1985 14 pp.

Report of a group run for young offenders whose offending was related to glue sniffing as a contributing factor in its causes. Describes in some detail the content of each session in which young people described the type of solvents they used, the effects and responses of and to sniffing, the causes of sniffing, the contract and token economy used to tackle this behaviour and the results.
Available from: Rotherham Adolescent Project, Havenhurst, Moorgate, Rotherham.

Groupwork with girls and young women

The Development and Operation of a Neighbourhood Based Intermediate Treatment Group for Adolescent Girls. The Barton Project, 1980, 14 pp.

Detailed account of a ten-week evening IT group for girls from a particular estate in Oxford, which aimed to improve their self-esteem and self-awareness. Includes details of the programme, notes on the problems experienced and makes an evaluation of the impact of the group on the girls and the effectiveness of the staff team.

Evaluation of girls (IT) Group by Colin Beckwith, Cumbria Social Services Department, 1986, 13 pp.

Account of the establishment and operation of an IT group for a small group of girls giving insights into agency responses to female delinquency and the individual responses of the participants to the programme.
Available from: Cumbria Social Services Department, Allerdale District, Park Lane, Workington, Cumbria CA14 2RR.

'Devising a treatment model built on "girls only" method' by Isobel Groves, *Social Work Today*, 11 (48), 19 August 1980, pages 12–13.

Report of a six-week, evening IT group for 13–15 year old girls in Camberley, focusing particularly on the problems of school non-attendance. Teachers and social workers co-operated in devising the programme using discussion and role play.

'Asians at risk' by Laxmi Jamdagni in *Youth in Society*, 64, March 1982, pages 22–23.
Description of a ten-week IT group in Birmingham for Asian girls who had committed offences. It was organised by two Asian women workers, who worked closely with families to enlist their support, and provided a programme which enabled the participants to examine issues of gender and race.

'Enabling mothers and daughters to reach a better understanding' by Lorraine Schaffer, in *Social Work Today*, 18 (12), 17 November 1986, pp. 16–17.
Description of a groupwork programme involving mothers and their adolescent daughters held over a six month period in Lambeth at the Old Library Project. The young women were mostly at risk of being received into care and the overall aim was to effect change in the relationship and improve communication and understanding. The article discusses some of the groupwork dynamics and the lessons learnt from this approach.

Setting Up Groups for Girls Who Have Been Sexually Abused. Taboo, 1985, 8 pp.
Account of a support group for girls who had been sexually abused. The group aimed to enable girls to share their experience of sexual abuse, enhance their self-esteem and confidence and give them a chance to meet other girls of a similar age, as many are socially isolated. The report gives details of the programme on offer at each stage of the group's life.
Available from: Taboo: Manchester Support Group for Incest Survivors, PO Box 38, Manchester, M60 1HG.

Working with Girls by Jean Trewhitt and Helen Zyskowski. Venture 12, 1986, 20 pp.
Detailed account of 'girls only' IT group provided for girls who are either on supervision orders for offending or felt to be at risk through school, family or community difficulties.

Using drama therapy in groupwork

'Dramatic recovery' by Anne Bannister in *Social Work Today*, 14 (18), 11 January 1983, pages 14–15.
Description of the use of drama therapy at an IT centre with groups of young people in the 13–15 age range. Discusses the benefits of this kind of work with adolescents.

'Sharing tears and laughter' by Michael La Borde and Judy Mckenzie in *Youth in Society*, 88, March 1984, pages 13–14.
Description of the use of drama therapy with an IT group on a ten-day trip to France. Outlines the techniques used to enable members to identify and work out individual and group problems. Notes an improvement in attitudes to displays of weakness or affection among group members after the experience.

'Psycho-drama as a medium for intermediate treatment' by Peter Rayner in *British Journal of Social Work*, 7 (4), 1977, pages 443–453.
Description of a weekly evening IT group using spontaneous drama as its only activity. Reviews the process by which the group determines how to proceed and how ideas can be turned into presentations. Discusses the value of this kind of approach and the role of adults in the group.

A Report on Psycho Drama Groups Run at Glasgote Probation Office, March 1981–March 1982 by Alan Swann, Sue Hunt and Elaine Leighton, Staffordshire Probation Service, 1982, 10pp.

Account of two groups provided for Probation Service clients aged 15–18, which aimed to improve individual levels of communication. The eighteen-week programme consisted of introductory sessions, role play around court appearances and job interviews, and the production of a mock TV commercial; it incorporated a trip to the theatre and sessions with a local drama group. Includes a specimen programme and details of lessons learnt from the experience.

Groupwork handbooks

Groupwork and IT by Lucy Ball and Theo Sowa, London IT Association, 1985, 74pp.
Practical handbook for workers involved in groupwork with young offenders, focusing on offending and related issues. Covers preliminary groundwork, aims and objectives, leadership, values clarification, planning, constructing programme content, assessment and evaluation. Includes practical examples of exercises to do with young people. The materials have been developed and used at the Junction Project over the past four years.

Intensive Intermediate Treatment with Juvenile Offenders: A Handbook on Assessment and Groupwork Practice by Gary Denman, University of Lancaster, Centre of Youth, Crime and Community, 1983, 103pp.
Substantial handbook intended for practitioners seeking to reduce delinquent behaviour in individual young people. The first half, on theory, reviews some of the social psychological literature on deviance and on the relation between attitudes and behaviour, emphasises cognitive and situational determinants of delinquent acts, and argues for understanding individual behaviour in very specific, rather than general, terms. The second half, on practice, provides the

outline of a correctional curriculum aimed at changing or improving the social skills, reasoning processes and general beliefs of young offenders. Includes a very detailed guide to individualised assessment in order to set objectives, and briefer guidelines on groupwork methods to meet these objectives.

Worth the Risk!? Creative Groupwork with Young Offenders by Kevin Ball, *et al.* West Yorkshire Probation Service, 1987, 60pp.
Well presented handbook on groupwork with young offenders setting out a philosophy of practice, a checklist of practicalities, a 22-session groupwork programme and ideas for games and exercises.
Available from: The Hilltop Project, Westwood Drive, Ilkley, West Yorkshire.

Caught in the System. A Handbook for Women Working with Young Women at Risk and in Trouble by Anita Mountain, National Youth Bureau, 1988 (reprint forthcoming).
Outlines a process for setting up a group for young women at risk and offers ideas for programme content, together with examples of games and exercises.

Working with Young People in Trouble by Tim Pickles, ITRC, 19 Elmbank Street, Glasgow G2 4PB, 1988, 96pp.
Offers a structure for clear planning, referral criteria, programme design and evaluation. The text includes over 30 exercises for use in applying the ideas in the book.

Working Out of Doors with Young People written and illustrated by Alan Smith, ITRC, 19 Elmbank Street, Glasgow G2 4PB, 1988, 128pp.
Offers a range of ideas for games and practice sessions based on the author's experience as a teacher of outdoor activities.

Greater Expectations: A Source Book for Working with Girls and Young Women by Tricia Szirom and Sue Dyson, Learning Development Aids, 1986, 196pp.
Series of worksheets and exercises on self-image, health, sex stereotypes, women and work etc for undertaking groupwork with girls and young women.

Groupwork with young people at risk and in trouble

Give 'Em a Break: Social Action By Young People at Risk and in Trouble by John Baldwin, *et al.* Dave Ward (ed.). National Youth Bureau, 1982, 28pp, ISBN 0 86155 058 7.
Collection of papers illustrating the social action approach to working with young people at risk and in trouble. Includes three case studies of social education groups in Nottingham where the young people acted collectively to improve conditions in their area. Background papers explore the implications for theory, practice, organisation and justice of this approach.

Working with Groups of Young People by Chris Cope, *et al.* Barnardo's North West Division, 1987, 67pp.

Report on groups run at the Speke IT Project in Liverpool during the past six years. Presents information on a care or custody at risk group, senior delinquents' group, young mothers' group, girls' group and boys' preventative group. Through the use of case histories offers insights into the difficulties of young people growing up in deprived circumstances in Merseyside and the successes and shortcomings of IT work with them.

Available from: The Librarian, Dr Barnardo's, Tanners Lane, Barkingside, Ilford, Essex IG6 IQG.

The RUTS File: Rural and Urban Training Scheme Off-Road Motorcycling and Groupwork with Young People – Report of the Pilot Scheme by Alan Dearling. Intermediate Treatment Resource Centre, 1982, 32 pp, ISBN 0 9506951 5 7.

Detailed description of a motorcycle project for young people in eastern Scotland providing maintenance and riding sessions, trips out and weekends away, group discussion and other activities. The project aimed to explore the value of motorcycles as a medium for working with young people at risk, motorcyle offenders and youngsters creating problems in conventional IT groups.

Intermediate Treatment: The Development and Operation of a 'Social Skills' group by Peter Howe. The Barton Project, 1979, 13 pp.

Account of a two-month, weekly evening IT group for 15–17 year olds organised by a neighbourhood project in Oxford. The group concentrated primarily on social skills, focusing particularly on job finding and various kinds of individual and community skills. Provides details of the programme and staff evaluations of individual group members.

Howgill Intermediate Treatment Development Group Evaluation Report. Howgill IT Project, 1981, 19 pp.

Description of a one-night-a-week IT group run by a voluntary agency in Whitehaven, Cumbria, focusing particularly on photography as an activity. Highlights the need for clear aims and objectives in IT work, clear referral criteria and detailed staff planning in advance.

Old Library Offenders Group Report May–December 1980, Lambeth Social Services Department, 1981, 43 pp.

Detailed report of a four-month, weekly evening group for young offenders in Lambeth using a behavioural points system and a mixed programme of games, activities and films. Gives details of programme content and a running commentary on reactions to it within the group, including some feedback from the young people themselves.

'Boys will be boys' by Lois Morgan and Saul Becker, in *Community Care*, 484, 20 October 1983, pages 24–26.
Description of a twelve-week evening IT group in Nottinghamshire with seven young people at risk of DC. The programme examined causes and consequences of offending and ways of handling people in authority, and made extensive use of games to enhance group cohesion and non-verbal methods of commenting on an individual's progress within the group.

Pilot Intermediate Treatment Group July 1983–October 1983 by David Mann, *et al.* Dr Barnardo's, Rotherham Adolescent Project, 1983, 17pp.
Description of a two-evenings-a-week, 16-week IT programme based on the correctional curriculum. Used games, role play, self-assessment, video and film making, counselling and family work. Outlines the process within the group and the experiences of individual members, and includes appendices giving details of the evening and the weekend residential programme.

Groupwork Review by Deirdre Quill, Leeds Alternatives to Custody and Care Scheme, 1986, 14 pp.
Account of the groupwork programme provided by the Leeds Alternatives to Custody and Care. Outlines programme content and includes appendices providing guidelines for volunteers on intensive groupwork, the induction group programme and the court information sheet.
Available from: Leeds Alternatives to Custody and Care Scheme. 134 Woodsley Road, Leeds LS2 9LZ.

Doncaster Probation Intensive Intermediate Treatment Programme, October 1979 to May 1980, South Yorkshire Probation Service, 1980, 16 pp.
Detailed description of an intensive seven-month, three-evenings-a-week programme designed to reduce the pattern of delinquent behaviour. Used activities, discussion and experiential learning as methods and gives some examples of practice. The staff team was interprofessional, drawn from the Probation Service, Social Services and the Youth Service. Includes a brief evaluation and guidelines for a future group.

Groupwork with school non-attenders

Pilot Scheme for School Leavers by M. Bietzk, Northants Social Services/ Southwood Upper School, 1982, 7pp.
Six week discussion group held in school with fifth form pupils who had underachieved during their school career, exhibited disruptive behaviour in class and were at risk of being suspended. The group aimed to discuss problems the pupils had encountered during their school careers and used self-assessment questionnaires, role play exercises and modelling. Staff comprised an EWO, two social workers and a teacher.

Starting Blocks by D. Burley, National Youth Bureau, 1982, 24pp.
Detailed account of a social education group for young people not attending school, referred by teachers, probation officers and social workers, sponsored by Nottingham Young Volunteers. The approach adopted focused on enabling young people to take collective action to meet their identified needs and describes their experiences in organising various events and the process within the group. Includes a series of guidelines to enable workers to plan, take part in and evaluate similar groups.

'The Ynys Mon intermediate treatment project' by Judy Hutchings *et al.* in *International Journal of Behaviour Social Work and Abstracts*, 1 (3), 1981, pages 187–198.
Article on IT work with a natural group of eight boys with problems at school and at risk of residential care, who attended a community centre one afternoon a week. The programme set targets for improving their relationships with specified individuals and reducing the amount of trouble they experienced, and it paid the boys for undertaking assignments and reporting back. Reports noticeable improvement in relationships at home, school and in the community.

'Breaking down the professional barriers' by D. Ward and J. Pearce in *Social Work Today*, 10 (36), 15 May 1979, pages 19–21.
Description of a school-based after hours group for seven boys on supervision. Involved the collaboration of a teacher and probation officer and provided a useful framework for discussing school-related problems.

'Dealing with disruptive pupils' by Jim Wilson, in *Community Care*, 658, 30 April 1987, pages 22–23.
Report of a joint initiative between Social Services and the Education Welfare Service in Wigan providing a groupwork programme one half day a week for non school attenders which has had some success in reducing the numbers of care orders made for this group of young people.

Note

Copies of local authority reports are available on loan from the National Youth Bureau. In the case of some of the older material, copies may no longer be available from the original local authority source. Up to six items at a time may be borrowed from the National Youth Bureau at a cost of 50 pence per item.

GROUPWORK (1988) 3, 278–281

BOOK REVIEWS

Groupwork with the Elderly: N. BENDER, A. NORRIS AND P. BAUCKHAM
Winslow Press
ISBN 0 86388 047 9

Without doubt anything that sets out to raise the status of work with older people has to be applauded. Groupwork has too often been seen as a method of work that is only employed with people who can be construed as productive, or who have the potential to be so. This is clearly based on a view of productivity that attaches value only to work to which we ascribe a simple economic value. Therefore, to begin to put older people, or more correctly work with older people, in a place which suggests that it needs skills and careful planning, is one very clear way of combating ageism and all that it imposes upon older people.

Nevertheless any material that deals with work with older people has a responsibility to combat ageism in every way and sadly this handbook fails to follow through some of the opportunities with which it is presented. This is not to say that, as a result, all of the content falls into disrepute, since there is much to take from it which, if implemented, would raise the standard of practice in many settings which older people use. The message that they offer is uncompromising and probably true for most workers currently in practice:

> ... your training and your work have made you, even forced you, to distance yourself from your elderly client and pretend they are very different from you. We hope by the time you have worked through this manual, you know that this is not true. (p.viii).

As a practitioner and now as a social work teacher, I always appreciate material that invites you to use it and the number of exercises that are provided will ensure that the repertoire of many workers and trainers will be increased by this manual. The manual is a course in itself but much of it can be used independently and that should be seen as a strength rather than a weakness.

It may be helpful to illustrate the useful material which points to a process that has been carefully thought out and tested with groups of staff. The manual starts with a 'Behaviours questionnaire', a mechanism which asks the user to do some thinking about what they know and what they might want to achieve. This is an aspect of the manual which is evident throughout, and it is possible to describe it as 'user-friendly', since there is plenty of opportunity for the user to evaluate what they have achieved, and learn from it. As they stress:

> ... recording and analysing the activities in your unit will give you a much clearer idea of what is going on (WE think it should be a continuous part of any unit and its self-review).

There is a lot of material on planning and a number of *aide-memoires* which workers could easily photocopy and leave pinned on staff room walls and notice-boards for ease of reference and to ensure that people follow good examples. I shall certainly remember the four major tasks which are suggested for the worker in a group: listen, learn, provide, and mediate. Not bad ground-rules for operating sensitively in many situations in which workers find themselves. Much of the foundation of this manual is relevant for all groups of people, and as such it may be that an opportunity has been lost to spread very worthwhile messages to a wider audience.

My major concern about this book is the way that insensitive and often quite ageist language is continually used. This is not inconsequential in a book about groupwork since ageist practice, and language that contributes towards such practice, is bad practice. For instance, the title *Groupwork with the Elderly* allows people to go on using a term like 'the elderly' as if it had real meaning. Are they really suggesting that it is possible to lump together people aged between 60 and 105 years? At least 'elderly people' should be used, but most writers, who have given some thought to the consequences of ageism prefer the term 'older people', if only because it implies no homogeneity to any specific group of people who may or may not be of pensionable age. Old age is socially constructed and unless we address what that means in our practice, we will continue some of the damaging consequences of ageism.

Two examples from Chapter 4, 'Which group, if any?', should serve to make my point. '*Never rush the elderly if you want to get the best from them*', and '*A good rule of thumb is to double the amount of time ... the interview itself will take*' (p. 28). Are the authors really saying that all older people, using the kinds of settings in which people who may use this manual will work, require twice the time of 'ordinary' people? Indeed it may be more accurate to say that one should never rush *people* if you want to offer them opportunities to make the most of any group experience. The issue for a groupworker is surely to help people take some control over what they want from a group, and therefore engender an atmosphere of reciprocity. This criticism could be countered by pointing to a sentence on the same page (p. 28) '*... creating enough time stresses the point that groups will only be as useful as the respect the regime of the unit shows the client generally*'. But it is a valid general point and not one that applies particularly to older people.

It would be hypocritical to conclude this review by saying that, some of the language apart, this training manual is fine. It is as if the authors knew what they wanted to achieve, but failed to consider the unintended consequences of much of the practice that currently goes on and some of what they are advocating. The process which it offers to workers is systematic and well planned. The exercises will make people think and some of them will help to challenge a view of older people that 'problematises' and labels. Any trainer/practitioner/manager interested in raising the standard of practice with older people will find much in this manual that is usable. However, anti-ageism will require that it is used selectively so as not to miss out on some of the subtleties, since however well intentioned, practice that continues to stereotype and generalise about older people, continues to oppress them.

Stewart Greenwell, Lecturer in Social Work, School of Social Sciences, University of Bath.

Groupwork in Adoption and Foster Care: JOHN TRISELIOTIS (Editor)
Batsford Academic
Price: Paperback £8.95

This book provides a much needed input about training in adoptive and foster care by the skillful use of groupwork processes. There is also the added bonus of descriptive pieces of work that have been undertaken with adolescents, and black children living in white foster homes. Part of the attraction for me as a trainer is the beneficial use of readable sections by several contributors who are able to identify the part of the groupwork that is successful and the areas that prove to be less desirable.

Part I concentrates on the preparation and selection of adoptive and foster parents. Being trainer to a scheme that uses groupwork to provide extra evidence and support to the assessment process, I know that the methods and ideas from the contributors to this publication are usable and translatable to my scheme setting.

The other benefits for me are that the text is easily readable and due to clearly identifiable sections can be used in a selective way. It can be read intermittently without losing the understanding of the process behind the text. I have read various sections as a means of alleviating other tedious tasks which beset me in my every day working life and even when travelling by train, it has proved a useful companion.

Part II concentrates on the use of groups to prepare and support children in placement. I have used groups with young people in residential care, but I have not used this method within my present scheme of work. The book gives plenty of practical ideas as to how to start such a group and, should the opportunity arise, I would feel more confident in proceeding with this idea.

As a CSS study supervisor, I have recommended this book to students for use when looking at the process and concepts of groupwork with young people.

Part III is concerned with post-placement and post-adoptive support groups. There is an expectation within my agency scheme that all foster/adoptive carers will attend a monthly support group. However there is the realisation that, once the adoption order is finalised, there is a reliance on the adoptive parents to attend of their own volition. This means the group members have to experience the benefits of group support and to feel that their own contributions are valid and important. This concept is extended in the book when examining the need for and the purpose of the post-adoptive support group. There is also a chapter about foster parent support groups in rural areas and the difficulties that have to be overcome when people live in isolated places and travelling to group venues is somewhat difficult.

Groupwork in a multi-cultural setting is the one specialism on which I found too little information. This could be attributed to my being white and having a small amount of knowledge in this field. I am probably expecting too much in order to improve my knowledge and skills in this very sensitive area, whilst identifying the need for our scheme to offer appropriate training for prospective black adopters/foster parents.

However, the chapter about groupwork with black children in white foster homes which is concerned with cultural identity is a positive contribution to the problems that face children and foster parents in this position. I liked the way that the writer made valid suggestions as to how to deal with the problem rather than being destructive about the appropriateness of such placements in the light of present day research about the placement of black children.

Finally I recommend this book to workers and students alike on the following basis:

i. It is easy to read.

ii. The tasks and the objectives of the groups are clearly identified.

iii. It is a valuable source of usable material based on a theoretical knowledge of groupwork principles and skills.

Averill Hammond, Training Officer National Childrens Homes; Associated Member of Institute of Training and Development; C.S.S. Study Supervisor.

FRENCH SUMMARIES

Short Term Groupwork in the Treatment of Chronic Sorrow: A Norwegian Experience

GERD KRAMM ENGEBRIGTSEN AND KEN HEAP

Le premier article de ce troisième numero est redigé par le Directeur de School of Social Work d'Oslo et traite de l'utilisation du travail de groupe dans le but d'apporter un soutien aux parents d'enfants souffrant de maladies incurables.

Revisiting Open Groups

MICHAEL HENRY

Le groupe ouvert, où un travailleur social oeuvre à l'interieur d'un groupe sans membership défini, a toujours tenu une place importante en service social, en soins à domicile ou, encore, lors d'intervention auprès des jeunes. Cet article traite de quelques des thèmes-clés de ce genre d'intervention.

Social Action Groupwork as Negotiation: Contradictions in the Process of Empowerment

EAMONN KEENAN AND JOHN PINKERTON

Dans ce premier de deux articles concernant un travail de groupe connu sous le nom de "social action", les auteurs, Keenan et Pinkerton, discutent des processus de perte de pouvoir des individus et de recouvrement de ce même pouvoir. Cet article a été rédigé à partir de consultations entre un chargé de cours en service social et un travailleur communautaire de Belfast, Irlande du Nord.

'Nowt To Do and Always Getting into Trouble'. The Bulwell Neighbourhood Project — A Social Action Response

BILL BADMAN, MICHAEL BENTE AND PAULINE HALL

Ce deuxième article sur le travail de groupe de type 'social action' nous illustre un travail social et communautaire dans une petite localité du Nottinghamshire, en Angleterre.

A Team Development Exercise

JOHN TAYLOR, DI MILES AND JOHN EASTGATE

Ce second article traitant de consultation nous décrit un exercice de formation avec un groupe de travailleurs sociaux oeuvrant avec des adolescents d'un ensemble résidentiel. Des méthodes de travail de groupe jusque là réservées à des interventions avec des adolescents ont été utilisées pour améliorer la communication entre les membres du personnel ainsi que leurs pratiques de travail.

'The Brothers and Sisters Group'. A Group for Siblings of Children with Physical Disabilities

ANNE BADGER

En complément à l'article de Heap *et al.*, ci-haut mentionné, cet article est consacré au travail d'un groupe de soutien aux frères et soeurs d'enfants handicapés.

Ce numéro renferme également un résumé specialisé du travail de groupe avec des adolescents.

GERMAN SUMMARIES

Short Term Groupwork in the Treatment of Chronic Sorrow: A Norwegian Experience

GERD KRAMM ENGEBRIGTSEN AND KEN HEAP

Die dritte Ausgabe dieses Fachblatts beginnt mit einem Artikel vom Direktor für Sozialarbeit am Institut für Sprachwissenschaften, Oslo. Der Artikel beschreibt die Anwendung von befristeter Gruppenarbeit, als Unterstützung für Eltern, deren Kinder an einer unheilbaren Krankheit leiden.

Revisiting Open Groups

MICHAEL HENRY

Offene Gruppen oder Gruppen mit Sozialarbeitern, deren Mitgliedschaft schwankt, haben von jeher der Sozialarbeit, Heimarbeit und Jugendarbeit angehört. Dieser Artikel versucht, die Schlüsselelemente dieser Formen der Gruppenarbeit zu beschreiben.

Social Action Groupwork as Negotiation: Contradictions in the Process of Empowerment

EAMONN KEENAN AND JOHN PINKERTON

Dieser ist der erste von zwei Artikeln, der sich mit der sogenannten "social action" Gruppenarbeit befaßt. Hier werden von Keenan und Pinkerton die Themen Machtlosigkeit und Machtbeschaffung untersucht. Der Artikel beruht auf der Zusammenarbeit zwischen einem Professor für Sozialwissenschaften und einem Sozialarbeiter, der in Belfast, Nord Irland arbeitet.

'Nowt To Do and Always Getting into Trouble'. The Bulwell Neighbourhood Project — A Social Action Response

BILL BADMAN, MICHEAL BENTE AND PAULINE HALL

Der zeite Artikel, der sich mit "social action" Gruppenarbeit befaßt, konzentriert sich auf eine kleine Gemeinde in Nottinghamshire, die sich ausschließlich mit gemeindebezogener Sozialarbeit beschäftigt.

A Team Development Exercise

JOHN TAYLOR, DI MILES AND JOHN EASTGATE

Das zweite konsultationspapier beschreibt eine Fortbildungsübung für Sozialarbeiter in einem Heim für Jugentliche. Um das theoretische Wissen zu erweitern und um ihre praktische Arbeit zu verbessern, machten die Gruppenleiter von einer Reihe von Gruppenarbeitspraktiken Gebrauch, die normaleweise eher bei Gruppenarbeit mit Jugentlichen verwendet werden.

'The Brothers and Sisters Group'. A Group for Siblings of Children with Physical Disabilities

ANNE BADGER

Im Gegensatz zum ersten Artikel von Heap et al, beschreibt dieses Papier eine Gruppe, die Unterstützung bietet für die Geschwister behinderter Kinder.

Diese Ausgabe bietet auch eine Abhandlung über Gruppenarbeit mit Jugendlichen.

NOTES ON CONTRIBUTORS

Anne Badger is a senior practitioner with Wandsworth Social Services, attached to both a child development centre and a pilot community team for adults with physical disabilities. Her colleagues for the group were Judith Bell, a child psychologist; Malcolm Conway, who is now with Croydon Probation service; and Leslie Turner, who was also formerly employed by Wandsworth.

Bill Badman has been a probation worker for five years.

Michael Bente was a sessional youth worker and residential worker in a young people's hostel and now works for a Nottingham housing association.

John Eastgate is a psychiatrist with Swindon Child and Family Guidance Service.

Gerd Kramm Engebrigtsen is a Norwegian medical social worker with experience from neurological, surgical and psychiatric settings as well as from social medicine. She also has earlier experience of work with refugees. The groupwork discussed in the present article is conducted during a long term co-operation between Frambu — the centre described — and the department of the National Teaching Hospital in Oslo where she is currently employed.

Pauline Hall was a social worker and intermediate treatment worker and is now a teacher in further education.

Ken Heap is a British social worker, who has been resident in Scandinavia since the early 1960s. He trained at the University of Nottingham, Tavistock Clinic and University of Bradford and has experience of probation, child psychiatry, marital counselling and gerontology. He has international consultative and teaching experience and has published books on groups and groupwork in most European languages. Currently, Ken Heap leads the Advanced Training Department of the Diakonhjemmet School of Social Work in Oslo, Norway.

Michael Henry is Deputy Project Leader at Lawrence Weston Family Centre (Barnardo's), Bristol and he has had experience of working with groups in residential, field and day care settings. His article is based on a Personal Social Services Fellowship study at Bristol University.

Eamonn Keenan has been employed by Save the Children since 1981, working primarily with adolescents in West Belfast. His current brief is working on the feasibility of 'social action' work in the Greater Belfast area. He is qualified in both social and youth community work.

Di Miles is the co-ordinator at Swindon Twelve-Eighteen Project (STEP) — a specialised voluntary organisation working with groups of young people with a variety of needs.

John Pinkerton was a social worker in Belfast's Northern suburbs and rural hinterland, prior to social work teaching, firstly in Ulster Polytechnic and, since 1984, at Queen's University, Belfast. His interest in groupwork is rooted in his everyday involvement in adult education, his trade union and political commitments and his active membership of Parents' Aid (Northern Ireland). He is a member of the support group established by Save the Children (NI) for their LIBRA Project, an alternative to custody initiative.

Alison Skinner is Information Officer at the National Youth Bureau, Leicester with specialist subject responsibility for intermediate treatment and services for young people at risk and in trouble. She has compiled two bibliographies, *Intermediate*

Treatment 1968-84 and *Disaffection from School: Issues and Interagency Responses*, both published by the NYB.

John Taylor is a social worker, Swindon Child and Family Guidance Service. He has particular experience in work with groups both in child guidance and in previous posts.

NOTES FOR CONTRIBUTORS

Potential contributors
Articles are welcome from all who have an interest in work with groups (whether as practitioner, trainer, researcher, user or consultant) and who wish to contribute to the development of groupwork theory and practice.

Types of articles
The journal will publish two main types of articles:
i. practice-based papers
ii. theory-building papers
Although these two types of article will differ in emphasis and perspective, both are seen as equally important. The intention is that the practice papers will draw out general principles and the theoretical papers will indicate their relevance to practice.

i. PRACTICE-BASED PAPERS
These articles will be based directly on groupwork practice experience, but written in a way which is evaluative as well as descriptive. The material will make a direct contribution to practice theory in a way which will enable groupworkers to learn from it, and to develop their practice competence. The journal would like to receive articles from groupworkers from a wide range of settings working in different ways with people having different needs and circumstances. This range includes statutory and voluntary agencies, fieldwork, residential, daycare and hospital settings; members of diverse age, race and gender; and methods varying between discussion, structured activity, therapy and action. We recognise that many practitioners may not be familiar with writing for journals, and we wish to suggest the following guidelines to assist in this process:
(a) A brief summary of the contents of the article (100-150 words), drawing attention to any particular theme or emphasis.
(b) Background to the group, the context, e.g. agency setting, type of group, workers and members; group aims and objectives; and the theoretical/philosophical perspectives i.e. any particular principles or values central to the approach taken.
(c) A brief review of the group, content, methods and process.
(d) Outcome and analysis, specific topics of interest relevant to the focus of the article, e.g. key issues arising from this piece of practice; and evaluation of the group drawing out learning points for other practitioners.

ii. THEORY-BUILDING PAPERS
Each issue will carry several theoretical papers ranging over groupwork concepts, theory, research, issues and values. These papers will have no set format, but contributors are asked to begin with a brief summary of the contents of the article (100-150 words) and to include a section at the end which indicates the specific implications of the theoretical material for groupwork practice. Papers on the following topics would be especially welcomed:
(a) The current 'state of the art' of groupwork.
(b) Papers analysing the significance for the groupwork process of race, gender, class, culture and other social factors.
(c) Papers analysing key group concepts and issues.
(d) Papers from different countries, sharing current developments and theoretical concerns and preoccupations likely to be significant for groupwork practice in Britain and elsewhere.
(e) New sources of research evidence.
(f) Groupwork training and skill development, consultation/supervision.

We recognise that some contributors may wish to write papers which do not fall neatly into one or other of these categories, e.g. papers drawing out general principles from groupwork practice programmes. Such papers will, of course, be just as welcome in the journal.

Length of papers

The normal range will be 2,500-4,000 words, with practice accounts not longer than 3,000 words. Exceptionally, longer articles will be accepted and there will be a place for briefer contributions on new developments, responses to previous articles and other material of special interest.

Form of submission

Articles should be submitted in one of two ways:

i. typed on A4 paper, 3 copies, double-spaced with wide margins

ii. on computer disc. Materials submitted in this way should be for use on either IBM-PCs and compatibles (e.g. Amstrad 1512, Apricot PCs, or Amstrad PCW 8256), and should use either Wordcraft, Wordstar or Smart word-processing packages. Those intending to submit material in other formats should first contact the editors.

References

These should be quoted in the text by giving in brackets the author's name and year of publication. They should then be listed in alphabetical order at the end of the article as follows.

Books – author's surname, initials, date, title of book, place of publication, publisher's name, page if relevant.

Articles – author's surname, initials, date, title of article, title of journal, volume and number. Only those references which occur in the text should be listed. Where appropriate, additional resources may be listed separately as further reading.

N.B. It is important that punctuation and the use of capital letters should accord with the style used in GROUPWORK.

Assessment for publication

Articles submitted will normally be passed to members of the journal's panel of assessors, and decisions as to publication made by the editors in the light of the assessors' comments.

Publication

The journal will be published three times a year, in February, June and October.

Abstracts and information section

Any information for inclusion in this section, e.g. notification of conferences, network meetings, recent groupwork publications of particular interest, should reach the editors not later than two months prior to the publication month of the relevant issue.

Authors

Authors should include brief information – two or three sentences – about themselves and their background.

Enquiries

Any potential authors who would like to discuss their ideas prior to writing or submitting an article are welcome to contact either of the co-editors . . .

Allan Brown, Dept of Social Work, University of Bristol, 40 Berkeley Square, Bristol BS8 1HY Tel: 0272-303030, ext. M208

Andrew Kerslake, School of Humanities, University of Bath, Claverton Down, Bath BA2 7AY Tel: 0225-826826, ext. 5815.

ALL TYPED ARTICLES AND INFORMATION FOR THE ABSTRACTS SHOULD BE SENT TO ALLAN BROWN.

ALL ARTICLES ON COMPUTER DISC AND MATERIAL FOR REVIEW SHOULD BE SENT TO ANDREW KERSLAKE.

Appendix: Contents of *Groupwork* Volumes I-13

Volume 1 (ISBN 9781861770554)
Groupwork practice with hard to reach clients: A modality of choice Lawrence Shulman
The worker and the group process: A dilemma revisited Ken Heap
Race and groupwork: Some experiences in practice and training Ros Muston and Jeremy Weinstein
A group for white women with black children Clare Rhule
Structured activities with adolescent boys Rod Craig
Supporting voices: Groupwork with people suffering from schizophrenia Lynda Randall and Wendy Walker
Groupwork books published in Britain 1980-86 Harold Marchant
Swimming upstream: Articles on groupwork in social work journals 1986-87 Nano McCaughan
Preparing the client for social groupwork: An illustrated framework Oded Manor
Groups for older people in residential and day-care: The other groupworkers Lorraine Bernard, John Burton, Phyllis Kyne and June Simon
'But I don't want to lead a group!' Some common problems of social workers leading groups Ken Reid
Programming skills in social groupwork. Sue Ross and Andy Thorpe
A model for evaluating groupwork Michael Preston-shoot
Groupwork as the method of choice with black children in white foster homes Audrey Mullender
Short term groupwork in the treatment of chronic sorrow. A Norwegian experience Gerd Kramm Engebrigtsen and Ken Heap
Revisiting open groups Michael Henry
Social action groupwork as negotiation: Contradictions in the process of empowerment Eamonn Keenan and John Pinkerton
'Nowt to do and always getting into trouble'. The Bulwell Neighbourhood Project: A social action response Bill Badham, Michael Bente and Pauline Hall
A team development exercise John Taylor, Di Miles and John Eastgate
'The brothers and sisters group': A group for siblings of children with physical disabilities Anne Badger
Groupwork with adolescents: Abstracts Alison Skinner

Volume 2 (ISBN 9781861770561)
Challenging familiar assumptions: Preparing for and initiating a self-directed group Audrey Mullender and David Ward
Doing something with our lives when we're inside: Self-directive groupwork in a youth custody centre. Bill Badham (Ed.). Bob Blatchford, Steph Mcartney and Malcolm Nicholas
Using contracts in groupwork Michael Preston-shoot
Targeted activities in group contexts: The analysis of activities to meet consumer need Julie Phillips
Designing cancer groups for maximum effectiveness Barry M. Daste
Decision-making in therapeutic groups Marian F. Fatout
Confronting human finitude. Groupwork with people with AIDS George S. Getzel and Kevin F. Mahony
Organising accountability for social groupwork: More choices Oded Manor
A group for black and white sexually abused children Marie Lebacq and Zaffira Shah
Learning about groupwork. Jenny Lumley and Harold Marchant
Establishing a feminist model of groupwork in the Probation Service Tara Mistry
A way forward: A group for refugee women Rachel Tribe and Jane Shackman
Searching the literature on women's groups Cathrine Fitzgerald
Open grief groups: the resolution of complicated loss Marianne Davidsen-Nielsen and Nini Leick
Groupwork with the spouses of seriously ill patients Janine Favier
Supportive groupwork for dialysis patients Lizzie Bollmann
Supportive groupwork with young arthritic mothers Amy Østertun Geirdal
Staff development through groupwork in Polish

community agencies: 'The Centres Of Culture' Jerzy Szmagalski
Self-help groups as basic care in psychotherapy and social work Jürgen Matzat
Family group treatment in drug abuse Anna Casanova Torras
Groupwork As Early Intervention In High Risk Families Rigmor Grette Moe

Volume 3 (ISBN 9781861770578)
Social work with groups in multicultural contexts Kenneth L. Chau
Siblings in groups: Children of separated/divorced parents Sandra Regan and Jan Young
Groupwork techniques in a residential primary school for emotionally disturbed boys Peter Clarke and Amanda Aimable
The role of groupwork in research with people with learning difficulties Jan Walmsley
Groupwork training: A case study Andrew Kerslake
Beulah Rothman: An appreciation Oded Manor
Starting the journey: Enhancing the therapeutic elements of groupwork for adolescent female child sexual abuse victims Eileen Craig
Evaluating success in groupwork: Why not measure the obvious? Anne Peake and Olive Otway
Investigating groupwork: A Case study using a group approach in the initial stages of child sexual abuse investigation Sarah Allum
The Forgotten parent: Groupwork with mothers of sexually abused children Helen Masson and Marcus Erooga
Work with male sex offenders in groups Malcolm Cowburn
Protection, control, treatment: Groupwork with child sexual abuse perpetrators Marcus Erooga, Paul Clark and Mai Bentley
Group treatment for women sex offenders against children Sharon Barnett. Francesca Corder and Derek Jehu
Selected article abstracts on child sexual abuse and groupwork Julia Cramp and Helen Armstrong
Self help groups: A minefield for professionals Ulla Habermann
Facing the challenge of developing group services for high risk families Alice Home and Lise Darveau-Fournier
Groupwork with parents of sleepless children Rona Robertson
Culture' groups in prison Graham Towl
Groupwork with a difference: The group 'mosaic' in residential day centre settings Allan Brown
Groupwork in residential settings for elderly people Audrey Mullender

Volume 4 (ISBN 9781861770585)
Empowerment through mutual aid groups: A practice grounded conceptual framework Judith AB. Lee
Making authority accountable: The experience of a statutory based women's group Helen Bodinham and Jeremy Weinstein
Towards a model of social groupwork practice with marginalised populations Margot Breton
Working creatively with children Eugene Clerkin and Belinda Knaggs
The termination phase in groupwork: Tasks for the groupworker Sue Ross
Miami, October 1990 Oded Manor and Dave Ward
Black/white co-working in groups Tara Mistry And Allan Brown
Groupwork and oral history: Raising the consciousness of young people during social transition Sandra Drower
The use of photographs as a projective and facilitative technique in groups Merav DeVere And Ossi Rhonne
Facilitation in self-directed groupwork Dave Ward and Audrey Mullender
Evaluative study of groupwork for stress and anxiety Rhona Birrell Weisen
A long-term support group for chronic schizophrenic outpatients: A quantitative and qualitative evaluation Julie Cwikel And Adina Oron
Using groups in working with offenders:
A survey of groupwork in the Probation Service of England and Wales Brian Caddick
A Miskin Model of groupwork with women offenders Marion jones, Mary Mordecai, Frances Rutter and Linda Thomas
Evolution and accountability Ten years of groups in a day centre for offenders
Judith Earnshaw
The Telford Motoring Offenders Education Project Kathryn Hutchins
Groupwork in the Luton Probation And Bail Hostel Catherine Mulvie
The Newcastle intensive probation programme
A centralised approach to groupwork Jane Mackintosh

Meeting prisoners' needs through groupwork Mike Ashe
Groupwork in the Probation Service: Care or control in the 1990s Paul Senior
Selected abstracts on groupwork with offenders John Hodge
Derek Carter 1934-1991

Volume 5 (ISBN 9781861770592)
Groupwork from across the Atlantic: Its identity and diffusion Catherine Pappell
Groupwork in Europe: Past, Present, Future Ken Heap, Diakonhjemmet School of Social Work, Oslo
The groupwork consultant's role in facilitating work groups Alan Turkie, Independent
Evaluation For The Improvement Of Groupwork Practice Kenneth H Gordon, School of Social Work, King's College, Western Ontario
Groupwork in a residential home for older people: Building on the positive aspects of group living Gun Lewis, Officer in Charge
Groupwork with Youth Gangs in Hong Kong T Wing Lo, City Polytechnic, Hong Kong
On empowerment, partnership and authority in groupwork practice: A training contribution Michael Preston-Shoot, School of Social Work, University of Manchester
Groupwork with involuntary clients: Remotivating strategies Cyrus S Behroozi, Indiana University School of Social Work
Handling conflict: Groupwork with violent offenders Rob Canton, Carolyn Mack and Jeff Smith, Nottinghamshire Probation
The dream in groupwork practice Iain Edgar, Dept of Social Work, University of Northumbria
Support groups for older people: Is homogeneity or heterogeneity the answer? Susan Rice and Catherine Goodman, Dept of Social Work, California State University, Long Beach
The group turns inward: A consideration of some group phenomena as reflective of the Northern Irish situation Jarlath Benson, Psychotherapeutic Groupworker, Belfast
Groupwork with bereaved children Nuala Harmey and Bernie Price, Medical Social Work, Temple Street Children's Hospital, Dublin
Reminiscence groupwork with older people Faith Gibson, Dept of Social Work, University of Ulster, Coleraine
Social workers and psychologists as facilitators of groupwork with adults with a learning difficulty: A survey of current practice Heno Schonfield and Mary C Morrissey, Senior Social Workers, Dublin
Groupwork with teenage cancer patients Nicola Martin Medical Social Worker in Oncology, and Eddie O'Neill, Paediatric Oncology Social Worker, Mater Hospital, Dublin
Bereaved by suicide: Setting up an 'ideal' therapy group in a real world Imogen O'Connor, Therapist, Dublin Rape Crisis Centre

Volume 6 (ISBN 9781861770608)
Groupwork versus *casework in a group* Roselle Kurland and Robert Salmon, Hunter School of Social Work, New York
Why groupwork is not put into practice: Reflections on the social work scene in Denmark Ulla Habermann, Director, Volunteer Centre, Denmark
Away with the experts? Self-help groupwork in Germany Jürgen Matzat, Psychologist, Klinik für Psychosomatik und Psychotherapie, Justus-Liebig-Universität, Gießen
Groupwork with siblings of children with special needs: A pilot study Georgina Ferraro and Julie Tucker, Senior Family Project Workers
Neutralisation of group control in youth gangs T Wing Lo, City Polytechnic, Hong Kong
The large group: The heart of the system in group care Adrian Ward, Dept of Social Work, University of Reading
Working with a family group of bereaved children Sheila Finlayson, Child Advisory Social Work Service, City of Birmingham Education Dept
A comparative study of four family bereavement groups Estelle Hopmeyer, and Annette Werk, McGill School of Social Work, Montréal
An asian mothers' group Lynne Muir Director, MEd Programme in Community Education and Hardev Notta, Acorns Hospice for Children, Birmingham
A Cruse family circle Joyce Rimmer, Birmingham Cruse
Coping with trauma Frank Parkinson, former Army chaplain
From group meeting to therapeutic group Bernadette Duffy. Social Care Worker, Dublin and Brian McCarthy, Lecturer in Psychology, Dublin Institute of Technology
Group therapy with adults with learning difficulties who have committed sexual offences Elisabeth

Cormack, Young People's Centre , Northern Ireland

Critical incident analysis and its application in groupwork David Henchman and Susan Walton, Avon Probation Service

Life history work with a group of people with learning disabilities Dorothy Atkinson, School of Health, Welfare and Community Education, Open University

Art therapy: Creative groupwork for women. Olive Otway, Lecturer in Social Work, University of Keele

Groupwork with parents of learning disabled adolescents. Helen Gobat, Independent Social Worker

Groupwork with deaf people. Kavita Kohli, Social Worker, Hounslow Social Services s

Combining activities and growth games: A systems approach Oded Manor, Middlesex University, and Miriam Dumbleton, Care Manager, Westminster Social Services

Volume 7 (ISBN 9781861770615)

The linguistic and cultural barriers to cross-national groupwork Paul Taylor, Lecturer in Community Education, University of Tours, France

Partnership in training and practice with refugees Jill Reynolds, School of Health, Welfare and Community Education, Open University and Jane Shackman, Social Worker, The Medical Foundation for Care of Victims of Torture

Men working with men in groups: masculinity and crime John Benstead, Gloucester Probation, Allan Brown, School of Social Work, Bristol University, Carlton Forbes, and Rick Wall, Avon Probation Centre

Working *with religious communities* Geraldine Grindley, Dublin City University

Issues of empowerment: Anti-oppressive groupwork by disabled people in Ireland Maire Ni Chorcora and Eddie Jennings, DET and Nuala Lordan, Dept of Applied Social Studies, University College Cork

A Psychotherapeutic group for boys who have been sexually abused Gary Dixon formerly South London FSU and Michelle Phillips, Clinical Nurse Specialist, Camberwell Child Guidance Centre

Groupwork and black women: Viewing networks as groups Marcia Francis-Spence Centre for Applied Social Studies, University of Durham

Staying alive in difficult times: The experience of groupwork with mothers of children who have been sexually abused Deb Dobbin and Sarah Evans, Independent Social Workers

A time for women: An account of a group for women on an out of city housing development in Leicester Claire Wintram, Independent Trainer, Kerry Chamberlain, National Health Service Administrator, Marlene Kuhn, Midwife and Jo Smith, Woman with a Disability active in support and campaign groups , Leicester

Groupwork for mental health: Providers utilising the enchanted self concept Barbara Becker Holstein, Psychologist, Long Branch, New Jersey, and Doreen Laperdon-Addison, Movement Educator and Professional Dancer

Promoting positive images:. The role of groupwork in promoting women managers within organisations Judy Fawcett, Independent Consultant and Trainer

Using a facilitated self help group for women whose children have been sexually abused Olive Otway, Dept of Social Work, Keele University, and Anne Peak, Principal Psychologist, Oxfordshire

'All I've got in my purse is mothballs' the social action women's group Sandra Butler, Dept of Social Work, University of Nottingham

Silence in working across difference: Groupwork in a youth and community work training context Janet Batsleer, Youth and Community Work Section, Manchester Metropolitan University

Ourselves and others Helen Gobat, Independent Social Worker

Groupwork with young mothers Caroline Norman, Project Worker, St Gabriels Family Centre, Brighton

Groupwork for parents of young people in trouble: A proposal Mark Drakeford, Dept of Applied Social Studies, University of Wales, Swansea

A dramatic view of groupwork Jeremy Weinstein, Dept of Social Work, South Bank University

Anger management groupwork with prisoners: An empirical evaluation Graham J Towl and Polly Dexter, Forensic Psychologists, HM Prison Service

Volume 8 (ISBN 9781861770622)

'Cycling Over Everest' Groupwork with depressed women Pamela Trevithick, Dept of Social Work, Bristol University

Groupwork in Croatia: Experiences with older refugees Marina Adjukovic, School of Social Work, University of Zagreb, Milena Cevcizovic

and Ksenija Kontak, Psychologists, Society for Psychological Assistance, Croatia
Group dialogue within prisons Peter Garrett, Centre for Action Research in Professional Practice, School of Management, University of Bath
Establishing community meetings in a children's home Adrian Ward, Dept of Social Work, University of Reading
Groups for children who have lived with domestic violence: Learning from North America Audrey Mullender, Centre for Applied Social Studies, University of Durham
Facilitating enquiry and action learning groups for social work education Hilary Burgess and Imogen Taylor, School for Policy Studies, University of Bristol
Developing critical conversations about practice Mark K Smith, Research Fellow and Tutor, YMCA George Williams College
Dialogue and reparation in the large whole group Alan Turkie, Independent and Lecturer in Youth and Community Work, Goldsmiths' College
Using groupwork methods in social work education Margaret O'Dee, Social Work Studies, Salford University
An outdoor treatment programme for a group of first year sixth formers Derrick Rowland Coverdale consultant
A Strategy for groupwork education and training in a social work agency Mark Doel, University of Sheffield and Catherine Sawdon, Training Officer, Wakefield Social Services
Managing the tension between being task-centred and being anti-oppressive Marcia Francis Spence and Beverley Prevatt-Goldstein, Centre for Applied Social Studies, University of Durham
Teachers, learning, ego and groups Leslie Silverlock and Marion Silverlock 'Groups Work'
Creative short term group therapy in a managed care environment Barry M Daste, Louisiana State University School of Social Work
Groupwork to facilitate family reconstitution: A social work response Jan Hadlow, Keynes College
Social groupwork practice in Hong Kong: Application of western ideas in an asian population Debbie O B Lam, University of Hong Kong
Time and space to grieve: A bereavement group for children Sister Margaret Pennels, Northampton General Hospital NHS Trust
An integrated feminist-socioeducational model: Groupwork with nurses in Hong Kong Elaine Au Liu, City University of Hong Kong

Volume 9 (ISBN 9781861770639)
Living with loss: A bereavement support group Sheila Thompson, School of Social Work, McGill University
A collaborative group approach for urban parents Mary McKernan McKay, Teresa Garcia, Joseph Scally and Lori Martinez, Institute for Juvenile Research, University of Illinois, Chicago
Groupwork with male 'domestic' abusers: Models and dilemmas Audrey Mullender, Professor in Social Work, University of Warwick
'Without the group, I'd still be eating half the Co-op': An example of groupwork with women who use food Jill Ball and Annemarie Norman, , Northern Initiative on Women and Food, Newcastle
The use of sculpt in social groupwork education Nuala Lordan, University College, Cork
Groupwork into the future: Some personal reflections Allan Brown, formerly University of Bristol
Ethical issues in practice: Participatory social research and groups George Taylor, Dept of Social and Community Studies, De Montfort University
Enhancing research usefulness with adapted focus groups Alice M. Home, Professor of Social Work, University of Ottawa
Focus groups and familiar social work skills: Their contribution to practitioner research Pat Walton, Lecturer in Post-Qualifying Studies (Child Care)
Focusing on groups in social policy research Paul Swift, Project Researcher, School for Policy Studies, University of Bristol
Exploitation or empowerment? Gaining access to young people's reflections on crime prevention Strategies Alan France, Research Fellow, University of Warwick University
A youth and community work approach to practitioner research into sensitive issues Steve Kenny, Dept of Applied Community Studies, Manchester Metropolitan University
Black community members-as-researchers: Working with community groups in the research process Simon Dyson and Mark Harrison, Director, Centre for Social Action, de Montfort University,
Empowering research process: Using groups in research to empower the people Asnarulkhadi

Abu-Samah, Doctoral student, University of Nottingham

Storming as transformation: A case study of group relationships Oded Manor, Middlesex University

An art therapy group for young people with eating difficulties Janet Fitzsimmons, Social Worker and Rosemary Levy, Art Therapist, Barnet Social Services Children and Families Health related Social Work Team

Intervention in the decision-making of youth gangs Francis W L Lee, Dept of Social Work, Chinese University of Hong Kong, T. Wing Lo and Dennis S W Wong, Dept of Applied Social Studies, City University of Hong Kong

Support groups for families of confused elders: Issues surrounding open peer-led groups Elizabeth Hughes Schneewind, Independent Social Worker

Drama and groupwork: Overcoming the 'double whammy' Philip Moore, Actor and Groupworker, Cumbria Probation

Psychosocial assistance to refugee and displaced women in Croatia Nina Pecnik, School of Social Work, University of Zagreb and Mira Miskulin, Programme for Refugee Women, 'Sunflower' Centre for Grassroots Relief, Zagreb

Volume 10 (ISBN 9781861770646)

Teleconferencing group counselling: Pre-group public phase Sandra Regan, Senior Lecturer in Groupwork, School of Social Work, University of New South Wales,

Suddenly the light went on: Using groupwork to empower returning students Roni Berger, Assistant Professor, School of Social Work, Adelphi University

A group's journey through separation and loss: Therapeutic groupwork with children as a social work intervention Maria Neary and Geraldine Brandon, Thamesmead Family Service Unit

Implementing a novel groupwork model: Application of an innovation-developmental process Jerome R. Kolbo, University of S Mississippi, Kimberly Horn, W Virginia University and Elizabeth Randall, University of S Mississippi

Applying a strengths, competence and empowerment model Anna Nosko, Family Services Association of Toronto and Margot Breton, University of Toronto

Effective groupwork packages and the importance of process David Henchman and Susan Walton, Freelance Trainers and Probation Officers

Using the sensory orientation group with a frail elder population Norma Thomas, Professor, Center for Social Work, Widener University, Pennsylvania and Suzanne Coleman, Social Worker, Bryn Mawr Terrace Nursing Home, Pennsylvania

Research into practice does go: Integrating research within programme development Rob Harry, Staff Dev't Manager, Patricia Heggarty, Probation Officer, Cathy Lisles, Freelance Researcher, Richard Thurston, Research Mgr, Mid-Glams Probation and Maurice Vanstone, Lecturer, University of Wales, Swansea

Brief group therapy and the use of metaphor Christian C Sunderland, Clinical Social Worker, Cardston Clinic, Alberta

We'd like you to come back Hilary Hopkin, Social Worker, Royal Liverpool University Hospital

The use of music in group work with out-patient alcoholic couples: A pilot investigation Wilfred A Gallant, Assoc. Professor of Social Work, Melanie D Galant, Research Asst Human Services Research Unit, Kevin M Gorey, Assoc. Professor of Social Work, Michael J Holosko, Professor of Social Work and Sammi Siegel, Director of Music Therapy, University of Windsor, Ontario

Exploring worker responses to critical incidents Marian F Fatout, Professor, School of Social Work, Louisiana State University, Baton Rouge

A Critical analysis of a support and clinical supervision group for interpreters working with refugees located in Britain Rachel Tribe, Senior Lecturer, Psychology Dept, University of East London, Romford

Feminist groupwork with lesbian survivors of incest Patricia A Groves, Director of Social Work Program and Connie Schondel, formerly Associate Professor, , University of Toledo, Ohio

Don't worry, it's just a stage he's going through: A reappraisal of the stage theory of group work as applied to an open model treatment group for men who abuse women Tom Caplan, Adj. Professor and Director, and Harle Thomas, Clinical and Groupworker, McGill University Domestic Violence Clinic

Active learning programmes to promote cognitive change Siu-Kau Cheung, Principal Lecturer,

Division of Social Studies, City University of Hong Kong

Volume 11 (ISBN 9781861770653)
Crossing bridges: Groupwork in Guyana Judith A B Lee, Professor, Dept of Social Work, Florida Gulf Coast University
Working with polarities, roles and timespirits: A process oriented approach to emotions in the Group Bogna Szymkiewicz-Komalska, Asst Professor, Inst of Applied Social Sciences, Warsaw University
It ain't (just) what you do: It's the way that you do it: Working towards effective practice in probation groupwork Alan Hayden, Jonathan Hopkinson, Janeen Sengendo and Elisabeth von Rabenau, Probation Officers, Cambridgeshire Probation
A Group intervention for children of incarcerated parents: Initial blunders and subsequent solutions David W Springer, Asst Professor, Elizabeth C Pomeroy, Asst Professor and Toni Johnson, Doctoral Student, School of Social Work, University of Texas, Austin
Expressing our anger: Hindrance or help in groupwork with adolescents? Andrew Malekoff, Director or Program Development, North Shore Child and Family Guidance Center, Roslyn Heights, New York
Technical errors or missed alternatives: An interview with Catherine Pappell
Groupwork with the mothers of teenage mothers Catherine Dennison, Research Psychologist and Helen Ingledew, Family Centre Worker, Trust for the Study of Adolescence
Men united: Fathers' voices Jennie Fleming, Research Fellow, Centre for Social Action, de Montfort University and Zbyszek Luczynski, Broader Initiatives Development Worker, Nottingham City Council
Parent education groups: Using cultural literature during engagement phase Gwenelle Styles O'Neal, Assoc Professor of Social Work, West Chester University, Pennsylvania and Janis Coombs Reid, Vice President of Academic Affairs, Atlanta Metropolitan College, Georgia
Action methods and interpersonal processes in groups: An exploration of psychodramatic concepts Annie Huntington, Lecturer, Dept of Social Work, Salford University
Building solutions in groupwork with parents John Sharry, Senior Social Worker, Dept of Child and Family Psychiatry, Mater Hospital, Dublin
Crossing the great gap: Groupwork for personal growth John Rowan, Group and Individual Psychotherapist
When actions speak louder: Groupwork in occupational therapy Linda Finlay, Associate Lecturer in Social Psychology, the Open University, Leeds
Help as mutual aid: Groupwork in mental health Oded Manor, Principal Lecturer in Social Work, School of Social Science, Middlesex University
No Group is an island: Groupwork in a social work agency Mark Doel, Professor of Social Work School of Social Work and RNIB Rehabilitation Studies, University of Central England and Catherine Sawdon, Training Officer, Wakefield Social Services
Breaking the culture of silence: Groupwork and community development Jacky Drysdale, Lecturer in Social Work and Rod Purcell, Lecturer in Community Development and Adult Education, University of Glasgow
Values as Context: Groupwork and social action Mark Harrison, Director, Centre for Social Action and Dave Ward, Professor and Head, Dept of Social and Community Studies, De Montfort University

Volume 12 (ISBN 9781861770660)
Punishment and the question of ownership: Groupwork in the criminal justice system Liz Dixon, Senior Lecturer in Criminal Justice Studies, University of Hertfordshire and Probation Officer, ILPS
Picking up the Pieces: Groupwork in Palliative Care Pam Firth, Senior Social Worker/Head of Family Support, Isabel Hospice, Welwyn Garden City
Developing the professionals: Groupwork for health promotion Ellen E Reverand, Senior Manager (Learning and Professional Development) and Louis B Levy, Acting Director, Health First, London
Learning beyond the classroom: A role for groupwork? Marion Silverlock, Education and Training Consultant, Somerset
Evolving the curriculum: Groupwork and community based learning Lynne Muir, Course Director, MA in Community Based Learning. , Centre for Education Development, Coventry
*Using workshops on loss for adults with learning

disabilities Sue Read, Vicky Papakosta-Harvey and Sal Bower

Groupwork with schizophrenia: Clinical aspects Susan E. Mason, Associate Professor of Social Work, Wurzweiler School of Social Work, Yeshiva University, New York

Multi-family group interventions with schizophrenia Jane Hanvey Phillips, Doctoral Candidate, and Jacqueline Corcoran, Assistant Professor, School of Social Work, University of Texas, Arlington

The mixed-based nature of self-help groups in Finland Marianne Nylund, Researcher, Doctor of Social Sciences, Dept of Social Policy, University of Helsinky

Teenagers' experiences of a health promotion project Frances Maggs-Rapport, Senior Research Fellow, Mary Seacole Research Centre, De Montfort University

Working with natural groups of youth-at-risk: An RGC approach Francis Wing-lin Lee Assistant Professor, Dept of Social Work, University of Hong Kong

The strengths perspective in reminiscence groupwork with depressed older adults Alison C. Rishty Advanced Standing MSW Candidate in Clinical Practice, Columbia University

Using fieldwork experience as a tool for teaching: A multi-layered approach Barbara Worden, Assoc. Professor of Social Work, Southern Conecticut State University

Volume 13 (ISBN 9781861770677)

Using technologies in groupwork . Part I: Face-to-face groups, and *Part II: Technology-based groups* Paul R. Smokowski, Director of Distance Education, Maeda Galinsky, Kenan Distinguished Professor, School of Social Work, University of North Carolina at Chapel Hill, and Kristin Harlow, Social Work Practitioner

Researching our own practice: Single system design for groupwork Paul Johnson, Asst Professor, Dept of Social Work, University of S. Maine. Aaron Beckerman, Professor Emeritus and Charles Auerbach, Professor, Wurzweiler School of Social Work, Yeshiva University

Facilitating group beginnings. I: A practice model, and *Part II: From basic to working engagement* Alf Lizzio, Lecturer, and Keithia Wilson, Senior Lecturer, School of Applied Psychology, Griffiths University, Brisbane

To share or not to share: Dilemmas of facilitators who share the problem of group members Marian Maram, Assistant Director of Field Education, and Susan Rice, Professor and Undergraduate Program Coordinator, Dept of Social Work, California State University, Long Beach

In their own voices: Play activities and art with traumatised children Bruce St. Thomas, Psychotherapist/Art Therapist, Westbrook Street Psychotherapy Associates, Portland, and Paul Johnson, Assistant Professor, Dept of Social Work, University of S. Maine

Groupwork with children and adolescents using lifegames Isabelle C. Streng, Chartered Clinical Psychologist, Erasmus Medical Centre, Rotterdam, The Netherlands

Closing a cultural divide: Enhancing mutual aid while working with groups in Hong Kong Fanny L.W.C. Liu, Senior Lecturer, Division of Social Studies, City University of Hong Kong

Strengths and weaknesses of self-help groups in mental health: The case of Grow Kam-shing Yip, Associate Professor, Dept of Applied Social Studies, Hong Kong Polytechnic University

Using groupwork in community mental health: Practitioners' views Ben Papps, Lecturer in Clinical Psychology, Institute of Psychiatry, London., Oded Manor, Principal Lecturer in Social Work, Middlesex University and Jerome Carson, Senior Lecturer in Clinical Psychology, Institute of Psychiatry, London

Hearing voices: Learning to engage the group Terry Conway, Senior Social Worker, Kneesworth House Hospital, Royston

An isle full of noises: Enhancing mental health through the Music Workshop Project Tony Gillam, Early Interventions Team Leader, Merdian Family Interventions Programme, South Worcestershire Early Interventions Service

Henderson Hospital: Greater than the sum of its sub-groups Dr Kingsley Norton, Director, Henderson Hospital and Reader in Psychotherapy, St George's Hospital Medical School

Groupwork fit for purpose? An inclusive framework for mental health Oded Manor, Principal Lecturer in Social Work, School of Health and Social Sciences, Middlesex University

Authors' professional affiliations are those at the time of original publication

www.ingramcontent.com/pod-product-compliance
Lightning Source LLC
LaVergne TN
LVHW101443200926
848483LV00001B/33